The Normative Web

Antirealist views about morality claim that moral facts or truths do not exist. Does this imply that other types of normative facts, such as epistemic facts, do not exist? *The Normative Web* develops a positive answer to this question. Terence Cuneo argues that moral and epistemic facts are sufficiently similar so that, if moral facts do not exist, then epistemic facts do not exist. But epistemic facts exist: to deny their existence would commit us to an extreme version of epistemological scepticism. Therefore, Cuneo concludes, moral facts do exist. And if moral facts exist, then moral realism is true.

It is sometimes said that moral realists rarely offer arguments for their position, settling instead for mere defenses of a view they find intuitively plausible. By contrast, *The Normative Web* provides not merely a defense of robust realism in ethics, but a positive argument for this position. In so doing, it engages with a range of antirealist positions in epistemology such as error theories, expressivist views, and reductionist views of epistemic reasons. These positions, Cuneo claims, come at a prohibitively high theoretical cost. Given this cost, it follows that realism about both epistemic and moral facts is a position that we should find highly attractive.

Terence Cuneo is Assistant Professor of Philosophy at the University of Vermont.

The Normative Web

An Argument for Moral Realism

Terence Cuneo

OXFORD
UNIVERSITY PRESS

BJ
1012
.C84
2007

OXFORD

UNIVERSITY PRESS

Great Clarendon Street, Oxford OX2 6DP

Oxford University Press is a department of the University of Oxford.
It furthers the University's objective of excellence in research, scholarship,
and education by publishing worldwide in

Oxford New York

Auckland Cape Town Dar es Salaam Hong Kong Karachi
Kuala Lumpur Madrid Melbourne Mexico City Nairobi
New Delhi Shanghai Taipei Toronto

With offices in

Argentina Austria Brazil Chile Czech Republic France Greece
Guatemala Hungary Italy Japan Poland Portugal Singapore
South Korea Switzerland Thailand Turkey Ukraine Vietnam

Oxford is a registered trade mark of Oxford University Press
in the UK and in certain other countries

Published in the United States
by Oxford University Press Inc., New York

© Terence Cuneo 2007

British Library Cataloguing in Publication Data

Data available

Library of Congress Cataloging in Publication Data

Data available

Typeset by Laserwords Private Limited, Chennai, India
Printed in Great Britain
on acid-free paper by the
MPG Books Group, Bodmin and King's Lynn

ISBN 978–0–19–921883–7 (hbk.); 978–0–19–958138–2 (pbk.)

10 9 8 7 6 5 4 3 2 1

For my wife Kari Anne,
our three daughters
Janina, Olivia, and Esther;
and to the memory of a fourth:
Jessica Elise
(10 September—10 September 1999)
ΑΙΩΝΙΑ ΜΝΗΜΗ

Contents

Introduction

The types of silence that punctuate ordinary conversation come in many varieties. There are awkward silences, pregnant pauses, and the types of silence that signal that two friends have understood each other perfectly well on some matter. This book is concerned to address a type of silence that characterizes not ordinary conversation, but philosophical conversation, at least the type of philosophical conversation one hears in contemporary ethics. The closest analogue in ordinary conversation to the type of silence with which I am concerned is one in which things are not said that one would expect to be said. Somewhat more precisely, it is that type of silence that signals that something has been passed over or otherwise ignored that one would not have expected to have been passed over or ignored. (The passing over or ignoring, of course, needn't be deliberate.) I can pinpoint still more exactly the sort of silence that I have in mind by furnishing several examples of it from discussions in contemporary metaethics.

On the first page of his influential book, *Ethics: Inventing Right and Wrong,* J. L. Mackie writes:

The claim that values are not objective, are not part of the fabric of the world, is meant to include not only moral goodness, which might be most naturally equated with moral value, but also other things that could be more loosely called moral values or disvalues—rightness and wrongness, duty, obligation, an action's being rotten and contemptible, and so on. It also includes non-moral values, notably aesthetic ones, beauty and various kinds of artistic merit. I shall not discuss these explicitly, but clearly much the same considerations apply to aesthetic and moral values, and there would be at least some initial implausibility in a view that gave the one a different status from the other.[1]

---

[1] Mackie (1977), 1.

In this paragraph, Mackie takes glancing notice of the fact that his antirealist position in ethics is likely to have far-reaching consequences. Given the similarities between putative moral and aesthetic values, Mackie notes that the arguments he marshals for believing that values of the former type do not exist will also provide strong reasons for believing that values of the latter kind do not exist. This implication appears not to worry Mackie; nothing in his brief discussion of the issue reveals that he views the rejection of objective aesthetic values as being particularly problematic. But at this point one may well sense that something has been unexpectedly passed over in silence. For, arguably, the moral domain bears close similarities to domains other than just the aesthetic. Epistemic values such as *being rational, being justified*, and *being warranted*, for example, appear to be no less similar to moral values than aesthetic ones. But if this is right, won't Mackie's arguments, if sound, also provide good reason to reject the existence of such values? And won't this be a good deal more theoretically problematic than the non-existence of aesthetic values?

Consider, as a second example, the discussion of moral realism in Crispin Wright's *Truth and Objectivity*. In this book, Wright argues that we ought to be 'minimalists' about moral facts (or truths), where minimalism implies that moral facts (or truths) exist, but don't enjoy a mode of existence such that they can be 'seriously' represented by moral thought; they are, to use Wright's terminology, mere 'semantic shadows' cast by the assertoric form of moral thought. (I'll have more to say about this view toward the end of Chapter 6.) This view implies, according to Wright, that moral shortcomings may be 'worthy of reproach'. But the reproach will have to come from a committed moral standpoint in which differences in moral opinion 'involve nothing worth regarding as a *cognitive* shortcoming'.[2] As Wright puts it:

In general, the immediate price of minimalism about morals is that the gravity of moral judgement will lack an external sanction. No discourse-neutral notion of objectivity will give value to moral truth. When one is asked, 'Why bother to try to arrive at correct moral opinion?', the only available answer will be: because such opinion informs better conduct—better, that is, from a moral point of view. The only value of moral truth will thus be an instrumental moral value. If we think there are, by contrast, intrinsic, general values associated with discovery,

---

[2] Wright (1992), 200.

understanding and knowledge, we must recognize, I believe, that they belong with the application of these notions within discourses that deserve realism.[3]

Wright's claim in this passage is that while moral values deserve a minimalist treatment, epistemic values such as understanding and knowledge do not; they deserve a realist treatment. That is to say, such values, if they exist, are not such that they are mere 'semantic shadows' cast by the assertoric form of epistemic thought and discourse.

Between Wright's position and Mackie's there are both difference and similarity. Unlike Mackie, Wright does not simply pass over the issue of whether there are theoretically important connections between the nature of moral and epistemic values. But like Mackie, Wright does not suppose that the reasons he offers in favor of an antirealist position with regard to moral values also yield an antirealist view with regard to epistemic values. And it is this latter point of similarity between Wright and Mackie that may provoke puzzlement. After all, on the face of it, epistemic values and reasons don't appear to be very different types of creatures from moral values and reasons. To draw attention to one feature that seems not to distinguish them:[4] Epistemic values or reasons do not appear to have any more direct causal or explanatory impact on the world than do moral ones—that is, causal or explanatory impact not dependent on our propositional attitudes. We don't speak, for example, of either moral or epistemic reasons as being causally responsible for the occurrence of events studied by physicists or chemists. And yet Wright himself advocates the view that we have prima facie reason to believe that moral facts only minimally exist because they fail to exhibit this very sort of direct causal or explanatory impact. In light of this, one may well sense that in the passage I have quoted from Wright something has been unexpectedly passed over in silence. If moral and epistemic facts are exactly alike in the respect just mentioned, one wonders: Could it really be that epistemic facts such as those that concern understanding and knowledge deserve a realist treatment while moral ones do not?

Consider, as a final case, the concluding paragraph from Mark Timmons's book, *Morality without Foundations*, in which Timmons develops what is

---

[3] Wright (1992), 201.
[4] I ignore Wright's claim that minimalism about moral truth implies that such truths are only instrumentally valuable. For I do not see why it should follow from the fact that moral truths minimally exist, that their goodness consists only in their bringing about other sorts of values. I will revisit issues regarding the explanatory efficacy of moral and epistemic facts in Chapter 3.

arguably one of the most sophisticated moral epistemologies presently on offer. After having developed a moral antirealist view that has close affinities with Wright's, Timmons says the following:

I have tried to develop a moral epistemology about justification that is largely independent of my irrealist moral metaphysics and associated semantics, so that the plausibility of the epistemology does not depend on the metaphysics or semantics. I should also mention that, as far as I can see, my epistemological contextualism in ethics and its analog with regard to other domains of inquiry does not make very many assumptions about the metaphysics and associated semantics of epistemic discourse. Granted, one sort of contextualism in epistemology—what I have called 'normative contextualism'—does, indeed, seem to presuppose some brand of epistemic irrealism … but I disavow this sort of contextualism. And granted, I have made use of Foley's schema for understanding the semantic workings of terms like 'rational' and 'justified' in the context of epistemic appraisal. But none of this commits one to any sort of epistemic irrealism with regard to the issue about the existence and nature of objective epistemic facts, and none of this commits one to descriptivist—as opposed to non-descriptivist—treatments of epistemic language.[5]

Timmons makes no claim about how one should view the ontological status of epistemic facts, averring that the views he defends in moral epistemology are 'largely independent' from the antirealist view he defends in ethics. And there is a sense in which this seems right. Neither Timmons's own views regarding the workings of moral language nor his employment of Richard Foley's understanding of the semantics of epistemic terms such as 'rational' implies that epistemic facts do not exist. Still, here, as before, one may well sense that something has been unexpectedly passed over or otherwise ignored.

Timmons's project (like Mackie's) is, after all, one that attempts to fit together a robustly naturalistic world view with a position that takes the assertoric-seeming cast of ordinary moral discourse and thought seriously. Naturalism, says Timmons, gives us excellent reason to believe that a complete, accurate, and perspicuous account of the world does not contain moral facts, for normative facts have no place in such a world. Consequently one asks: How could it be that this broadly naturalistic position also fails to yield an antirealist position regarding epistemic facts, which are also robustly normative in character? Won't it be the case, then, that even if

---

[5] Timmons (1999), 246.

certain things that Timmons says needn't imply epistemic antirealism, and even if the plausibility of the epistemology he develops is independent of his favored moral antirealist position, the sort of *rationale* he offers for moral antirealism will also yield an antirealist view with regard to the existence of objective epistemic facts?

I. An argument for moral realism

Cases of the type I have just adduced could be multiplied. What such cases bring to the fore are two (largely implicit) assumptions that characterize much (though certainly not all) of the recent discussion among philosophers working in the foundations of ethics. The first assumption is that among the various normative features the world may contain, there is something especially objectionable about the existence of moral features. (One can find a good many books in contemporary Anglo-American philosophy arguing for the thesis that there are no robust moral truths. One is hard-pressed to find, by contrast, books dedicated to arguing that there are no robust aesthetic or epistemic truths.[6]) The second assumption is that the arguments offered against the existence of robust moral facts (or truths) do not have particularly objectionable consequences for other normative domains such as the epistemic domain. I believe both these assumptions are mistaken. The overarching aim of this book is to explain why.

To state the argument I want to develop more precisely, it will be helpful to offer a somewhat more exact account of some of the terminology that to this point I have employed freely. Suppose we assume that within the broadly normative domain there are different subcategories, among which are the moral and epistemic domains. (I assume that these domains are not identical; if they are, my argument will be considerably simplified. Later I shall have more to say about how we might demarcate them.) Suppose we assume, moreover, that among the putative denizens of these respective domains are moral and epistemic facts (or as I shall say in Chapters 1 and 2 'irreducible' moral and epistemic facts. This qualification needn't concern

---

[6] I use the term 'robust' to contrast with the expression 'minimalist', as it was used earlier to describe Wright's views. For more on the qualification, see Chapter 6. Some of the more prominent attempts to argue that there are no robust moral facts include Blackburn (1984), (1993), and (1998), Gibbard (1990), Joyce (2001), Mackie (1977), and Timmons (1999).

us here). We can think of entities of these sorts as having two central characteristics.

In the first place, moral and epistemic facts are what are represented by true moral and epistemic claims. The true moral claim that Sam's treatment of Margaret is wrong, for example, represents the moral fact *that Sam's treatment of Margaret is wrong*. Likewise, the true epistemic claim that engaging in a particular plan or inquiry is manifestly irrational represents the epistemic fact *that engaging in this plan of inquiry is manifestly irrational*. In the second place, if facts of either sort exist, then at least some such facts are, imply, or indicate categorical reasons for agents to behave in certain ways. To stay with our examples, according to the present understanding of moral and epistemic facts, the fact *that Sam's treatment of Margaret is wrong* implies that there is a moral reason to disapprove of Sam's behavior that applies to properly situated agents, regardless of the desires, projects, or concerns those agents may have. Similarly, the fact *that engaging in a particular plan of inquiry is manifestly irrational* implies that there is an epistemic reason not to engage in that particular plan of inquiry that applies to properly situated agents, regardless of the cares, projects, or concerns such agents may have.[7] Fundamental to what I call 'paradigmatic' moral and epistemic realism is the claim that moral and epistemic facts thus understood exist. Definitive of paradigmatic forms of moral and epistemic antirealism, as I understand these views, is the denial that moral and epistemic facts thus understood exist.

The core argument I will develop in what follows can be stated simply enough. It runs thus:

(1) If moral facts do not exist, then epistemic facts do not exist.
(2) Epistemic facts exist.
(3) So, moral facts exist.
(4) If moral facts exist, then moral realism is true.
(5) So, moral realism is true.

If the core argument is on-target, there is nothing particularly objectionable about moral facts; epistemic facts, if they exist, are no less objectionable

---

[7] In what follows, I remain neutral on the issue of whether these facts directly imply such reasons or do so only because they fall under more general bridge principles to the effect that 'if engaging in a plan of inquiry is manifestly irrational in circumstances of type C and someone is in C, then that person has epistemic reason not to engage in that plan of inquiry in C'. For a defense of the former view, *see* Thomson (1990), Introduction.

than moral facts. (To use a phrase of Bernard Williams's: morality may be a peculiar institution, but is not more so than epistemology.) And contrary to a widespread assumption embedded in much of the work in contemporary ethical theory, the arguments ordinarily offered for moral antirealism, if sound, have some fairly sweeping results that are not innocuous, but are deeply theoretically problematic.[8] In any event, the real work lies not with simply formulating the core argument, but in arguing for its three premises. I divide this work as follows.

Having offered an account of what I mean by the phrase 'moral realism of a paradigmatic sort' in the first chapter, I then develop a two-stage argument for the core argument's first premise. The development of the argument's first stage takes place in Chapter 2. My aim in this chapter is to lay the conceptual groundwork for the argument's second stage (and, indeed argumentation subsequent to this) by highlighting several salient respects in which putative moral and epistemic facts are similar. At the same time, I want to respond to the worry that facts of both sorts are sufficiently disanalogous that any attempt to argue for the core argument's first premise is doomed to fail. In this discussion, I emphasize that the similarities between moral and epistemic facts are not limited to certain ways in which facts of both sorts resemble one another in certain theoretically interesting respects. Moral and epistemic facts, I contend, also bear theoretically interesting relations to one another other than resemblance, such as implying and presupposing each other. To employ the metaphor that figures in the title of this book, the moral and epistemic domains are like a web with their denizens paralleling, intertwining with, and mutually supporting one another in a variety of theoretically interesting ways. As I argue later, it is this phenomenon of both domains being entangled in various manners that makes it difficult, if not impossible, to excise certain strands of the web while leaving the others intact.

The second and principal stage of the argument for the core argument's first premise occurs in Chapter 3. In this chapter, I maintain that there is a class of standard objections ordinarily leveled against the claim that moral facts exist. These objections purport to establish that were moral facts to exist, then they would display what I call the 'objectionable

---

[8] When suitably modified, would these arguments have implications for domains other than epistemology such as aesthetics or practical rationality? Perhaps so. But I won't pursue the issue here.

features'—properties such as *being intrinsically motivating, being categorically reason-giving, being explanatorily idle*, and so forth. Were the standard objections to establish this, I contend, then, when suitably modified, they would also establish that were epistemic facts to exist, then they too would exhibit the objectionable features. These two claims allow us to formulate a direct argument for the core argument's first premise, which goes like this: If moral facts do not exist, then presumably this is simply because they would display the objectionable features. But there is nothing about moral facts in particular that makes their having these features objectionable; it is the character of the *features themselves* that renders moral facts problematic. Accordingly, we can affirm:

If moral facts do not exist, then nothing has the objectionable features.

However, if epistemic facts exist, then there is something that has the objectionable features. Or, otherwise put:

If nothing has the objectionable features, then epistemic facts do not exist.

From this it follows that the core argument's first premise is true:

(1) If moral facts do not exist, then epistemic facts do not exist.

If what I contend in this chapter is on the right lines, then we should accept the core argument's first premise. Having argued for this claim, Chapters 4, 5, 6, and 7 press the case that we have strong reason to believe that epistemic facts exist. My argument for this claim is one from elimination. I claim that, if we model epistemic antirealist views on the dominant moral antirealist positions, we can divide views of the former sort into three types: epistemic nihilist, epistemic expressivist, and epistemic reductionist positions, respectively. Antirealist views of all three types, I contend, encounter serious difficulties. In short, I contend that views of the first two types imply a sweeping version of epistemological skepticism according to which there is no epistemic reason to believe anything, whereas views of the latter sort fail to capture some theoretically entrenched and highly plausible positions regarding the nature of epistemic merits. If the argument in these chapters is correct, then there is at least a prima facie case that we ought to accept the core argument's second premise or the claim that epistemic facts exist.

In the final chapter—Chapter 8—I attempt to strengthen the argument by addressing three objections that might be raised against what I say in the preceding chapters. The first objection is directed toward the core argument's first premise. It maintains that the existence of epistemic facts should lead us to believe not that moral facts exist, but that the first premise of the core argument is false. The second objection concerns the core argument's second premise. It states that, even if the arguments in Chapters 4 through 7 are sound, we do not have better reason than not to believe that epistemic facts exist. Finally, the third objection rejects the core argument's fourth premise. It asserts that, even if it is true that moral facts exist, we cannot conclude that moral realism is true, for the latter position is also composed of claims regarding the nature of moral discourse and truth. I contend that these objections can be answered. And, thus, I conclude that we should accept both the claims that moral facts exist and that moral realism is true.

II. Assumptions

The details of the argumentation, as they say, come later. However, I should at this point highlight two features of these details. First, although the argument I develop is intended to establish that moral realism is true, my attention in the bulk of this book is focused primarily not on moral realism, but on the claim that epistemic facts exist. So, there is a sense in which much of the subsequent discussion is primarily dedicated not to issues in metaethics, but to issues in the foundations of epistemology. Indeed, since epistemic antirealist views have generally not been developed at all by philosophers, much of the subsequent discussion is dedicated to investigating issues in the foundations of epistemology that have been by and large left unexplored. And, second, although I view what follows as being an argument for, and not merely a defense of moral realism, it should be noted that the strategy I will employ, especially in Chapters 4 through 7, where I argue that we should reject epistemic antirealism, is thoroughly polemical and defensive in character. Indeed, most of the argumentation in these chapters is geared to highlight the weak points of epistemic antirealist views, thereby throwing epistemic and moral realism in a positive light vis-à-vis their competitors. I feel somewhat apologetic about proceeding thus, but I believe there is no alternative to employing a strategy such as this. In fact, in seems to me that explicitly acknowledging the defensive character of some of the subsequent argumentation can help us to see an important methodological assumption implicit in the ensuing discussion.

The assumption to which I refer is probably best approached by considering a different branch of the realist/antirealist debate, viz., that between realists and antirealists regarding the external world. Realists regarding the external world—roughly, those who believe that the external world of mountains, fish, and the like exists independent of our cognitive activity—frequently point out that theirs is a position we do not generally argue ourselves to, but is one that we ordinarily take for granted in our ordinary doings and believings.[9] Or, if we distinguish between realism about the external world itself and a realist conception of the world—roughly, a way in which ordinary agents conceive of the external world that appears to commit them to the existence of entities such as mountains and fish realistically understood—realists are best understood as saying this: A realist conception of the world is something that, all else being equal, ordinary mature human agents whose cognitive faculties are functioning adequately in a world such as ours take for granted in their everyday doings and believings. According to the realists, so deeply ingressed is this way of viewing reality in our shared world picture, that it is difficult to find propositions more obvious than those constitutive of realism itself that can be employed to formulate a non-question-begging argument in favor of it. This, so realists aver, is why positive arguments for realism regarding the external world are so difficult to come by. And it is also why, when arguments are offered for realism, they generally have the form of teasing out the implausible implications of its rivals rather than citing the theoretically positive characteristics of realism itself.

Realists about moral and epistemic features also point out that theirs is a position that we generally do not argue ourselves to, but is one that we generally take for granted in our ordinary doings and believings.[10] Or, if we distinguish between a realist position regarding moral and

---

[9] See, for example, Searle (1995), Ch. 8.

[10] See, for example, Brink (1989), 23 ff., McNaughton (1988), Ch. 3, and Nagel (1986), 143–44. I should note, however, that these authors are concerned only with moral realism and understand this view somewhat differently than I do.

epistemic features and a realist conception of putative moral and epistemic features—roughly, a way in which ordinary agents conceive of the world that appears to commit them to the existence of such features realistically understood—we can interpret realists as saying at least the following: A realist conception of moral and epistemic features is something that, all else being equal, ordinary mature human agents whose cognitive faculties are functioning adequately in a world such as ours take for granted in their everyday doings and believings. It is because this way of viewing things is rather firmly entrenched in our shared world picture that it is difficult to formulate arguments for moral or epistemic realism that appeal to premises more obvious than the positions themselves. (Imagine trying to make sense of our ordinary moral and epistemic practices while also assuming that those who sincerely engage in these practices do not think that there are moral or epistemic reasons or that such reasons can be shrugged off if we fail to have the appropriate desires.) This, or so it is suggested, is why positive arguments for realism regarding moral and epistemic facts are also difficult to come by. And it is also why, when arguments are offered for moral and epistemic realism, they generally have the form of eliciting the implausible implications of their rivals rather than citing the theoretically positive characteristics of the realist views themselves.

I want to suggest, then, that what accounts for the largely defensive character of the subsequent argument for moral realism is also what accounts for the largely defensive character of the arguments for realism regarding the external world. Given the depth to which a realist conception of the moral and epistemic realms is entrenched in what John Searle calls 'the Background', it is extraordinarily challenging to find other ways to argue for such views in a non-question-begging fashion.

To this broadly methodological point, let me add three caveats. (I shall have more to say about such matters in Chapters 1 and 2.)

First, while what I have just said about a realist conception of the moral and epistemic domains may be controversial in some contexts, I judge it not to be in the context of the present discussion among philosophers in the Anglo-American analytic tradition regarding the foundations of ethics and epistemology. Indeed, I believe that nearly all the prominent antirealist views presently on offer in contemporary Anglo-American metaethics would accept the claim that ordinary thinking is by and large realist in cast and that an adequate moral theory should do its best to preserve these appearances. (One thinks especially of Simon Blackburn's 'quasi-realist' view in this regard.) At any rate, if there are positions that deny what I have said about the realist-seeming appearances of ordinary ethical and epistemic thought—and I deem there are, though I take them not to be the prominent positions in Anglo-American metaethics—I will on this occasion not be concerned with them. I realize that failing to consider such positions is a limitation of the present discussion. Nevertheless, I believe that the most fruitful way to carry on a discussion concerning moral and epistemic objectivity is to engage with positions that share some important methodological assumptions. And, quite frankly, I am not sure what to say in response to more radical versions of moral and epistemic antirealism that deny either that ordinary moral and epistemic discourse and practice is realist in appearance or the claim that an adequate theory should try to preserve these appearances. Where could one gain a theoretical foothold in such a discussion?

The second qualification I would like to make is this: to claim that a realist conception of entities of some kind is part of a widely shared world picture is not thereby to deny that such a conception may be deeply mistaken. So, I do not assume at the outset of theorizing that a realist conception of the moral and epistemic domains is *true*. I assume only that, when we theorize about the moral and epistemic domains, we begin by taking the appearances seriously and ascertain whether they can withstand the various types of worries—some very substantial in nature—we may have about their veracity.

And, finally, to claim that ordinary moral and epistemic thought appears to be realist in cast is not thereby to imply that such thought commits ordinary agents to the conviction that there are moral or epistemic facts realistically understood. The appearances may, after all, be just that: mere appearances that commit ordinary agents to nothing that could be adequately characterized as objective values. Indeed, if I understand aright the character of the most sophisticated versions of contemporary moral antirealism, their aim is to concede the realist-looking appearances of ordinary moral thought, but to deny that these appearances commit ordinary agents to thinking there are moral facts realistically understood. Much of the argument in Chapters 5 through 7 is concerned with arguing that, in the realm of epistemology, this is an unstable view.

In sum: The subsequent argument is predicated on the assumptions that ordinary moral and epistemic thought and discourse are by and large realist-seeming and that any adequate moral theory ought to preserve these appearances as best as possible. These are fairly conservative-looking assumptions. Nor are they the only such assumptions I shall make. Let me close this section by noting four other conservative-looking claims that my discussion will presuppose, but not defend in any detail.

I will assume, in the first place, that a fairly traditional, rich ontological scheme is correct. I assume, then, that there are entities such as properties, propositions, states of affairs, and facts. With an exception that I will note in a moment, the subsequent discussion is not predicated upon any particular understanding of the nature of these entities. It may be, as Roderick Chisholm thought at one point, that facts and propositions are simply states of affairs, the latter being abstract objects of a type.[11] Or it may be that properties are sets of resembling tropes (i.e. property instances), as some nominalists suggest. I assume only that outright nihilism regarding entities of any of these types and reductionist views that claim that they are merely figures of speech are false. (If one is squeamish about this assumption, one can view the conclusion of the core argument as being implicitly hedged in the following way: General misgivings about facts aside, moral realism is true.[12])

The exception to this policy of neutrality regards what I will assume about moral propositions. I assume that there are three main ways in which a moral realist can plausibly think of the class of moral propositions. This class can be understood as being comprised of only broadly Fregean propositions (according to which propositions are complexes of objective ways of conceiving objects and properties), only broadly Russellian propositions (according to which propositions are complexes that include concrete individuals such as persons), or a combination of Fregean and Russellian propositions. The assumption I shall make is that at least some moral propositions are of the Fregean variety. My reasons for assuming this are two. First, I find it very plausible to assume that thoughts incorporate ways of thinking about entities, while (many) facts do not—the latter being constituted not by concepts, but by 'worldly' objects and properties. If Russelian propositions are facts, then at least some thoughts are going to be

---

[11] See Chisholm (1977).   [12] Here I borrow from Enoch (2003), 11.

too fine-grained to be plausible candidates for being facts. Second, a central rationale in favor of believing that there are Russellian propositions is rooted in an allegiance to a robust externalist view of mental content according to which worldly facts and their concrete constituents are the contents of our thoughts. But, even if sound, arguments for externalist views of this kind imply only that thoughts that are completely expressible with proper names, demonstratives, and natural-kind terms count as 'external' content. Since, however, not all moral propositions are completely expressible in such terms, not all moral propositions are of the Russellian variety. And, on the assumption that propositions are either Fregean or Russellian, it follows that, if there are any moral propositions, then some of them are Fregean propositions.[13]

The second conservative-looking assumption I shall make is that the concept of being is univocal and that this concept is captured by the existential quantifier in formal logic. So, when I claim that there are moral facts, I mean to say that such entities exist in the same sense of 'exist' as do mountains or persons. (Of course I would say these things have drastically different natures, but that is a different issue.) To put the matter in a broadly Fregean vein, to say that there are moral facts is to say something very much like the number of moral facts is greater than one.[14] I assume, then, that there are not different types of 'being' that an entity might have, mountains having one sort and moral facts having another. Accordingly, I find myself disagreeing with philosophers such as Hilary Putnam (whose views in ethics I generally find very congenial) who claim that moral facts exist, but not in the broadly Fregean sense of 'exist' just specified.[15] I am prepared to agree that Putnam says something true when he argues that we can see that we needn't posit entities such as mathematical objects or moral

[13]   By assuming that some moral propositions are Fregean, I do not mean to minimize the importance of how one thinks of the nature of propositions, for how one thinks of propositions will have a direct bearing on how one views the nature of facts, truth, and representation. For example, if propositions are Russellian, it is very plausible to believe that true propositions are identical with facts. And if true propositions are identical with facts, it is very plausible to believe that propositions don't correspond with facts, but are identical with them. It follows from this, however, that it is likely that some form of the 'identity' theory of truth is correct. Finally, if true propositions are identical with facts, it is difficult to see in what sense propositions represent facts; rather, propositions look to be what are represented. I have been helped here by David (2001a).

[14]   Here I echo van Inwagen (2001), Part 1.

[15]   See Putnam (2002), Ch. 2 and (2004). I should emphasize that in earlier work, Putnam has defended an argument similar to that which I defend in this book. See, for example, Putnam (1987), Lecture IV and (1990), Ch. 9.

facts in the sense that realists think of them because, were such objects to cease to exist, our mathematical or moral practices would not work one bit less well.[16] But I think that such a claim is true only in the sense that a claim such as 'Since a God who could actualize impossibilities is more powerful than one who cannot, then God must be able to actualize impossibilities' is true. Such claims are true only because their antecedents are necessarily false.

Third, I will make two assumptions regarding the nature of the truth property. In the first place, I assume that although truth is a property, it is not a scheme-relative property. Accordingly, I assume that if some moral propositions are true, then they are not true relative to some conceptual scheme. (Likewise, I assume that if there exist moral facts, then they do not exist relative to some conceptual scheme.) I do not deny, incidentally, that some moral propositions may be true *within* some conceptual scheme; that is, I do not deny that propositions may be such that only within some conceptual scheme are there the concepts that constitute that proposition. But I deny that this implies that, if any such proposition is true, then it should be analyzed as having the logical form of 'p is true relative to scheme C'. Rather, any such proposition, I submit, is true *überhaupt*.

In the second place, I shall assume that epistemic conceptions of truth are false. That is to say, I will assume that a proposition's being true does not consist in its having some sort of exalted epistemic status such as being ideally justifiable or part of an ideally coherent system of propositions. I believe this assumption would be largely unremarkable if it were not for the fact that some philosophers seem to believe that, if moral propositions are true, then they are true in an epistemic sense. For example, Crispin Wright maintains that 'there seems no sense to be attached to the idea that ... the moral significance of an act might lie beyond human recognition'.[17] It follows from this, says Wright, that 'a presumption is established that moral ... truth can be taken as [a] species of superassertibility'.[18] And by saying this, Wright means to claim that 'the morally true is that which can be morally justified and which then retains that justification no matter how refined or extensive an additional consideration is given to the matter'.[19]

---

[16] See Putnam (2002), 17. Here Putnam's claim concerns mathematical objects. But the lesson is extended to ethical objects in Putnam (2004).

[17] Wright (1992), 58.   [18] Ibid., 60.   [19] Wright (1995), 218.

I find this suggestion perplexing, mostly because I fail to see what is nonsensical about assuming that some domains of moral truth might lie beyond human recognition. Indeed, if one takes seriously the idea that human persons are endowed with cognitive capacities that are limited in certain fundamental ways, it is not very hard to accept that there might be realms of value that are simply inaccessible to human persons no matter how much information is available.[20] Moreover, it is difficult to see why, if moral reality is not evidence-transcendent, this creates a presumption in favor of the claim that a moral proposition's being true *consists* in its being superassertible. One reason for thinking that the connection between evidence transcendence and superassertibility cannot be that tight is the following: The claim that some realms of fact cannot outstrip our cognitive capacities is perfectly compatible with a robust correspondence theory of truth, according to which truth consists in a proposition's corresponding to a correlative fact. So, as far as moral realism is concerned, it may be that moral facts are always, in principle, accessible to us.[21] If they were, this would be an interesting feature of the nature of moral facts, but it would not have any implication for that in which the truth of moral propositions consists.

Finally, I shall assume that the questions 'Do moral facts exist?' and 'Do we have adequate reason to be moral?' are different, and that an adequate answer to the first needn't supply an adequate answer to the second. I acknowledge that if moral realism were unable to offer an adequate answer to the second question, this would be a problem for the view. However, I see no reason why it cannot. I find myself, then, disagreeing with a Kantian such as Christine Korsgaard when she claims that, by appealing to the existence of 'intrinsically normative entities', realists render themselves unable to address adequately what she calls 'the normative question' or the question of what reasons we have to be moral. As Korsgaard writes:

And that is the problem with realism: it refuses to answer the normative question. It is a way of saying it cannot be done. ... The metaphysical view that intrinsically

[20] McGinn (1993) develops this theme at length. Of course if a position such as theism were true, it would not be at all surprising that there are realms of value—say, those contained in the mind of God—that are inaccessible to human agents.

[21] Foot (2002a), 58, appears to claim that such a view is incompatible with moral realism. David Brink's official characterization of moral realism in Brink (1989), 17, strongly suggests that the realist must reject this view too. But I think that a closer look at Brink's position reveals that he means to say something different.

normative entities or properties exist must be *supported by* our confidence that we really do have obligations. It is because we are confident that obligation is real that we are prepared to believe in the existence of some sort of objective values. But for that very reason the appeal to the existence of objective values cannot be used to support our confidence. And the normative question arises when our confidence has been shaken, whether by philosophy or by the exigencies of life. So realism cannot answer the normative question.[22]

As I understand it, this passage says that the realist position is vitiated by an objectionable type of explanatory circularity. In particular, the realist's claim *that there are intrinsically normative entities* is evidentially supported by the realist's antecedent conviction that there are such entities. But if this is true, then the claim *that there are intrinsically normative entities* cannot evidentially support the realist's belief that there are any such entities. (I assume that the support relation to which Korsgaard refers is evidential. If it isn't, it is hard to see how the ostensible circularity could be objectionable.[23])

I think that what Korsgaard says about the realist position in this passage is not true. This is in large part because it is difficult to see why realists 'must' be committed to the type of explanatory circularity on which Korsgaard appears to have her eye.[24] Korsgaard notes that realists such as Thomas Nagel don't seem to be much concerned to answer the normative question and simply claim that it is self-evident that there are objective moral reasons.[25] In my estimation, however, it would be very uncharitable to say that because some realists say such things they are thereby committed to the claim that their belief *that it is true that there are moral reasons* is evidence in favor of there being moral reasons. To make a second-order epistemological claim about a moral proposition—for example, that an action's causing

---

[22] Korsgaard (1996), 39–40. What Korsgaard calls 'realism' here is only one version of the view that I call 'realism.'

[23] The passage I have quoted can be read in such a way that Korsgaard intends to give a psychological explanation of why the realist accepts the view that there are objective values. In this case, we're told that the explanation of why the realist believes *that there are intrinsically normative entities* is that she is confident that there are such entities. This doesn't seem right for two reasons, however. Believing a proposition arguably just is a matter of having a certain degree of confidence in its truth. So, it can't be that an agent's having a high degree of confidence in a proposition psychologically *explains* why she believes that proposition. Moreover, even if this psychological observation were true, it would not be terribly interesting for our purposes. It doesn't give us any reason to believe that the realist position is vitiated by any type of objectionable circularity.

[24] Actually, I don't think the circularity is even objectionable. See Cuneo (unpublished). FitzPatrick (2005) offers a detailed response to Korsgaard's concerns regarding moral realism.

[25] See Nagel (1986), 159–60.

gratuitous pain provides a reason not to perform it is self-evident—does not perforce commit the agent who makes this claim to the view that her *taking* that proposition to have this epistemic status is evidence in favor of its being true. That would be like saying that an agent's claim that a simple arithmetical proposition is self-evident thereby commits that agent to the view that her belief that that proposition is self-evident is evidence in favor of that proposition's being true.

At any rate, so ends the list of conservative-looking assumptions I shall make in what follows. If one situates the type of moral realist view I wish to defend within the history of western philosophy, I suppose it wouldn't be inaccurate to say that these conservative-looking assumptions are being employed to defend a fairly conservative-looking position. But in moral philosophy a great deal has changed in the last one hundred years, as moral antirealist views have been increasingly defended with zeal and ingenuity. These changes make it a lively and interesting period to work on the foundations of ethics. They also can make it seem as if a moral realist view such as the one I will develop in this book is anything but philosophical orthodoxy.

III. Acknowledgments

I began work on this book in 2001 while a research fellow at the Vrije Universiteit in Amsterdam. At the Vrije, I have numerous people to thank, including Martijn Blaauw, Wim DeJong, Ron Rood, Sabine Roeser, Mariëtte Williamson, and, especially, René van Woudenberg, for their comments on early drafts of some of the material in this book. I also wish to thank the Rev. Hans Schouten, who hosted our family at his house during our second year in the Netherlands.

In the United States, I have my former colleagues at Seattle Pacific University, Phil Goggans, Ken Himma, Pat McDonald, and, in particular, Steve Layman, to thank for their helpful input into this project. I am also pleased to acknowledge my colleagues at Calvin College, David Billings, Kelly Clark, Kevin Corcoran, Rebecca Konyndyk DeYoung, Ruth Groenhout, Matt Halteman, Lee Hardy, Greg Mellema, Del Ratzsch, Jamie Smith, C. J. Van Dyke, and Steve Wykstra, for their feedback on parts of this book, and for making our department a congenial environment in which to do philosophy. In one way or another, Paul Bloomfield, Todd Buras, Chris Eberle, Steve Finlay, Chris Gowans, John Hare, Tom Kennedy, Ben Lipscomb, Ryan Nichols, Nathan Nobis, Sarah Stroud, Nick Wolterstorff, Linda Zagzebski, and Nick Zangwill were kind enough to offer help with material that found its way into the content of this book. David Enoch, John Greco, Brad Majors, Mark Murphy, Russ Shafer-Landau, Christian Miller, Pekka Väyrynen, and Fritz Warfield were generous with their time, offering comments on either a complete draft of the book or large sections thereof. Two anonymous referees for Oxford University Press also provided penetrating feedback on the book, prompting numerous changes. Finally, two outstanding Calvin undergraduates, Josh Armstrong and Michael Schwiegger, provided comments on an entire draft of the book. Of these people, I should make special mention of Russ Shafer-Landau in particular for his friendship, encouragement, and philosophical help.

Two institutions, the Vrije Universiteit and Calvin College (the latter of which granted a course reduction during the fall of 2004), also provided support that has been invaluable to this project. In particular, I would like to thank Jim Bratt at the Calvin Center for Christian Scholarship. When I requested help to proofread this manuscript in its final stages, Jim was kind enough to provide the funds to make it possible. Luke Reinsma generously provided that help.

Finally, I wish to express my thanks to the editors at Oxford University Press, Peter Momtchiloff and Catherine Berry. They have been a delight to work with.

Writing a book is often a solitary affair in which one is for many hours tucked away in an office or immobile at the keyboard. It can be made considerably less so, however, by the presence of small children whirring around one's feet while working! For my active and curious daughters—Janina, Olivia, and Esther—and, especially, my wife Kari Anne (the most active of us all), I am immensely grateful. They humor a father and husband frequently distracted from the cares of the ordinary day.

1

Moral Realism of a Paradigmatic Sort

In the opening pages of *Truth and Objectivity*, Crispin Wright says that:

if there ever was a consensus of understanding about 'realism', as a philosophical term of art, it has undoubtedly been fragmented by the pressures exerted by the various debates—so much so that a philosopher who asserts that she is a realist about theoretical science, for example, or ethics, has probably, for most philosophical audiences, accomplished little more than to clear her throat.[1]

Hyperbole aside, I believe that what Wright says here is fundamentally correct. A quick glance at the recent literature in moral philosophy reveals that 'moral realism' comes in a dizzying array of guises. Some philosophers characterize realism as the view that some of our moral beliefs are true; others maintain that it is the position that there are moral facts. Some claim that realism is simply the view that moral propositions are true independent of our best evidence for them; others maintain that it is the position that moral propositions are true independent of our ability to assign truth conditions to them. Some philosophers claim that realism is committed to the thesis that entities have moral properties independent of facts about the attitudes of moral agents; others maintain that realists hold that entities have moral properties independent of persons responding to those entities. And to this we could add still other ways of characterizing the view. Given the present state of disagreement, I believe that it would be fruitless to sift through these various proposals in the hope of fixing upon a more nearly adequate characterization of moral realism. So, I shall take a different route. This route consists in limning the contours of the view I will defend in the

[1] Wright (1992), 1.

remainder of this book—a view I call 'moral realism of a paradigmatic sort'. The sense in which this view is a paradigmatic realist view, I hope, should emerge soon enough. But for present purposes we can understand it to be composed of three theses: first, a thesis about the nature of moral discourse; second, a thesis about the truth of moral claims; and, third, a thesis about the nature of moral facts. In the next chapter, I offer a framework for developing a more specific version of this type of position. My present aim, however, is to develop the view broadly construed.

My discussion in this chapter has two parts. In the first part, I present the lineaments of paradigmatic moral realism, unpacking each of its three components. In the second (and considerably shorter) part, I explain why this view is not committed to other claims often attributed to moral realists, such as the claim that moral facts are mind-independent.

I. The speech act thesis

Perhaps the only feature common to those views that have flown under the banner of moral realism is 'moral cognitivism' or the claim that moral discourse is assertoric. Accordingly, I shall assume that constitutive of moral realism of a paradigmatic sort is:

The Moral Realist's Speech Act Thesis: Some moral discourse is assertoric.

Since I intend the speech act thesis to be understood in a specific way, I need to introduce some terminology that will help us to capture its sense.

Consider an atomic sentence of the form 'a is F'. Suppose we call the general predicate term 'F' and the singular term 'a' contained in this sentence 'simple' terms (because they are not compound).[2] Suppose we also assume that general predicative terms function to pick out properties, while singular terms stand for particular objects. (I will assume that the class of particular objects does not include abstracta such as properties and sets, but only their non-abstract tokens or members.) Call any property picked out by such a general predicative term a 'simple property' and any object

---

[2] In restricting the discussion to simple or non-compound terms, I wish to avoid the consequence that a position satisfies the realist claim that some predicative moral discourse is true in the realist sense simply in virtue of the fact that that discourse expresses analytic propositions such as *that Smith's murder of Jones is either morally permissible or not morally permissible.*

denoted by such a singular term a 'particular object'. Given an atomic claim 'a is F', then, the role of the predicate term 'F' is to pick out the simple property *being F* or the *F-ness* of some particular object *a*.

A 'moral sentence', as I use the expression, is a sentence whose surface logical form is that of either (i) predicating a simple moral property of a particular or (ii) a universal generalization to the effect that, if something has a given feature, then it has a simple moral property. So, for example, 'Smith is kind' and 'Stealing money from the poor is wrong' are examples of moral sentences as I am thinking of them.[3] For ease of reference, call sentences of the first type 'predicative moral sentences' and those of the latter type 'general moral sentences'. 'Moral discourse', in its present usage, is simply discourse that consists only in the sincere utterance of moral sentences.

A 'moral claim' (or 'judgment'), as I shall use the phrase, is whatever mental state that is expressed by the sincere utterance of a moral sentence. A 'moral proposition', accordingly, is the content (or, if you like, the object) of a moral claim that purports (in some cases at least) to represent a moral fact. (I'll have more to say about moral facts in a moment.) Moral propositions can be divided into two types. As I will think of them, 'predicative moral propositions' are those whose logical form corresponds to the (surface) semantic components of predicative moral sentences. *That Smith is kind* is an example of a predicative moral proposition. According to a fairly traditional analysis, the proposition can be thought of as being composed of Smith (or the individual concept of Smith) and the property of *being kind* bound together by the 'predicative tie'.[4] By contrast, 'general moral propositions' are those whose logical form corresponds to the (surface) semantic components of general moral sentences. So, for example, *that stealing money from the poor is wrong* is a case of a general moral proposition. One might think of it as being a distributive function that specifies that any token of the act-type *stealing money from the poor* is bound together by the predicative tie to the property *being wrong*. That said, we can now identify

---

[3] Two points: First, for the sake of manageability, I will not be concerned with discourse that consists in the utterance of moral sentences that have the logical form of so-called impredicative existential statements (e.g. 'It is not the case that Smith's murder of Jones is wrong') or negative generalizations (e.g. 'No murder is wrong'). Second, while I distinguish between predicative and general moral sentences, there are views according to which sentences of the latter type are a species of sentences of the former type (see Fantl [2006]). I have no objection to this way of viewing things.

[4] For more on the nature of this correspondence, see Alston (2000), 118.

what assertoric moral discourse is. As I shall define it, a speech act counts as an instance of assertoric moral discourse if and only if it consists in the explicit presentation of a moral proposition by way of uttering a correlative moral sentence.[5]

Putting this together, the speech act thesis tells us that moral discourse consists only in the sincere utterance of moral sentences and that at least one such sentence is used explicitly to present a moral proposition.

To this let me now add several clarifications.

First, I do not have any suggestions for how we might offer precise boundaries for what counts as genuinely 'moral' discourse. Accordingly, I will simply assume that there is a stock of simple predicative expressions that (in a wide range of common usage) we commonly recognize as moral. For example, I assume that evaluative expressions such as 'is wrong', 'is just', 'is kind', 'is vicious', 'is evil' and deontic expressions such as 'is (morally) forbidden', 'is (morally) required', 'is (morally) obligatory', or 'is a (moral) reason' are good examples of simple predicative moral expressions. As such, I assume that discourse that consists only in the sincere utterance of well-formed predicative or general sentences that contain such predicative expressions counts as moral discourse.

Second, I do not have any suggestions as to what extent moral discourse is assertoric. I assume only that the speech act thesis is best interpreted as implying that ordinary moral discourse is such that its participants commonly use moral sentences to assert moral propositions. However, I do not take this to imply that, were the speech act thesis true, moral sentences would be ordinarily used merely to assert moral propositions. Perhaps, as some philosophers have claimed, moral sentences are typically used both to assert moral propositions and to express pro or con attitudes of various kinds.[6]

Third, I do not have any suggestions as to what range of speech acts counts as moral assertions. I assume only that genuinely assertoric moral discourse can take the form of informing, alleging, reporting,

---

[5] Here I draw upon the account of assertion that Alston (2000), Ch. 5, defends. Let me note that I regard this account of assertion as only an approximation of a more nearly correct account. It may be, for example, that there are cases of assertoric moral discourse that do not consist in a moral proposition's being explicitly presented (e.g. cases in which one conversationally implies a moral proposition).

[6] I assume that the attitudes in question are not ones with moral propositional content. See Ross (1939), Copp (2001), and Hare (2001), who defend views in which moral discourse ordinarily has both an assertoric and expressive function.

insisting, agreeing, and so forth. It follows that, while the speech act thesis can be fairly characterized as a 'descriptivist' account of moral discourse, this label needs to be understood aright. To say that the view is descriptivist is not thereby to claim that moral discourse consists primarily in the description of moral facts (say, in the way one might describe an antique vase to a friend), but only that it purports to represent such facts.[7]

Fourth, and finally, I do not have any suggestions for what an informative analysis of representing moral facts consists in. I assume only that when the realist claims that moral claims (or their content) represent(s) moral reality, representation is to be understood as a robust 'aboutness' relation that obtains between the claim (or its content) and moral facts.[8]

These clarifications having been made, let me now highlight two implications of the speech act thesis that are important for our purposes. The first implication is that the speech act thesis entails that so-called nondescriptivist or expressivist views are not moral realist positions. In its paradigmatic form, expressivism tells us that, although moral sentences appear as if they are used to express moral propositions, they do not. Rather, their primary function is to express 'sentiments' or 'attitudes' toward non-moral states of affairs or objects. For example, according to expressivists, while the sentence 'murder is wrong' may appear in the ordinary case to express the proposition *that murder is wrong*, it does not express any moral proposition. Rather, its primary function is to express an attitude of disapproval toward killings of a certain type or to endorse norms that prohibit killings of that type.

The second implication is that so-called deflationary accounts of moral discourse are not compatible with the realist's speech act thesis. For present purposes, we can understand 'assertoric deflationism' to be comprised of the following two claims: First, a sentence p is assertible if p displays syntax of such a type that it fulfills certain grammatical and logical roles—roles such

---

[7] The exact sense of 'purports', as it is used here and in similar contexts, is difficult to identify. For more on the matter, see Quine (1960) and Wolterstorff (1970), Ch. 2.

[8] I'll have more to say about what distinguishes robust from minimalist or deflationary accounts of representation in Chapter 6. Also, in what follows, I will regularly speak of *claims* representing reality. I intend this to be a less than precise way of saying that claims, or their contents, or the sentences that express this content represent reality.

as embedding in conditional, propositional attitude, and truth ascription contexts; and, second, the use of p is subject to communal standards of 'discipline' according to which it is deemed appropriate or inappropriate in one or another way. To fill this out a bit more, suppose 'p' stands for the sentence 'It is wrong to steal'. According to assertoric deflationism, if we can appropriately say such things as, 'If it is wrong to steal, then John ought not to steal', 'I believe that it is wrong to steal', and 'It is true that it is wrong to steal', then p is assertible. Nothing more is needed.

In Chapter 6, I will have more to say about this position. For now, let me indicate why it falls afoul of the realist's speech act thesis.

As I have formulated it, the realist's speech act thesis tells us that some moral discourse is assertoric. I have also claimed that assertoric discourse is to be understood in a fairly robust sense; when a person asserts a proposition, a person thereby commits himself to the world being as that proposition says it is. It is compatible with assertoric deflationism, however, that no moral discourse is assertoric in this sense. Indeed, it is possible according to the deflationary view that a sentence-type such as:

'Socrates is just'

is always used merely to express the attitude:

Yes! to Socrates.

The first sentence has the right syntax to be minimally assertoric. And we may suppose that its use is governed by standards of communal discipline. However, *what* this sentence expresses is not a proposition. In uttering it, a person does not thereby express anything that is truth-evaluable, nor does that person purport to predicate a moral property of anything. It follows that assertoric deflationism is compatible with a robust form of expressivism and is thus incompatible with the realist's speech act thesis.[9]

---

[9] Some philosophers advocate so-called quietist positions about speech according to which the availability of deflationary views about assertion collapses the distinction between robust and deflationary accounts of assertion. I am going to assume without much argument that these views are false. (I address the issue briefly in Ch. 6, n. 45.) That is, I am going to assume that there really are substantive differences between deflationary and non-deflationary views of speech (and other topics such as truth and facthood). For more on the matter, including a treatment of 'global quietism', see Zangwill (1992) and Fine (2001).

II. The alethic thesis

To the speech act thesis, (paradigmatic) moral realists add a claim about truth. Suppose we call a moral claim that expresses a predicative proposition a 'predicative moral claim'. We can then state:

The Moral Realist's Alethic Thesis: The contents of some predicative moral claims are true and, if the contents of such claims are true, then they are true in the realist sense.[10]

Following William P. Alston, I shall say that the content of a claim that p is true in the realist sense just in case there is a fact *that p*. The content of the claim that Smith is kind, for example, is true just in case it is a fact *that Smith is kind*. In what follows, I will adopt the simplifying assumption that the contents of claims—namely, propositions—are the primary 'truth-bearers' according to a realist scheme. (By assuming that propositions are the primary truth-bearers, I do not intend to deny that sentence types or tokens are also truth-bearers.) Furthermore, I assume that (in a certain range of cases at least) what makes the content of a claim true are facts. Facts are (in a certain range of cases) the 'truth-makers' according to a realist conception of truth.[11] As I indicated in the Introduction, I shall remain largely neutral concerning the ontological status of both propositions and facts (one could, for example, think of the latter as being states of affairs that obtain or complex unities that include entities-having-properties.)

   There are several ways to misread the realist's alethic thesis. So, let me make some clarificatory comments that should help to avoid both 'deflationary' and 'inflationary' readings of it.

   Begin with potentially deflationary readings of the realist's claim. One potentially deflationary reading of the realist's alethic thesis is to say that it does not imply that truth is a genuine or a 'substantial' property. That is, it might be claimed that the realist's alethic thesis is compatible with the view according to which the apparently predicative expression 'is true' fails to refer to the property *being true* or refers only to a 'non-substantial' property—that is, a property that fails to admit of any type of informative

---

[10] I assume that, if true, this thesis holds with respect to worlds in which we are not utterly deceived about the nature of morality.

[11] I hedge this claim because, as I suggested in the Introduction, I want to allow for the possibility that in some cases moral facts are moral truths.

elucidation. (This gloss calls for further refinement. I'll have more to say about deflationary views of truth in Chapter 6.)

I intend to preclude any such reading of the alethic thesis. I shall assume that truth—at least as it is predicated of moral propositions—is a substantive property picked out (when all goes well) by the predicative expression 'is true'. My reason for assuming this is as follows: The realist's alethic thesis tells us that the content of some moral claims is true. It is, however, a platitude accepted by deflationists and realists alike that true claims represent or correspond to reality.[12] As deflationists gloss this platitude, it amounts to no more than an anodyne gloss on the claim that p is true if and only if p. But the realist's speech act thesis makes this deflationary gloss on the so-called correspondence platitude unattractive. For fundamental to the realist's speech act thesis is the claim that the content of some moral claims purports to represent moral reality—where 'representation' in this case is understood in a fairly robust sense. This (together with the alethic thesis) entails that some predicative moral claims are true and that they represent reality aright—represent reality aright in a fairly robust sense of 'represent'.

Admittedly, it doesn't follow from this that the truth property *consists* in a truth-bearer's representing reality aright. Nevertheless, to deny this claim would be peculiar, for it is difficult to see why, if true predicative claims do not consist in representing reality aright, they are nonetheless such that they necessarily accurately represent reality. If deflationism were true, this coincidence, as David Lewis says in another context, would be magical; there would be no accounting for why it obtains.[13] How best, then, to explain the coincidence? Without much argument, I will assume that the most promising explanation is this: Truth is a genuine property such that when it is exemplified by a predicative claim (or its content), it consists in that claim's (or its content) representing a correlative fact. If this is right, it follows that truth is also a 'substantial' property in the sense that we can give an informative account of that in which its instantiation by a predicative claim (or its content) consists.

---

[12] See Horwich (1998), Ch. 7, Wright (1992), Ch. 1, and McGrath (2003) for examples of deflationists who make this claim.

[13] See Lewis (1986), Ch. 3, Sect. 4. Horwich (1998a) writes that 'the truth predicate exists solely for the sake of a certain logical need' (p. 2). I am suggesting that, if this is its *raison d'être*, it is mysterious why predicative claims that exhibit the truth property should also correspond to correlative truth-makers.

If a deflationary reading of the alethic thesis is one that denies either that truth is a property or a substantial property, an inflationary reading is one that attempts to offer a fairly specific account of the nature of the truth property, one which, say, attempts to spell out the nature of the correspondence relation between proposition and fact. I wish also to resist an inflationary reading of the realist's alethic thesis.

Perhaps the most tempting inflationary reading of the alethic thesis is broadly Russellian in nature.[14] According to this view, realism about truth commits us to a correspondence theory such that there is a structural isomorphism between truth-bearers and truth-makers in which truth-bearers 'mirror' truth-makers. (The isomorphism is often thought of as holding between the conceptual content of a proposition and the non-conceptual components of a correlative fact.) While nothing I say is meant to rule out the possibility that moral realists can avail themselves of such a correspondence theory, I wish to deny that accepting the alethic thesis as such does, for there is nothing about this thesis that implies that true propositions must be structurally isomorphic with their truth-makers. I don't think that this implies that the alethic realist is without resources to illuminate the relationship that obtains between true propositions and facts. As Alston has pointed out, what the alethic realist can say is that, in her view, a particularly intimate relation holds between a true proposition that p and the correlative fact *that p*. It is in virtue of a fact's sharing the same 'informational content' as a given proposition that that fact guarantees that the proposition in question is true. Or to put the point in an admittedly more stilted manner: According to the alethic realist's position, for any true proposition that p, what the proposition that p is a proposition *that* is the same as what the fact *that p* is a fact *that*.[15] It is this phenomenon of proposition and fact sharing the same content that ensures that there is the right sort of satisfaction relation between a particular proposition and fact.

III. The ontic thesis

Thus far I have suggested that paradigmatic moral realism is committed both to the claims that some moral discourse is assertoric and that the contents

---

[14] See, for example, Russell (1997), Ch. 12.

[15] Alston puts it thus; see Alston (1996), 38. Alston (2002), 24, appears to want to resist a position according to which the sameness in question is identity. By contrast, I have sympathy with this position, at least when the proposition in question is a Russellian one.

of some such discourse are true in the realist sense. Moreover, in my presentation of these claims, I have maintained that the realist understands the notions of assertion and truth in a decidedly non-deflationary fashion. An immediate implication of the realist's claims about moral discourse and truth is that there are moral facts. What the realist of a paradigmatic sort adds is a claim about the character of these facts. More exactly, she defends:

The Moral Realist's Ontic Thesis: There are irreducible moral facts.

The ontic thesis lies at the heart of moral realism of the type I wish to defend. It is also the least perspicuous of the realist's claims. The main problem here is that 'reduction' talk is notoriously slippery in contemporary philosophy. So, I need to say just how I am using it. Let me turn to this task by first explaining what I mean when I claim that something 'irreducibly exists', and then describing the sense in which moral facts irreducibly exist.[16]

Reductionism

My use of the term 'irreducibly exist' is borrowed from longstanding debates between metaphysical realists and antirealists. Roughly, the idea is this: Suppose we think of metaphysical antirealist views concerning entities of kind K as falling into two basic types. On the one hand, there are what we might call 'nihilist' views. To be a nihilist with respect to Ks is simply to deny that Ks exist. For instance, to be a nihilist about beliefs is just to deny that there are beliefs. This, I take it, has traditionally been the focal meaning of the term 'metaphysical antirealist'. On the other hand, there are what are sometimes called 'reductionist' positions. The reductionist concerning Ks does not deny outright that Ks exist. Rather, she claims that Ks exist, though, contrary to the appearances, Ks are really Ys—where Ys are supposed to be less 'ontologically problematic' than, and significantly different from, what we intuitively or commonsensically assume Ks to be. Consider (psychological) behaviorism concerning beliefs in this regard. Behaviorists find our ordinary supposition that beliefs are mental states deeply problematic. They cannot see how a mental state could possess such mysterious qualities as being about the world or having a qualitative 'feel'. Still, behaviorists do not simply deny that there are beliefs. Rather, they

---

[16] What I say in this next section has been helped by Alston (1996), Ch. 2 and Plantinga (1987).

maintain that there are entities such as beliefs, but that contrary to the appearances, beliefs are not mental states. Beliefs, say behaviorists, are really just certain complex behavioral dispositions: The belief that it is snowing, for example, is simply a complex behavioral disposition to do such things as put on gloves when venturing outside, answer 'Yes' to the question 'Is it snowing?' and so on. Behaviorists, in effect, 'reduce' beliefs to complex behavioral dispositions.

Suppose we use the schematic letter 'C' to stand for our ordinary or commonsensical conception of Ks. While I will have more to say in a moment about what I take a commonsensical conception of an entity to be, for present purposes we can think of it as a way of thinking about that entity that incorporates (or is constituted by) a cluster of platitudes or truisms regarding the character of that entity.[17] (For example, a platitude regarding colors is that we usually can't detect them simply by smell.) The account of reduction I am proposing tells us that:

The Ks reduce to the Ys if and only if the Ks are identical with the Ys and the Ys fail to satisfy C.

As I am thinking of them, then, reductions are always a species of so-called type-type reductions. Classic behaviorists are reductionists about beliefs inasmuch as they identify beliefs with complex behavioral dispositions.[18]

Let me now make two qualifications about what I have said. First, although I have spoken of metaphysical antirealisms as falling into two different kinds, I do not suppose that the distinction between these two kinds of metaphysical antirealism is a sharp one. It might be that, in some cases, it is unclear whether a view is best categorized as a nihilist view or a reductionist one. It might be, for example, that a proponent of a given view claims that Ks exist. On reflection, however, it might become apparent that

[17] Although I will speak of our commonsensical conception of an entity as being constituted by platitudes of various sorts, I don't assume that all of these platitudes are essential to our commonsensical conception of that entity.

[18] Two points: First, does this view about reduction imply that if a behaviorist view were to say that beliefs are not identical with behavioral dispositions, but *constituted* by such dispositions, that her view fails to be reductionist? No. A view such as this would still count as reductionist so long as beliefs—whatever they may be according to this view—fail to satisfy our commonsensical conception of a belief. Second, does this view imply that a behaviorist view that advocates a token-token reduction of beliefs to behavioral dispositions does not count as reductionist? No. A view such as this would still count as reductionist so long as beliefs—whatever type they belong to according to this view—fail to satisfy our commonsensical conception of a belief.

this person is using the term 'exist' in less than its strict and proper sense (perhaps she is a Meinongian of a certain kind). And, thus, rhetoric aside, it might be more illuminating to classify this view as a species of nihilism rather than reductionism.

Second, I have also spoken as if sufficient for being an antirealist with respect to entities of some kind is being a reductionist concerning entities of that kind. But that is not quite right. Most philosophers would agree that only some reductionist positions are best viewed as being antirealist positions. The reason, I surmise, is that reductionist positions can be more or less revisionary in substance. The more revisionary the content of some reductionist position—the farther away it leads us from our intuitive, 'shared picture' of entities of some kind and approximates nihilism with respect to those entities—the more likely it is to be classified as an antirealist view concerning entities of that kind. The less revisionary the content of some reductionist position—the greater the degree to which it preserves the platitudes concerning the nature of entities of some kind—the more likely it is to be viewed as a realist position concerning entities of that kind. So, reductionist positions with respect to entities of some kind K are best thought of as falling along a spectrum: those that do less violence to our intuitive, commonsensical view of Ks and those that more violently overturn our commonsensical view of Ks. Needless to say, those reductionist views that fall toward the middle of the reductionist spectrum will be difficult to categorize as either realist or antirealist positions. That having been said, in what follows, I shall use the term 'reductionism' to pick out those positions that are best categorized as *antirealist* forms of reductionism.

With these qualifications noted, I can now offer an initial account of what I mean when I claim that entities of a kind irreducibly exist. To say that Ks irreducibly exist is to claim, first, that there is a commonsensical conception of Ks, fundamental to which are platitudes of various kinds that concern the nature of Ks. Second, it is to claim that Ks exist if and only if they satisfy these platitudes and that some such entities satisfy these platitudes. As such, Ks cannot be reduced to facts of a type that fail to satisfy platitudes central to our commonsensical conception of Ks. I need to emphasize, however, that this does not imply that a non–reductionist with respect to Ks must deny that Ks supervene on entities of some other kind or even that they are identical with entities of that kind. (I, for one, do not wish to deny that moral facts supervene on merely descriptive features.) It implies only that the non-reductionist must hold that, if Ks exist, then they are not reducible to entities that fail to satisfy the platitudes central to our commonsensical conception of Ks.

On common sense

What I have said about the concept of a reduction thus far presupposes that, with respect to entities of some kinds, there is something like an 'ordinary' or 'commonsensical' idea of what those entities are like. This sort of language is bound to arouse suspicion. If I am to fill out this account of what it is for something to irreducibly exist, I need to say something more about it. What, after all, could we mean by the claim that there is an ordinary or commonsensical conception of a kind? And what could be meant by the claim that there is an ordinary or commonsensical conception of specifically moral features?

These are delicate questions. And perhaps any answer to them is better off being vaguely right than precisely wrong. Accordingly, I shall offer two types of reply to these questions—a less determinate and a more determinate one.

The less determinate answer to the second question is as follows: When we talk of a commonsensical conception of a putative moral feature, we mean to pick out a way of thinking about that feature that incorporates various platitudes concerning the content and objectivity of that feature that are sufficiently entrenched in the beliefs and practices of ordinary folk that moral realists and antirealists ordinarily attempt to accommodate them in their respective theories. A reductionist account of a putatively moral feature, then, is one that claims that that moral feature is instantiated, but offers an account of that moral feature without genuinely honoring these platitudes. Of course some philosophers deny that there is any shared fund of platitudes that characterize moral features—such platitudes always being specific to one or another tradition or conceptual scheme. I myself find the arguments for these views unpersuasive; the mere fact that we often do not talk past one another on moral matters, but genuinely agree and disagree with each other, strongly suggests that we do have something like a stock of very general shared moral concepts. But suppose that I am wrong about this. Then what I say can be easily recast as saying that our 'commonsensical' conception of moral features is constituted by a certain stock of platitudes that are sufficiently entrenched in the beliefs and practices of some subset of the ordinary folk, and that philosophers have typically found these platitudes plausible enough to want to try to preserve them in their moral theories.

The more determinate reply takes its inspiration from an unlikely pair of philosophers—David Lewis and Thomas Reid.[19] The proponent of this reply maintains that there are what we might call 'commonly conceived kinds'. Commonly conceived kinds are kinds of which most properly functioning, paradigmatically situated adults (e.g. those who live in social groups) at some time have the concept. Fundamental to our concepts of at least some commonly conceived kinds are various platitudes. For example: Most adults of this sort have the concept of *being a colored thing*. And constitutive of our concept of *being a colored thing* are platitudes such as '(nearly) all objects that we see appear to be colored', 'things don't usually look the color they are in the dark', 'one usually cannot tell what color an object is just by touching it and smelling it', and so forth. If a person were not explicitly to believe or take for granted these platitudes in her ordinary activities of judging, questioning, blaming, praising, inquiring, predicting, and so forth, that would be prima facie grounds for believing that that person lacks the concept of *being a colored thing*, or suffers from some cognitive malfunction, or occupies (or has occupied) some highly unfavorable epistemic situation. (Perhaps, for example, she has been massively deceived about the nature of colors.)

What I am calling 'the more determinate reply' tells us that some putatively moral features are commonly conceived kinds. They are the sorts of thing of which most properly functioning, paradigmatically situated adults have the concept. It is further claimed that fundamental to our concept of certain moral features are platitudes of various sorts. If a person were not explicitly to believe or take for granted these platitudes in her ordinary activities of judging, questioning, blaming, praising, inquiring, predicting, and so forth, this would be prima facie grounds for believing

---

[19] As some might see it, an odd coupling of a less-than-ardent-advocate and a steadfast defender of common sense! See Lewis (1983d), Ch. 6 and Reid (2002). It was reading Smith (1994) that helped me see how the Lewisian view could be of help in moral philosophy. Although the views I present are compatible with the position that the platitudes with respect to the moral domain fix the meaning of moral terms, I do not, in what follows, assume that they do. For an alternate view, see Jackson and Pettit (1995).

that this person lacks the concept of that putatively moral feature, or suffers from some cognitive malfunction, or is the victim of (or has been the victim of) some highly unfavorable epistemic situation. (Perhaps, for example, she has been massively deceived about the nature of morality.) For example, it is plausible to believe that kinds such as *being a just action* or *being a wicked action* are commonly conceived kinds. It is also plausible to believe that fundamental to our concepts of these kinds are various platitudes. It seems to be constitutive of our concept of justice that no action could be just that simply randomly discriminates against some group of persons. Accordingly, if a person were not to believe or take for granted this platitude in her ordinary activities of judging, questioning, blaming, praising, inquiring, predicting, and so forth, this would be prima facie grounds for believing that this person lacks the concept of justice, or suffers from some cognitive malfunction, or has been misled by her teachers about the nature of justice.

If we wish to work with this more determinate answer to our questions, then we can say that a reductionist account of some moral feature is one that claims that that moral feature exists, but that it is not characterized by the platitudes that are constitutive of the commonsensical concept of that kind.

I add to this three clarifications. First, it will often be the case that among the platitudes constitutive of our commonsensical conception of a K some are more central than others insofar as they are more important or have more explanatory power than others. Thus, it may be that our commonsensical conception of a K undergoes revisions over time in which some less central platitudes fall away, while a central core remains.[20]

Second, if a person possesses the concept of some commonly conceived kind, it will ordinarily be the case that that person only consciously and occurrently believes a rather small number of the platitudes constitutive of the concept of that kind. In most cases, the possessor of the concept of the kind *being a colored thing* will *take it for granted* that a great many of the platitudes concerning colors are true. The platitudes concerning

---

[20] One is reminded of Wittgenstein's metaphors for the Background in *On Certainty* in which the Background is likened to a river bed of hard rock over which the river flows (§99). Incidentally, if we concede that our commonsensical conception of a K can change, it need not follow that what counts as a realist position concerning Ks will change. One might claim that the phrase 'realism with respect to Ks' rigidly designates what properly functioning, paradigmatically situated adults in the actual world at some time take for granted or explicitly believe in their ordinary activities. Understood thus, common sense is not merely a statistical notion, but a *normative* one.

colored things whose truth a person takes for granted form a 'background', 'substratum', or 'horizon' against which color discourse (among other things) takes place. It follows that, according to the present account, what a person who possesses the concept of a certain kind takes for granted in her ordinary activities can commit that person to the truth of various propositions—even when those propositions never form the content of any intentional attitude that that person may have. A professor may have never consciously entertained the proposition that the ordinary blackboard in his classroom is solid. But when he slaps his blackboard in exasperation, he cannot—consistently with his behavior—deny the platitude that ordinary blackboards are solid.

Third, although what I am calling our commonsensical conception of a kind clearly has a great deal in common with what Reid called 'common sense', what Wittgenstein termed our 'shared world picture', and what John Searle has recently called the 'Background', it is important to emphasize that I will not assume that our commonsensical conception of a kind is certain, indubitable, infallible, incorrigible, or even true of that which it purports to be about.[21] Indeed, according to the present account, if a person were not to believe or take for granted the platitudes constitutive of our concept of a commonly conceived kind K, this would give us only a prima facie ground for believing that she lacks the concept of a K or suffers from some epistemic setback. It might be that, though she has our ordinary concept, she has very good reasons for thinking that it does not apply to anything because she sees that it is incoherent.

Commonsensical moral realism

Suppose, then, there is a commonsensical conception of moral features such as justice, kindness, and benevolence. Our commonsensical conception of these features, I've said, is comprised of various platitudes that (when all goes well) are indicative of the nature of these features. The realist claims that these platitudes are pregnant with important implications for what

---

[21] See Reid (2002), Wittgenstein (1969), Searle (1983), (1992), and (1995). There are differences in substance and emphasis between Reid's conception of common sense, Wittgenstein's notion of our shared world-picture, and Searle's conception of the Background. Moreover, I should stress that my use of 'common sense' mirrors only one—but arguably central—manner in which Reid uses the term. Wolterstorff (2001), Ch. 9, illuminates some of the parallels between Reid's thought and Wittgenstein's later thought.

might be called our 'commonsensical conception of moral facts'. The idea is that, if anything is a genuinely moral fact, then we have prima facie reason to believe that it would have to be such that it satisfies a certain set of platitudes. However, to this it is important to add a qualification: It is not the realist's claim that we can, as it were, pull out a highly determinate account of what a moral fact is from these platitudes. It may well be the case that the content of the platitudes constitutive of our most central moral concepts has very modest implications for what moral facts are. That said, I submit that lying at the heart of our commonsensical conception of moral facts are platitudes of two sorts—platitudes that concern the *content* and the *authority* of morality. I want now to elucidate these platitudes, and then say why I believe we have good reason to maintain that they are fundamental to our commonsensical conception of moral facts.

The content and authority platitudes

To understand the platitudes that concern the content of morality, it is useful to return to some considerations that Philippa Foot pressed against emotivist and prescriptivist views several decades ago.[22] Foot argued that not just any action could count as wicked, benevolent, compassionate, or wrong; there are conceptual limits to what sorts of action could admit of these moral predicates. And though it was not her aim to offer a comprehensive account of what should fall under the concept 'moral', Foot contended that acts that have one or another positive moral status are generally concerned to promote, sustain, or contribute in some fashion to genuine human well-being or the states and activities that are components thereof. Likewise, acts that have one or another negative moral status are typically concerned to frustrate, undercut, or destroy authentic human flourishing or the states and activities that are components thereof.[23] Indeed, we might add that some

---

[22] See Foot (2002), Chs. 7 and 8 and also Frankena (1973).

[23] In claiming that moral facts are ordinarily intimately intertwined with the realization and frustration of human well-being or the goods that are components thereof, I don't mean to claim that they aren't intimately intertwined with the realization and frustration of the well-being of creatures other than humans. Nor do I mean to rule out the possibility that there are content platitudes that indicate that some moral features are not intimately intertwined with the flourishing of humans or other creatures. I might add that what I am calling the 'content' platitudes should be amenable to Kantians. What Kantians will add is a deeper explanatory claim: It is wrong to intend to destroy human well-being (or the goods that comprise such flourishing) because and insofar as this expresses disrespect for persons; and, it is right to intend to foster human well-being because and insofar as it expresses respect for persons.

actions have such an intimate connection to causing serious harm—e.g. torturing others for mere pleasure—that they are plausibly viewed as being *necessarily* wrong.[24]

In my judgment, Foot's contention regarding the conceptual limits as to what could count as a moral fact is correct. And if we add the qualification that there are conceptual limits on what could plausibly count as authentic human flourishing, there appear to be substantial restrictions on both what could count as a moral fact and what could count as the instantiation of particular types of moral property such as justice, mercy, benevolence, and so forth.[25]

I have also claimed that, in addition to there being platitudes concerning the content of morality, there are various platitudes that concern the authority of morality. I divide the platitudes concerning the authority of morality into two sorts.

First of all, there are various platitudes to the effect that moral features of the world are *prescriptive* insofar as they are, imply, or indicate reasons for us to behave in certain ways. Consider the fact that an action is wicked. It is an apparent platitude to claim that, necessarily, the fact that an action is wicked provides persons in the appropriate circumstances with a reason to despise it, attempt to stop it, or the like. The truth of this platitude is guaranteed by what appears to be a conceptual truth about reasons and evaluative moral facts, viz., that if an entity has some evaluative moral property (e.g. wickedness), then (all other things being equal) there is a reason for persons in the relevant circumstances to respond to that entity in an appropriate fashion. To which we should add that moral facts (or the reasons they indicate) on some occasions appear to provide persons with a *decisive* reason to act as they direct.[26]

---

[24] See Thomson (1990), Introduction, for a defense of this claim.

[25] It is a consequence of my view that, if a person championed a sufficiently unorthodox conception of human well-being (or the components thereof) and claimed that actions acquire positive moral status by virtue of their promoting, honoring, or respecting the well-being of persons in this unorthodox sense, then that person does not espouse moral realism of a paradigmatic sort.

[26] It is sometimes asked: What sort of reason is implied by evaluative facts of this kind? A moral reason, an all-things-considered reason, a prudential reason, or something else? My short answer is: A reason such that, were one not to respond to it appropriately, one would thereby suffer from a normative defect such as being inconsiderate, wicked, malevolent, obtuse, or the like. Since these defects can fall into different normative categories, I do not think the question admits of a streamlined answer.

Second, there are platitudes that tell us that moral features are authoritative insofar as they inescapably govern our conduct. The idea here is twofold. In the first place, the claim is that, necessarily, some moral reasons apply to persons and thereby give persons reasons to act (or indicate such reasons) regardless of whether they want to act in a morally upright fashion, or whether they belong to a certain social group, or whether they have entered into certain agreements with others, and so forth. Whether I am under an obligation, say, to stop the occurrence of a wicked action is independent of whether I desire to stop the occurrence of that wicked action, whether I care about acting in a morally upright fashion, whether stopping it serves any of my interests, whether I belong to a certain social group, or the like. (Consequently, if it is a conceptual truth that moral reasons govern 'appropriately situated' agents, being thus situated needn't include having concerns or social standings of certain kinds.) As such, some moral reasons are categorical and stand in contrast to so-called hypothetical and institutional reasons, which apply to persons only insofar as they have certain goals or are committed to institutions or social practices of certain kinds. (Think of the norms of etiquette as a contrast.[27]) In the second place, moral reasons are authoritative inasmuch as the decisiveness of some such reasons for appropriately situated agents is not a function of whether such agents want to act in a morally upright fashion, or belong to a certain social group, or have entered into certain agreements with others, and so forth.[28]

In both these respects, what I am calling 'moral realism of a paradigmatic sort' differs markedly from other types of views that are called realist, but deny that moral reasons are authoritative in the sense just specified. For example, common to many so-called naturalist versions of moral realism is the claim that moral facts exist in a fairly 'objective' sense. Moral facts,

---

[27] On the assumption that the goals, desires, and commitments that generate hypothetical and institutional reasons are possessed contingently by moral agents, this view implies that moral reasons categorically merit our concern independently of any particular goals we have. In this sense, moral facts have non-derivative normative significance. For an argument that moral facts would have non-derivative normative significance even if we assumed that the goals, desires, etc. that underwrite hypothetical reasons were not contingent, see FitzPatrick (forthcoming). For a more elaborate defense of the inescapability of moral obligations by a moral antirealist, see Joyce (2001), Ch. 2.

[28] I am not assuming that, if a given norm applies to a person, it thereby gives a person a reason to act. Rather, I assume that, for a norm to *govern* a person's behavior, that norm applies to that person and gives her a reason to act (all other things being equal). Incidentally, while this implies a type of moral rationalism according to which there is always reason to act morally, it does not imply that immoral behavior is as such irrational. More argument would be needed to establish that claim.

according to these views, are not the product of social convention or of our being disposed to react to the non-moral world in certain ways. Nonetheless, these philosophers maintain that moral facts generate reasons for agents to act as they direct only if acting in this way is conducive to satisfying desires those agents possess, such as living a long and flourishing life. While there may be a perfectly respectable sense in which views such as this deserve to be called 'realist', they are not paradigmatic realist views as I use this phrase. For these views deny the categoricity of moral reasons.[29]

At any rate, I suggest that we call the platitudes concerning the content and authority of morality the 'central platitudes concerning moral facts'. Having the central platitudes concerning moral facts before us allows us to develop a more definitive account of what realists mean when they say that moral facts irreducibly exist. Definitive of moral realism of a paradigmatic sort is the thesis that there is a commonsensical conception of moral facts, fundamental to which are platitudes that concern the content and authority of such facts. Moral facts irreducibly exist just in case such facts exist that satisfy the content and authority platitudes fundamental to our commonsensical conception of moral facts. They cannot be reduced to the sorts of fact that lack these characteristics.

An assessment of the realist's claims

I have claimed that it is plausible to believe that there is something like a commonsensical conception of moral facts and that this conception implies that moral facts have a certain kind of content and authority. I now want to address the doubt that what I have claimed is false.

Let me begin by noting that I have not claimed that it is part of our commonsensical conception of the moral realm that there *are* moral facts. I have only claimed that, if there are moral facts, then we have prima facie reason to believe that they must be the sort of thing that satisfy the central platitudes concerning moral facts. It would be misguided, then, to object to the present account that our ordinary views of morality do not assume

---

[29] See Railton (1986 and 1992) and Brink (1989) for views such as this. Railton adds that his use of the term 'moral realism' is not 'proprietary' and that 'other positions...may have equal claim' to the name (p. 165). The position defended in Boyd (1995) is sometimes cited as a naturalist view that denies that moral reasons are categorical (see Hampton [1998], Ch. 3, for example). For reasons that I won't go into here, it is not clear to me that Boyd's view is committed to this denial, however.

that there are moral facts. That said, I should emphasize that it is commonly agreed by realists and antirealists alike that most of us appear to believe or take it for granted that some actions really are wicked, unjust, gracious, or kind. These appearances, however, are plausibly interpreted as implying that we typically believe or take it for granted that there are moral facts or truths—or at least that we typically harbor attitudes that appear to be beliefs concerning something resembling such facts or truths. Indeed, it is instructive to note that even 'quasi-realists' such as Simon Blackburn who deny that there are moral facts in any robust sense are keen to capture the purported objectivity of morality by claiming that our putative responses to moral reality are really a matter of our 'projecting' our attitudes on the world and reading them off the world as if it already contained moral features.[30]

In any case, the real issue is whether the realist is correct to contend that we commonly assume that there are conceptual limits of a certain sort on what could count as wicked, benevolent, or kind actions and whether some moral facts are categorical in the sense I have specified. I believe that the answer to these questions has to be that we do commonly assume these things. In subsequent chapters, I will try to tease out some of the ways in which the content and authority platitudes concerning moral facts are interconnected. For now, it is sufficient to point out that the realist seems not to be exceeding the bounds of theoretical modesty by claiming that morality and human well-being are intimately intertwined. It appears, for example, to be constitutive of our concept of wickedness that paradigmatic examples of wicked actions are those actions that are intended to harm others. Similarly, it appears constitutive of our concept of kindness that the kind person is one who is habitually inclined to aid others out of concern for their well-being. Severing the tight connection between moral features and human well-being is something for which we should need a convincing argument.

In like fashion, I take it to be essential to the nature of moral features that they are normative in this sense: They are the sorts of thing that

---

[30] Blackburn (1984), Ch. 6 and (1981). John Greco has suggested to me that it is no less a part of our commonsensical conception of moral facts that such facts exist than it is that they satisfy the content and authority platitudes. But since the existence of such facts is at issue, the realist simply brackets this component of our commonsensical conception of moral facts. While I have no objection to this way of viewing things, I will persist in not assuming that our commonsensical conception of such facts is committed to their existence.

either direct us to respond in certain ways or are appropriate responses to such directives. It is constitutive of our concept of a wicked or kind thing—to return to our previous example—that it is *worthy* of or *demands* various kinds of response on our part. If someone agreed that an action is thoroughly wicked, but also claimed that that action does not merit any sort of response on our part, we would find ourselves deeply puzzled; we would doubt whether this person possessed the concept of wickedness, or was sincere, sober, or sane. (Although I should note that this sort of case is different from one in which the person recognizes that the thoroughly wicked action demands a certain response on his part but does not *care* that that response is demanded of him.)

Perhaps the most controversial of the realist's claims is that it is part of our commonsensical conception of moral facts that moral facts inescapably govern our conduct. Judith Jarvis Thomson quips that it 'is a good heuristic in philosophy to be suspicious of views that would shock your grocer'.[31] Denying that moral facts of certain kinds inescapably govern our conduct, I believe, fails Thomson's test. Suppose, for example, a man were sincerely to tell his grocer that he could have easily prevented the occurrence of a thoroughly wicked action aimed at a family member, but also to deny that the wickedness of this action provided any reason for him to try to prevent it since he himself did not have any desires that would be satisfied by trying to prevent it. This man's view of morality would be enough to shock his grocer. I imagine that his grocer would find himself baffled; he would wonder whether this man had the concept of wickedness, or was joking, or had all his wits about him.

Most realists and antirealists alike, I believe, would concede the bulk of what I have claimed thus far about the nature of putative moral facts. Indeed, the ordinary antirealist strategy is to say that moral antirealism can satisfy the central platitudes about moral facts (or something very close thereto), but without incurring the realist's ontological baggage. Nevertheless, it should be admitted that there are some philosophers who appear to deny that the authority of morality is any part of our ordinary conception of morality. Consider the following passage from Gilbert Harman:

I have always been a moral relativist. As far back as I remember thinking about it, it has seemed to me obvious that the dictates of morality arise from some sort of

---

[31] Thomson (1996), 211.

convention or understanding among people, that different people arrive at different understandings, and that there are no basic moral demands that apply to everyone. For many years, this seemed so obvious to me that I assumed it was everyone's instinctive view, at least everyone who gave the matter any thought 'in this day and age'.[32]

It is not easy to know what to make of this since it is not entirely clear what Harman means by 'moral relativism' here. But it is worth noting that the sort of moral relativist view that Harman has defended in print elsewhere seems to be of the grocer-shocking variety.[33] Moral relativism of this sort says that a person has a moral reason to Φ only if that person has desires of the appropriate kind that would be satisfied by his Φing. Accordingly, if I don't have any desires that would be satisfied by my attempting to stop the occurrence of a wicked action, then I have no moral reason to do so. Despite what Harman says, then, I find myself unable to believe that our ordinary moral view is anything like what he says. Of course I do not dispute that Harman himself may find moral relativism of this variety to be *his* instinctive view. But that is not in conflict with what I have claimed.

Connections

To this point, I have been chiefly concerned to sketch the main lines of moral realism of a paradigmatic sort. I have claimed that there are three components to such a view: a thesis regarding the nature of moral speech, a claim about moral truth, and a thesis about the character of moral facts. I assume that affirming these three theses is both necessary and sufficient for being a moral realist of a paradigmatic sort. Thus, I will assume that sufficient for not being a paradigmatic moral realist is denying any of these three claims. That said, I maintain that the three components of paradigmatic moral realism come in a hierarchy. In particular, I maintain that the last claim we've considered—i.e. the ontic thesis—occupies the heart of the realist position. Let me explain.

The ontic thesis does not directly imply nor is it directly implied by the speech act thesis or the alethic thesis. Nonetheless, the connections between it and the other claims are intimate. In the first place, affirming the ontic thesis undercuts a major motivation for rejecting the speech act thesis. This is because philosophers who reject the speech act thesis

---

[32] Harman (1984), 27.   [33] See Harman (1975), (1977), and (1984).

ordinarily do so because they believe that there are no moral facts to which we can refer. The reasoning on the part of these philosophers is fairly plain: Suppose there are no moral facts. Suppose also that moral claims purport to represent these facts. If these two suppositions are true, then moral discourse is systematically mistaken, for it purports to represent that which does not exist. An attractive way to avoid this result is to accept expressivism, rejecting The Realist's Speech Act Thesis in favor of the claim that moral discourse is non-assertoric.[34] Were a realist to mount a successful argument for the ontic thesis, however, then this would undercut the foregoing rationale for denying the speech act thesis.

Second, there is also a sense in which the ontic thesis and the negation of the speech act thesis are not 'co-assertible'. By saying this I mean to claim that there is a sense in which one could not rationally believe the ontic thesis and deny the speech act thesis. To see the point, it is helpful to recognize that the denial of the speech act thesis is simply the expression of a particular position about the nature of moral thought—what I've referred to as 'expressivism'—according to which moral thought does not consist in the believing or accepting of moral propositions and, hence, moral discourse does not consist in the expression of these propositions. To deny the speech act thesis, then, is to adopt expressivism. (I'll offer a more precise account of this position in Chapters 5 and 6.) But, according to the present realist view, to believe or assert a predicative moral proposition p is to believe that there is a fact in virtue of which p is true. It follows that to affirm expressivism is to accept that one does not believe that there are any moral facts that correspond to the content of moral discourse. But if this is right, a person's affirming the ontic thesis and denying the speech act thesis (as they are understood by the realist) commit her to a Moorean paradox of the following sort:

There are moral facts, but I don't believe any exist.

Although there has been some controversy among philosophers about why accepting a proposition such as this is absurd, the correct answer seems to me the following: The person who sincerely utters this claim is committed to both its conjuncts. However, the claim expressed in its second conjunct ('I don't believe there are moral facts') undercuts his justification or warrant

---

[34] See Blackburn (1993), Ch. 8 and (2002) for this line of thought.

for accepting the claim expressed in its first conjunct ('there are moral facts') and vice-versa. Hence, the paradox.

So, accepting the ontic thesis is not something that sits comfortably with denying the speech act thesis; if one accepts the former thesis, then one can deny the latter only on pain of being committed to a host of Moorean paradoxical claims. If this is right, however, then it is a short step toward establishing the realist's alethic thesis. For, suppose we have established that the ontic thesis is true and, thus, that there are moral facts of various kinds. And suppose we conclude from this that the speech act thesis is true and that some moral claims are in the business of representing such facts. Finally, suppose we assume that some moral claims are not systematically malformed, but in fact represent moral facts. (It is hard to see why, given their other commitments, realists would deny this.) If we assume this, then it follows that the alethic thesis is true, for a sufficient condition of a predicative moral claim's being true in the realist sense is that claim's representing a correlative moral fact.

Of considerable interest for our purposes, then, is the following method-ological point: If one wants an economical way of arguing for moral realism of a paradigmatic sort, then one should argue for The Moral Realist's Ontic Thesis. As the statement of the core argument I offered in the Introduction will have indicated, this is precisely the strategy I will employ in what follows. In any case, for ease of exposition, I will use the term 'moral antirealist' to stand for any view that rejects The Moral Realist's Ontic Thesis. But I should emphasize that any such view is best understood to be antirealist only in the sense that it rejects a fundamental tenet of paradigmatic moral realism.

IV. What paradigmatic moral realism is not

The three claims that comprise paradigmatic moral realism, I have claimed, form a package in which the ontic thesis enjoys a certain pride of place. Affirm the ontic thesis, I argued, and the rest of the package comes in tow. In the remainder of this chapter, I want to consider two further claims that some philosophers maintain are definitive of moral realism. The first claim is that moral facts, according to the realist view, are in some sense mind-independent. The second is that moral facts must be explanatorily efficacious in some yet-to-be-specified sense. I will argue that neither claim is implied by paradigmatic moral realism.

Mind-independence

All moral realists believe that moral facts exist. But many stipulate that to be a realist with regard to these facts, then they must, in some suitable sense, be 'mind-independent'.[35] In this section, I am going to discuss two different versions of the claim that moral facts are mind-independent. I shall argue that moral realists of a paradigmatic sort are committed to neither of them.

Let's call the claim that a realist account of moral facts implies that such facts are mind-independent the 'mind-independence constraint'. The mind-independence constraint comes in a strong and weak form. The strong version of the claim says that moral facts are mind-independent inasmuch as they are existentially independent of the attitudes of actual or hypothetical human moral agents. The thought in this case is that moral realism implies that, even if there were no actual or hypothetical human agents exemplifying attitudes at some time or other, some things would be right or wrong, good or bad, just or unjust, and so forth. By contrast, the weak version of this constraint says that moral facts are mind-independent insofar as they are not a function of human agents having (or being disposed to have) intentional attitudes toward non-moral features of certain kinds. According to this way of understanding the constraint, some entities instantiate moral properties, but not in virtue of some (human) agent's (or agents') having (or being disposed to have) one or another intentional attitude (or attitudes) toward that thing. Let's consider each version of this constraint.

Here are some recent statements of the strong mind-independence constraint. Mark Timmons says that the moral realist holds:

that there are moral facts (and properties) that are independent of human attitudes, conventions, and the like.[36]

---

[35] Here is a sample of where this claim can be found: Boyd (1995), Brink (1989), Butchvarov (1996), Foot (2002a), Ch. 3, Kupperman (1987), Lemos (1994), McNaughton (1988), Milo (1995), Oddie (2005), Quinn (1993), Ch. 1, Railton (1996), Rawls (1980), Shafer-Landau (2003), Ch. 1, Sturgeon (1986), Timmons (1996), Wong (1986), Wright (1995), and Zimmerman (1985). The distinction I make between different senses of mind-independence uses terminology borrowed from Milo (1995).

[36] Timmons (1996), 106.

Writing for the *Encyclopedia of Philosophy*, Panayot Butchvarov says that:

moral realism holds that there exist moral facts and therefore moral properties that … are independent of our awareness, the manner in which we think or speak, our beliefs and attitudes, and our feelings and desires.[37]

Finally, Thomas Carson and Paul Moser maintain that:

moral realism implies that some things are good or bad or right or wrong independently of facts about the attitudes (for example the beliefs and desires) of moral agents—even under ideal conditions.[38]

There are some ambiguities intrinsic to and differences between these characterizations of moral realism. Common to them all, nonetheless, is the claim that the moral realist is committed to the existential independence of moral facts from the attitudes of human agents.

In order to evaluate this version of the mind–independence constraint, let me introduce a distinction that corresponds to the distinction introduced earlier between predicative and general moral propositions. The distinction I have in mind is that between 'particular' and 'general' moral facts. Particular moral facts are those that correspond to true predicative moral propositions. The facts *that Smith is kind* or *that this murder is wrong* are good examples of particular moral facts. These are facts that consist in some particular's having some moral property at a time. General moral facts, by contrast, are those that correspond to true general moral propositions. The facts that *stealing money from the poor is wrong* and *that murder is morally bad* are good examples of general moral facts. They are facts that have the logical form: If x is a token of some intention, action, etc., type y (e.g. murder), then x has some moral property F.

What this distinction makes clear is that any suggestion that moral facts are existentially independent of the attitudes of human agents cannot plausibly be understood to be the claim that particular moral facts are existentially independent of the attitudes of human agents. For example, I take it to be evident that a particular moral fact such as *that this murder is wrong* cannot exist unless there is (or was) an agent who has the intention to kill another person. And something similar holds for many other particular moral facts; they are entities that are essentially constituted by the cognitive

---

[37] Butchvarov (1996), 361.   [38] Carson and Moser (1996), 277.

activity of human agents. In light of this, I suggest that the claim that moral facts are existentially independent of human attitudes must be the claim that (some) general moral facts are existentially independent of human attitudes. Is this, however, something to which the moral realist of a paradigmatic sort is committed?

One argument for an affirmative answer to this question is this: It is plausible to believe that some moral facts exist necessarily. For instance, it is plausible to believe that the fact *that it is wrong to torture infants for the mere fun of it* is a necessary moral fact. If this is right, then the moral realist of a paradigmatic sort is committed to there being necessary moral facts. But necessary moral facts are the sorts of entity that would exist even if no human agents were to exemplify attitudes at any time. Hence, the moral realist is committed to there being some moral facts—general moral facts—which are existentially independent of the attitudes of human agents.

This argument depends on two premises, viz., that the realist is committed to there being necessary moral facts and that necessary facts do not existentially depend on the attitudes of human agents. I think that the first premise is true; realists are committed to the existence of necessary moral facts. (These facts may only be general ones such as *that right actions are those that maximize value.*) But I doubt realists are committed to the second. A moral realist might, for example, be a modal antirealist—perhaps because he accepts D. M. Armstrong's claim that all modal facts existentially depend on the occurrence of contingent states of affairs in the actual world.[39] Or, perhaps more commonly, a realist might claim that putatively necessary moral facts existentially depend on the attitudes of hypothetical human moral agents. For instance, according to some views, the putatively necessary fact *that gratuitous killing is wrong* supervenes on the necessary fact *that ideally rational human agents in epistemically ideal conditions would disapprove of gratuitous killing.* If such a view were correct, the putatively necessary moral fact *that gratuitous killing is wrong* would existentially depend on the attitudes of hypothetical

---

[39] See Armstrong (1997). Armstrong maintains that 'modal truths, therefore, while not contingent truths, have nothing but these contingent beings as truthmakers. ... The truthmaker ... for a particular modal truth will make that truth true in virtue of nothing more than relations of *identity* (strict identity) and *difference* holding between the constituents of the truthmaker' (p. 150). One wonders how we can elucidate the concepts of identity and difference without recourse to modal concepts, however.

human beings. To be sure, so-called constructivist views of this variety are commonly labeled 'antirealist'.[40] But, according to the way I understand paradigmatic moral realism, these views needn't be viewed as non-realist. If such a position were to preserve the central platitudes concerning moral facts and accept the realist's speech act and alethic theses, then it would, in my view, deserve to be called a paradigmatic moral realist view.

The Realist's Ontic Thesis, then, does not commit the realist to the claim that moral facts are strongly mind-independent. Does it commit the realist to the claim that such facts are weakly mind-independent? I believe not. I do not deny that affirming this second version of the mind-independence constraint has respectable motivations. After all, prominent versions of idealism about the external world imply that entities such as mountains and trees are a function of our having (or being disposed to have) attitudes of various kinds toward some type of noumenal stuff. Since idealist views are ordinarily labeled antirealist because of their allegiance to a mind-dependence thesis of this kind, one might think that moral realism ought to mirror non-idealist positions with respect to the external world by claiming that moral facts are not similarly mind-dependent.[41]

I think that this line of thought should give us pause. Implicit in the discussion so far has been the assumption that realism and antirealism of any sort are typically categoreal in nature. One is ordinarily a realist *relative to* entities of a particular kind. And I think that there is no obvious reason for thinking that being a realist or antirealist with respect to entities of some kind will always closely resemble being a realist or antirealist with respect to entities of some other kind. (Of course there will be some resemblances between different types of realist views: A realist view regarding Ks is perforce committed to the existence of Ks.) So, for example, it is plausible to believe that an account of the nature of trees and mountains that renders these entities strongly mind-dependent is properly termed a metaphysical antirealist view concerning these entities. (According to the view I favor, it is an antirealist view in virtue of being reductionist.) But it is not obvious that a strongly

[40] See Shafer-Landau (2003), Ch. 2, for example.
[41] The assumption is explicit in Brink (1989), Ch. 1 and Wright (1995).

mind-dependent account of, say, colors is best thought of as an antirealist view of colors. Indeed, I believe that few philosophers think of dispositionalist accounts of colors as versions of antirealism. It might thus be wondered whether it is better to model an account of moral realism on a realist account of colors rather than a realist account of mountains or trees.[42]

Be that as it may, I maintain that there is in principle no incompatibility between accepting paradigmatic realism, on the one hand, and the claim that moral facts are a function of the attitudes we have toward non-moral reality, on the other. As far as I can see, there is no reason to believe that every position that affirms mind-dependence of this sort thereby fails to capture the platitudes with respect to the content and authority of moral facts (although, no doubt, some will). My strong suspicion is that constructivist views of this variety are not the *best* type of realist position to adopt. But this is a weaker thesis than the claim that any such position is not a realist view in the first place.

The explanatory criterion

The thesis that moral facts are either weakly or strongly mind-independent, I have argued, is not constitutive of moral realism of a paradigmatic sort. In this sense at least, paradigmatic moral realism is a fairly capacious position, admitting of both constructivist and non-constructivist varieties. In closing, I wish to consider briefly a second claim that is frequently made about moral realism. The claim is that moral facts exist only if they can satisfy one or another version of 'the explanatory criterion'. In the hands of some philosophers, the criterion says that moral facts exist only if they are causally efficacious. In the hands of others, it says that moral facts exist only if they can figure in our best scientific explanations. In the hands of yet others, it says that moral facts exist only if they would explain why rational inquirers converge on the belief that entities of some kind are moral facts.[43]

---

[42] It is something like this thought, I believe, that is driving John McDowell's development of moral qualities in McDowell (1985).

[43] For some of the relevant literature, see Harman (1977), Sturgeon (1985), Williams (1985), Ch. 7, and Shafer-Landau (2003), Ch. 4. I myself defend the thesis that moral facts are explanatorily efficacious in Cuneo (2006) and (unpublished a).

I assume that a realist of a paradigmatic sort needn't embrace any of these formulations of the explanatory criterion. This is because I assume that none of the three theses that comprise moral realism of a paradigmatic sort implies that a necessary condition of a putative entity's existing is that entity's being causally efficacious, its pulling its explanatory weight in the sciences, or the like. If any such claim is constitutive of, say, a naturalist view in ethics, then I assume that moral realism of a paradigmatic sort is not committed to a naturalist view in ethics (although it is, I believe, compatible with it). That said, I do deny that paradigmatic realism is compatible with a type of epiphenomenalism according to which moral facts play *no* type of explanatory role. For at the heart of paradigmatic moral realism is the thesis that moral facts of certain sorts give persons reasons to conduct their behavior in certain fashions. Thus, it is a conceptual truth according to the realist that moral facts enter into justificatory or 'rationalizing' explanations. When asked why I should give money to help aid the starving, realists can avail themselves of this answer: Because it is just that I do so. If I were to fail to do so, I would (all other things being equal) suffer from one or another moral defect such as being callous, selfish, or complacent. Accordingly, its being just to give money to help aid the starving gives me a reason of a sort to act. It explains why I ought to send in my money. There is, then, a perfectly good sense in which realism of a paradigmatic sort satisfies a version of the explanatory requirement—albeit not a version that has much animated philosophers working in the foundations of ethics!

V. Conclusion

This completes my account of what moral realism of a paradigmatic sort is. In summary, any such view implies that some moral discourse is assertoric, that some moral claims are true in the realist sense, and that moral facts irreducibly exist—where this latter claim is understood to imply that moral facts satisfy what I've called the 'content' and 'authority' platitudes constitutive of our commonsensical conception of moral facts. I trust it is evident why the view I have developed is a paradigmatic version of moral realism: It is, I submit, the type of view to which moral realists such as Plato, Aristotle, Aquinas, Butler, Reid, Sidgwick, Ross, Moore, and others subscribe. I need to emphasize, however, that I don't mean to claim that, if a position were to reject some feature of moral realism of a paradigmatic sort, it thereby follows that such a position would not be a moral realist view. My claim is simply that any such position would not be a *paradigmatic* moral realist view. At any rate, it is moral realism of a paradigmatic sort for which I shall offer an argument in the subsequent chapters.

2

Defending the Parallel

In the last chapter, I suggested that there is a commonsensical conception of moral facts, fundamental to which are platitudes of two kinds. In the first place, there are what I called the 'content' platitudes. These platitudes tell us that there are intimate relations that obtain between moral facts and human well-being. For example, according to the content platitudes, actions of a certain range generally display moral properties only inasmuch as they foster or undercut (or express intentions to foster or undercut) human flourishing or the participation in the states and activities that are components thereof. In the second place, there are what I called the 'authority' platitudes. According to these platitudes, moral facts of certain types are, imply, or indicate categorical reasons for agents to behave in certain ways. To return to an example I used earlier, these platitudes imply that whether I have a moral reason to try to stop the occurrence of a wicked action that I can easily prevent is not contingent upon whether I desire to stop the occurrence of that action, whether I care about acting in a morally upright fashion, or whether I belong to a certain social group. Definitive of the position I have labeled 'moral realism of a paradigmatic sort' is the thesis that there are moral facts if and only if there are such facts that answer to platitudes of these kinds.

My aim in the subsequent chapters is to argue that moral facts thus understood exist and, thus, that moral realism of a paradigmatic sort is true. (From now on, unless I indicate otherwise, when I speak of moral facts I will mean moral facts as they are understood by the paradigmatic moral realist.) As I indicated in the Introduction, the strategy for doing so is to develop an argument from parity, one that exploits commonalities of a certain kind that exist between putative moral and epistemic facts. These commonalities, the suggestion is, give us excellent reason to believe that:

(1) If moral facts do not exist, then epistemic facts do not exist.

There are two stages of argument for this claim. The second and principal stage of argument, which is the concern of the next chapter, defends the thesis that there is a range of so-called objectionable features such that (i) were they displayed by moral facts, they would also be displayed by epistemic facts, and (ii) were their being displayed by moral facts to imply that moral facts do not exist, then their being displayed by epistemic facts would also imply that epistemic facts do not exist. The first stage of argument, which is the concern of this chapter, provides the conceptual backdrop for this argument. At this stage, my primary concern is to provide evidential support for several (in some cases implicit) assumptions made in the argument's second stage. I do this in two ways. In the first place, I identify four theoretically important respects in which moral and epistemic facts are similar. I then reply to several objections to the effect that moral and epistemic facts are sufficiently disanalogous that the case for premise (1) of the core argument cannot be made.

I. What epistemic realism is

To set the stage for identifying the first area of similarity between moral and epistemic facts—and, indeed, for developing the core argument sketched in the Introduction—let me begin by introducing the view that I shall call 'epistemic realism of a paradigmatic sort'. As I understand it, epistemic realism of a paradigmatic sort bears a close structural resemblance to its moral counterpart inasmuch as it is also comprised of three claims that concern the nature of epistemic discourse, truth, and facthood, respectively.

The speech act thesis

In the first place, the epistemic realist defends:

The Epistemic Realist's Speech Act Thesis: Some epistemic discourse is assertoric.

Suppose we assume that an 'epistemic sentence' is any sentence whose surface logical form is that of either (i) predicating a simple (i.e. non-compound) epistemic property of a particular entity or (ii) a universal generalization to the effect that, if something has a given feature, then it has a simple epistemic property. According to this account, sentences such as 'Sam's belief about UFOs is irrational' and 'Beliefs based on good evidence are justified' are examples of epistemic sentences. Call sentences of the first type 'predicative epistemic sentences' and those of the latter sort 'general epistemic sentences'. Epistemic discourse, as I shall understand it, is discourse that consists only in the sincere utterance of epistemic sentences.

Let's stipulate that an 'epistemic claim' (or 'judgment') is whatever mental state that is expressed by the sincere utterance of an epistemic sentence. An 'epistemic proposition' is the content (or, if you like, the object) of an epistemic claim that purports (in some cases, at least) to represent an epistemic fact. Propositions of this type can be divided into two kinds. 'Predicative epistemic propositions' are those whose logical form corresponds to the (surface) semantic components of predicative epistemic sentences. *That Sam's belief about UFOs is irrational* is an example of such a proposition. 'General epistemic propositions' are those propositions whose logical form corresponds to the (surface) semantic components of general epistemic sentences. *That beliefs based on good evidence are justified* is an example of a general epistemic proposition. A speech act counts as a case of assertoric epistemic discourse, I will assume, just in case it consists in the explicit presentation of an epistemic proposition by way of the sincere utterance of an epistemic sentence.

Let's now bring these claims together. Assuming that epistemic discourse is as I have described it, The Epistemic Realist's Speech Act Thesis tells us that discourse of this kind consists only in the sincere utterance of epistemic sentences and at least one such sentence is used explicitly to present an epistemic proposition.

In the last chapter, I developed a moral analogue to The Epistemic Realist's Speech Act Thesis, added several clarifications regarding it, and then pointed to some of its implications. I will proceed as if parallel clarificatory comments had been made regarding The Epistemic Realist's Speech Act Thesis. I assume, then, that The Epistemic Realist's Speech Act Thesis is incompatible with both expressivist and deflationary accounts of epistemic discourse, that it should be understood to tell us that epistemic sentences are commonly used to assert epistemic propositions, that assertoric epistemic discourse is best understood to include a fairly diverse lot of speech acts, and so forth. I pause only to acknowledge that I do not have any suggestions for how we might offer precise criteria for what counts as epistemic discourse. For present purposes, I assume only that there is a stock of simple predicative expressions that (in common usage) we commonly recognize as epistemic. Evaluative expressions such as 'is unjustified', 'is warranted', 'is rationally entitled', 'is conscientious', 'is insightful', and deontic expressions such as 'is (rationally) required', 'is (rationally) obligatory', 'is a(n) (epistemic) reason', and so forth are good examples of such expressions. I assume, accordingly, that only discourse that consists simply in the sincere utterance of well-formed predicative or general sentences that contain such predicative expressions counts as epistemic discourse.

The alethic thesis

Suppose we call an epistemic claim that expresses a predicative epistemic proposition a 'predicative epistemic claim'. We can then identify:

The Epistemic Realist's Alethic Thesis: The contents of some predicative epistemic claims are true and, if the contents of such claims are true, then they are true in the realist sense.

As with its moral counterpart, the idea here is that in some cases in which we say such things as 'Sam's belief about UFOs is irrational' or 'Sam ought to consider carefully the available evidence for Margaret's claim', we are saying something true. These claims are true, according to the realist conception of truth, just in case there are facts such as *that Sam's belief about UFOs is irrational* and *that Sam ought to consider carefully the available evidence for Margaret's claim*. A more extensive discussion of The Epistemic Realist's Alethic Thesis would indicate that qualifications hold parallel to those made about its moral analogue. For example, a more extensive discussion of The Epistemic Realist's Alethic Thesis would indicate that it should not be understood in either a deflationary or an inflationary manner. I will proceed as if these qualifications had been made explicit.

The ontic thesis

The thesis that some of our epistemic claims are true in the realist sense straightforwardly implies that there are epistemic facts. But, like moral realists, epistemic realists maintain that epistemic facts are of a special character. Epistemic realists thus defend this further claim:

The Epistemic Realist's Ontic Thesis: There are irreducible epistemic facts.

In the last chapter, I introduced a stylized account of what it is for facts of a certain kind to exist irreducibly. Recall the account went roughly like this: Suppose that Ks are putative facts of a certain kind. To say that Ks irreducibly exist is to claim, first, that there is a commonsensical conception of Ks, fundamental to which are platitudes of various kinds that purport to concern the nature of Ks. Second, it is to claim that Ks exist and satisfy the platitudes central to our commonsensical conception of Ks; they cannot be reduced to facts of a type that fail to satisfy central elements of our commonsensical conception of Ks. Characteristic of moral realism of a paradigmatic sort, I suggested, is the thesis that there is a commonsensical conception of moral facts, fundamental to which are platitudes that concern the content and authority of such facts. Moral facts irreducibly exist, I said, just in case such facts exist that satisfy the content and authority platitudes fundamental to our commonsensical conception of moral facts.

I propose a similar gloss on the claim that epistemic facts irreducibly exist. To say that epistemic facts irreducibly exist is to say, first, that there is a commonsensical conception of epistemic facts, fundamental to which are platitudes that concern the content and authority of such facts. And, second, it is to claim that epistemic facts exist if and only if such facts exist that satisfy the content and authority platitudes fundamental to our commonsensical conception of epistemic facts.

Let me unpack this account of the ontic thesis first by focusing on the content platitudes with respect to epistemic facts and then by turning to the authority platitudes. I'll then assess whether these platitudes genuinely belong to our commonsensical conception of epistemic facts.

The content and authority platitudes

The content platitudes with respect to epistemic facts tell us that there are conceptual limits as to what could count as an epistemic fact. Necessarily, were epistemic facts to exist, then they would have a certain type of nature. What might this be?

As a preliminary step toward answering this question, let me introduce a threefold distinction. Suppose we say that an entity x is *representational* with respect to y just in case x purports to represent y. Suppose, moreover, we say that an entity x *represents* y if and only if x is representational with respect to y and in fact is about, true of, or refers to y. Finally, let's say that an entity x is *representative* only insofar as it is representational and represents that which it purports to represent, or is likely to do so, or is the product of an agent's having done a sufficiently adequate job of trying to ensure that it represents reality aright. The answer I propose to the question raised above is that the content platitudes with respect to epistemic facts indicate that there is an intimate relationship between an entity's having one or another positive or negative epistemic status and the way in which it represents (or fails to represent) reality. More exactly, the suggestion I wish to make (which I shall refine in Chapter 5) is that the content platitudes with respect to epistemic facts tell us that representational entities such as the propositional attitudes display one or another epistemic merit (or positive epistemic status) such as *being a case of knowledge, being warranted, being an instance of understanding, insight,* or *wisdom,* and the like, only insofar as they are representative in some respect. That is, these entities display such merits only insofar as they represent reality aright, are likely to represent it aright, are the product of an agent's having done a sufficiently adequate job of trying to ensure that her attitudes represent reality aright, or the like. Likewise, entities such as the propositional attitudes have one or another epistemic demerit (or negative epistemic status) such as *being a case of ignorance, being shortsighted, unjustified,* or *irrational* only insofar as they fail to be representative in some respect.[1] That is, these entities display these demerits only insofar as they fail to represent reality aright, are unlikely to represent reality aright, are the product of an agent's having done an inadequate job of trying to ensure that her attitudes represent reality aright, or the like.

If this is correct, the content platitudes with respect to epistemic facts cluster around the notion of accurate representation in a similar fashion to the way in which the content platitudes with respect to moral facts congregate around the notion of human well-being. (I will have something more to say about this connection toward the end of this chapter.) In the interests of ensuring that the content platitudes are indeed platitudinous,

---

[1] A putative epistemic merit such as *being part of a coherent system of beliefs* might seem to be an exception to this claim. Given the way coherentists think of the concept of coherence, however, I doubt this is true. Lehrer (1986), for example, defines coherence in terms of the notion of its being more reasonable for an agent S to accept a proposition p on the assumption c than to accept a proposition q on the assumption d. Lehrer doesn't explicitly say what 'being more reasonable' consists in. But presumably it means something like 'it seems more likely to be the case to S than not'. If so, coherence is a notion that is intimately tied with representation.

I shall not adopt any particular account of what it is that representation consists in. So, while I assume for the moment that representation is a genuine 'substantive' relation that obtains between entities of various kinds, I aim to remain neutral on the question of how best to analyze this relation (or whether it can be analyzed).[2] Although to this let me add a clarification: While I have elucidated the content platitudes in terms of the representational function of the propositional attitudes, I do not mean thereby to suggest that epistemic merits attach only to the propositional attitudes. It may be that there are non-propositional modes of representation such that objects, maps, graphs, diagrams, and the like can properly be said to be representational and display in some derivative sense epistemic merits of certain kinds.[3] Moreover, I shall not assume that epistemic merits are one and all *alethic* merits—merits the presence of which in an agent's attitude indicates that the content of his attitude is true, that the content of his attitude is likely to be true, or that he has done a good job of trying to get at the truth. It may be, for example, that merits such as wisdom and insight cannot be analyzed in terms of truth. However, I shall assume that at least some epistemic merits are best understood as being alethic merits. Epistemic merits such as being justified, entitled, warranted, a case of knowledge, and so forth are almost always understood to be alethic merits, and I shall follow philosophical convention in thinking of them as such.

I turn now to the second platitude that figures in our commonsensical conception of epistemic facts, which concerns the claim that epistemic facts are authoritative. In what follows, I will assume that epistemic facts are authoritative in the following twofold sense. They are authoritative, in the first place, insofar as they are *prescriptive*. That is to say, epistemic facts are, imply, or indicate reasons for properly situated agents to behave in certain ways. It appears, for example, to be a conceptual truth that, if a certain plan of inquiry is manifestly irrational, then its being irrational provides appropriately situated persons with an epistemic reason not to engage in it. It is similarly platitudinous to say that, if a person investigates a matter with appropriate care and thoroughness, then she is deserving of approbation of a certain kind—approbation that we express by saying she is conscientious or scrupulous. To which we should add that it is the realist's

---

[2] I address these issues at greater length in Chapter 6.

[3] For more on this, see Zagzebski (2001).

conviction that epistemic facts of certain kinds (or the considerations they imply or indicate) on some occasions provide agents with a *decisive* reason to believe certain propositions or conduct their cognitive behavior in a particular fashion. (Here and elsewhere I use the term 'behavior' in its widest sense to stand for either the intentional or non-intentional activity of agents.)

The second sense in which epistemic facts are authoritative is that some such facts inescapably govern our conduct. The fundamental idea in this case is that some epistemic facts are, imply, or indicate categorical reasons for agents to behave in certain ways. As such, these facts are, imply, or indicate reasons for agents to behave in certain ways regardless of whether these agents care about conducting their behavior in a rational way, whether they belong to a social group of a certain kind, or whether they have entered into social agreements with others. (Consequently, if it is a conceptual truth that epistemic reasons govern 'appropriately situated' agents, being thus situated needn't include having concerns or social standings of certain kinds.) So, for example, according to the authority platitudes, whether I have an epistemic reason, say, to believe a proposition for which I have compelling evidence is not contingent upon whether I care about believing what is true. To this, realists add that epistemic reasons are authoritative inasmuch as the decisiveness of some such reasons for an agent is not a function of whether she wants to act in an epistemically commendable fashion, or belong to a certain social group, or has entered into certain agreements with others, and so forth. Like moral reasons of certain kinds, a wide range of epistemic reasons stands in sharp contrast to the norms that govern activities such as chess and tennis and bear a closer kinship to the norms of logic or mathematics. Indeed, arguably some of them *are* norms of logic and mathematics.

In sum, fundamental to the epistemic realist's ontic thesis is the claim that epistemic facts exist if and only if there are such facts that satisfy the content and authority platitudes fundamental to our commonsensical conception of epistemic facts. These platitudes tell us that entities such as the propositional attitudes display epistemic merits and demerits only insofar as they are representational and that some epistemic facts are, imply, or indicate categorical reasons. I suggest that we call these platitudes that concern the content and authority of epistemic facts 'the central platitudes concerning epistemic facts'.

An assessment of the realist's claims

The claim that the content and authority platitudes are fundamental to our commonsensical conception of epistemic facts will play a significant role in the case I make for the claim that epistemic facts exist, so I want to pause for a moment to assess the plausibility of what epistemic realists say.

In the first place, I will not assume that our commonsensical conception of epistemic facts implies that there are such facts. That there are such facts is something for which an argument will be offered. It is, however, part of the realist's claim that it *seems* as if ordinary agents believe or take it for granted that some of our beliefs have features such as being rational, entitled, and warranted. A very natural interpretation of these appearances is that ordinary agents believe or take it for granted that some of our beliefs display these epistemic merits—or at least these agents harbor attitudes that appear to be beliefs concerning entities that appear to display features that appear to be epistemic merits. It is instructive to note that philosophers such as Allan Gibbard who reject the existence of epistemic facts don't deny these claims.[4] In Gibbard's view, any adequate account of the epistemic realm needs to account for these appearances; accordingly, the antirealist who denies the existence of epistemic facts should be in the business of developing theories in which there are entities 'robustly mimicking facts'.[5] Nor, might I add, does it seem exceptionally controversial to say that epistemic concepts are sufficiently bound up with the notion of representation that these concepts properly apply only to those entities that are representative (although, as I indicated earlier, this will be subject to a qualification in Chapter 5). To be sure, some philosophers have suggested that we do away with the notion of truth or accurate representation in favor of broadly pragmatic goals for belief (e.g. whatever satisfies what you intrinsically value).[6] But I judge that the best way to interpret these philosophers is not as explicating our ordinary epistemic concepts. Their project is iconoclastic; they wish to do away with the discipline of epistemology altogether. After all, it is difficult to see how evaluating beliefs wholly in terms of how they contribute to health or happiness or whatever a person may value can be properly called *epistemic*. If this is right, what these philosophers say is not in conflict with the platitudes concerning the content of epistemic facts.

---

[4] At least this is true of Gibbard during his 'norm-expressivist' stage in Gibbard (1990). Gibbard's views have shifted recently, however; see Gibbard (2003).

[5] Gibbard (1992), 971.   [6] See Stich (1990) and Rorty (1984).

Perhaps the most controversial feature of the realist view is the claim that epistemic facts are authoritative in the sense just specified. The controversial feature of this claim is not so much that epistemic features are, imply, or indicate reasons to believe propositions or to conduct our behavior in certain ways; few have been keen to dispense with epistemic reasons altogether. The more controversial claim concerns whether the reasons in question are categorical. I intend to investigate this matter at some length in Chapter 7. For present purposes, however, it is worth emphasizing that the denial of this claim seems not to have mustered the same level of support in the epistemic realm as it has in the moral one.[7] There are probably numerous reasons for this, one of which is that any such view offers a highly strained interpretation of our practices of assessing epistemic conduct. Suppose, for example, I were to reproach you for having ignored considerations at your disposal that indicate that p is true. Suppose you were to reply by saying that, since you don't care about believing whether p is true, these considerations don't give you any type of reason to believe that p is true. Strange response! In so replying, we would rightly wonder whether you were being sincere, intent on provoking, or worse, in a lucid state of mind.

At any rate, the three claims we have considered—The Epistemic Realist's Speech Act, Alethic, and Ontic Theses—are the components of epistemic realism of a paradigmatic sort. I shall assume that embracing its three claims is necessary and sufficient for adopting the view. And, accordingly, I will assume that denying any of its claims is sufficient for not being a paradigmatic epistemic realist. That said, I add to this two provisos.

First, while paradigmatic epistemic realism is comprised of a cluster of theses, there is a clear sense in which The Epistemic Realist's Ontic Thesis lies at the heart of the view. For, as I highlighted in our earlier discussion of moral facts, if one establishes the ontic thesis, then one will be well along the way to establishing the other claims that comprise epistemic realism—these other claims being more or less natural consequences of

---

[7] Indeed, some philosophers who endorse the claim that moral reasons are hypothetical reject the claim that epistemic reasons (of certain kinds) are. Railton (1986) is an interesting example of this. After having introduced the claim that practical reasons are instrumental, he states that 'epistemology need not follow', for 'epistemic warrant may be tied to an external criterion—as it is for example by causal or reliabilist theories of knowledge' (pp. 169–70). Railton's position (in this essay, at least) appears to be that we should adopt a view according to which moral reasons are hypothetical, but epistemic ones (at least of certain kinds) are not.

the truth of the ontic thesis. Accordingly, I will assume that *paradigmatic* versions of epistemic antirealism are ones that deny the realist's ontic thesis—the rejection of the other two claims that comprise epistemic realism ordinarily being driven by the rejection of this thesis. Indeed, in what follows I will reserve the term 'epistemic antirealist' to stand for any position that rejects The Epistemic Realist's Ontic Thesis. So—and this is the second point—the general strategy that I shall implement in the subsequent chapters will be to argue that we have good reason to believe that epistemic antirealist positions are likely to be false because they reject the existence of such facts. (Unless I indicate otherwise, when I speak of epistemic facts, I shall mean epistemic facts as they are understood by the paradigmatic epistemic realist.)

The first similarity

The upshot of our discussion thus far is that paradigmatic epistemic realism bears a close structural resemblance to paradigmatic moral realism. While our discussion has located numerous points of resemblance between these two positions, I want now to highlight the first main area of similarity between moral and epistemic facts in which I am interested, one to which I have now regularly drawn attention: On the assumption that we understand moral and epistemic facts to be those entities that our commonsensical conceptions of moral and epistemic facts purport to pick out, then facts of both kinds are authoritative. If such facts exist, then some facts of each kind are, imply, or indicate categorical reasons for properly situated agents to behave themselves in certain ways.

II. A framework for thinking about normative facts

So far forth, I have been working with a fairly thin account of the nature of moral and epistemic facts. Facts of these kinds, I've said, can be thought of simply as that which is represented by true moral and epistemic claims and what (in a range of cases) are, imply, or indicate categorical reasons for agents to behave in certain ways. It will be helpful for our purposes to thicken this account somewhat. Doing so will allow us both to identify further areas of similarity between moral and epistemic facts and to introduce some claims that will bear importantly upon subsequent argumentation, especially that contained in Chapters 7 and 8. Accordingly, I want in this section to sketch a conceptual framework that can help us think about the nature of moral and epistemic facts. Let me emphasize at the outset that what I shall present is a *sketch* of such a framework; there are important issues regarding the nature of moral and epistemic facts that I will be unable to address. My aim at present, however, is not to offer a highly elaborate account of the ontology of moral and epistemic facts, but to indicate the ways in which moral and epistemic facts are similar in certain respects relevant for the subsequent argument.

Facts and reasons

I begin by introducing a twofold distinction between different types of normative fact. (I use the appellation 'normative' here in a restricted sense to range over only moral and epistemic features.) Harkening back to the last chapter, let's distinguish, in the first place, between particular and general normative facts. And, for ease of explication, let me employ the concept of a state of affairs to explicate the notion of a normative fact. (In a moment, I will address the distinction between states of affairs that exist and those that obtain. In the schemata I state below, I will use the term 'state of affairs' to refer to a state of affairs that obtains. I also assume that talk of states of affairs can be translated into different idioms that others may prefer.)

In the first place, let's say that:

X is a *particular normative fact* if and only if X is a state of affairs that is comprised of a particular entity's having a simple normative property.

That Sam's humiliating Margaret is wrong or *that Sam's belief regarding UFOs is irrational* are examples of particular normative facts. Facts such as these are represented by true predicative normative claims.

By contrast, let's say that:

X is a *general normative fact* if and only if X is a state of affairs that specifies that if a particular entity were instantiated, then it would have a simple normative property.

That humiliating others for mere pleasure is wrong or *that believing in UFOs is unjustified* are cases of putative general normative facts. Facts such as these correspond to true general normative claims.

Having distinguished particular from general normative facts, let's now distinguish between deontic and evaluative normative facts. Suppose we use the term 'response' in a fairly loose way to refer to either a single type of response or a range of such responses (and what we would also consider failures to respond). And suppose we similarly use the term 'agent' to refer to a particular agent or group thereof. Deontic normative facts can be thought of disjunctively:

X is a *deontic normative fact* if and only if X is a state of affairs that (i) consists in an entity's morally or epistemically favoring a response of a properly situated agent or (ii) specifies that an entity would, if instantiated, morally or epistemically favor that response of a properly situated agent.[8]

For example, *that Sam ought to apologize to Margaret* and *that agents should exercise care when forming and maintaining beliefs of certain kinds* are deontic normative facts.

Evaluative normative facts can also be thought of disjunctively. More exactly, let's stipulate that:

X is an *evaluative normative fact* if and only if X is a state of affairs that (i) consists in an agent's responding at some time (or being reliably disposed to respond) in an appropriate or inappropriate fashion to an entity that morally or epistemically favors a given response or (ii) specifies that an agent would respond at some time (or would be reliably disposed to respond) in an appropriate or inappropriate fashion to an entity that morally or epistemically favors a given response, were it to be instantiated.

That Margaret is kind and *that believing that UFOs exist is unjustified* are evaluative normative facts. As will have been evident from these character- izations, deontic and evaluative normative facts can be either particular or general in character.

Ever since John Rawls's *A Theory of Justice*, philosophers have been very interested in tagging some normative concept as explanatorily basic and explicating others in terms of that concept. I am skeptical of this project. For I doubt there is some one basic normative concept in terms of which we can informatively explicate all other normative concepts—all such attempts, in my estimation, ultimately being either uninformative or revers- ing what appear to be the proper orders of explanation between different

---

[8] I remain noncommittal with respect to the issue of whether the reasons in question are pro tanto, prima facie, ultima facie, or the like.

normative concepts.[9] Still, we can trace some theoretically interesting relations between different types of normative concepts, and I suggest that
one of the more illuminating ways to do so is in terms of the notion of a
reason.[10]

For present purposes, let's think of a reason as a consideration that counts
in favor of a given type of response of an agent. (I shall have more to say
about the range of types of response in the next section.) And when I say
that a consideration 'counts in favor of' a given response, I mean this to
cover a rather wide swath of conceptual territory. Something can count
in favor of a response insofar as the thing *commends* a given response. But
it can also count in favor of a response insofar as it *demands* or *requires* or
dictates that one *ought* to have that response. However, to this I should add
that I will not assume that something's being demanded of one just *is* for it
to be most favored.

Lying just beneath the surface of this account of a reason is the thesis
that reasons are relational entities of a sort. A reason ascription always has
as its components the following quartet:

Consideration G → Favors → Response R of S in Circumstance C

I.   II.   III.   IV.

Suppose we call the consideration that favors the 'ground'. And suppose we
call that which is favored the 'response'. Reasons, as I shall think of them,
are grounds that favor responses of certain kinds of properly situated agents.
Let it be noted that I have claimed that it is the *grounds* themselves that are
reasons. I have not said that reasons are the favoring relation or that they
are the grounds in addition to the favoring relation. That this appears to be
the right way to think of reasons can be brought out by example. Imagine
you were to ask Sam what reason he has to engage in a particular plan
of inquiry. It wouldn't be very informative for Sam to answer: 'Because
I ought to.' This isn't what favors Sam's engaging in this plan of inquiry.
At best, Sam's reply succeeds in locating not *what* favors his engaging in

[9] In an unpublished piece, 'The Evaluative and the Deontic', Michael Smith attempts to define
deontic concepts in terms of evaluative ones. Central to Smith's argument is the assumption that a
concept is deontic just in case it grounds the possibility of criticism and the allocation of responsibility.
It seems to me, however, that agents can fail to fulfill their obligations and not thereby be blameworthy.
I take up the matter at more length at the end of this chapter.
[10] I thus find myself in some sympathy with Scanlon (1998), Chs. 1 and 2 in this respect. I've found
Dancy (2000), Ch. 1 helpful for thinking about the notion of a reason.

that plan of inquiry, but the *type* of favoring in question. Nor, it should be added, would it be informative for Sam to offer this reply: 'The fact *that it is important I keep my promise favors my engaging in this plan of inquiry* is my reason to engage in this line of inquiry.' That would, as it were, be to offer one ought too many. It would be in effect to say that Sam ought to do what Sam ought. This statement may be true, but does not identify—at least in any perspicuous way—what favors his engaging in this particular plan of inquiry.

Think back now to the twofold distinction made between different types of normative fact. I suggest we can illuminate these different types of fact in terms of the notion of a reason thus understood. To begin with the most obvious case, particular deontic facts (or particular 'norms', if you like) are simply facts that consist in a ground's favoring a certain type of response. If the type of response falls under a positive moral concept such as *being compassionate* or *being just*, then the fact in question is a deontic moral fact and the ground that favors this type of response is a moral reason. Likewise, if the type of response falls under a positive epistemic concept such as *being rational* or *being intellectually careful*, then the fact in question is a deontic epistemic fact and the ground that favors this type of response is an epistemic reason.

Particular evaluative facts, by contrast, can be thought of in terms of the reasons that constitute deontic facts. (I do not deny the reverse is also the case.) 'Non-dispositional' facts of this kind consist in an agent's responding in an appropriate or inappropriate way to reasons. For example, the fact *that Sam's behavior toward Margaret is unjust* consists in an item of behavior's being an inappropriate response of a certain kind to considerations that morally favor Sam's not behaving in that fashion. Similarly, the fact *that Sam's belief about UFOs is irrational* consists in Sam's belief's being an inappropriate response of a certain kind to considerations that epistemically favor its being formed or maintained in a certain way. 'Dispositional' evaluative facts, by contrast, consist not in an agent's actually appropriately or inappropriately responding to reasons, but in her being reliably disposed to respond appropriately or inappropriately to reasons. *That Margaret is kind*, for example, consists in Margaret's being reliably disposed to respond in certain types of appropriate ways to moral reasons of a certain range. Likewise, the fact *that Sam is irrational* consists in Sam's being reliably disposed to respond in certain types of inappropriate fashion to reasons of certain kinds.

Turning now from particular to general normative facts, we can think of general deontic facts (or 'general' norms) as being distributive functions from possible or actual instantiations of reasons to types of appropriate response. Unpacked a little, the fact *that agents should exercise care when forming and maintaining beliefs of certain kinds* is the conditional state of affairs that, if any belief is of a certain type, then all mature agents in circumstances C have epistemic reasons to exercise care when forming and maintaining beliefs of this type. In this case, were a belief to be a token of that type, then that is what would favor any relevantly situated agent's exercising care if she were to form or maintain it. Similarly, general evaluative facts are naturally viewed as functions from possible or actual instantiations of reasons to types of appropriate or inappropriate response. The putative fact *that believing in UFOs is unjustified* is the conditional state of affairs that, if something is a belief that UFOs exist, then it is unjustified. Were a person to respond to the evidential grounds regarding the existence of UFOs by believing in their existence, then that would constitute an epistemically inappropriate response to these grounds.

Philosophers think of the interplay between general and particular normative facts differently. Some, such as Kantians and divine command theorists, hold that general normative facts generate particular normative facts. Paradigmatic versions of the divine command theory, for example, tell us that, in some cases, a particular person has a reason to act on a given occasion just in case and because there is a general norm or rule that issues from God (e.g. if someone is an innocent, then you ought not to kill him) and that this norm applies to this person on this occasion. Other philosophers, such as so-called particularists, reject this picture, denying that general normative facts generate reasons in this way.[11] In what follows, I take no stand on this issue. I simply emphasize that general normative facts are not themselves very plausible candidates for being reasons; it is difficult to see, after all, how a conditional state of affairs could itself favor one or another response of an agent. At best, facts of this sort are (as the divine command theorist believes) components of reasons or, perhaps better, simply reason-indicators, telling us what types of ground actually favor certain types of response. Once we see this, it can help us to make better sense of the phrase, which I have used

---

[11] For more on particularism, see Dancy (1993), (2000a), (2004), and Little (2000).

frequently, that some moral and epistemic facts are categorical reasons inasmuch as they are, imply, or indicate categorical reasons. If what the realist says is true, particular deontic and evaluative facts of certain kinds are or imply reasons for agents to respond in certain ways. The particular deontic fact *that Sam ought not to humiliate Margaret*, for instance, implies that there are considerations that count in favor of Sam's not acting in a certain way toward Margaret. But the general deontic fact *that one ought not to humiliate others for mere fun* does not imply that there are reasons, but simply indicates that, were something a case of humiliating others for fun, then it would count in favor of not engaging in such activity.

Let me now add three points. First, there are live controversies among philosophers as to what sorts of things reasons are and whether they are 'complete'—that is, whether they have among their constituents everything necessary and sufficient to favor a response of a certain kind.[12] I aim to keep relatively neutral on these debates, assuming only that some reasons constitute (or are) moral and epistemic facts.

Second, I assume that there is a distinction between something's *being* a reason to Φ and someone's *having* a reason to Φ. Something is a reason for someone to Φ, I will assume, just in case it favors his Φing. By contrast, someone has a reason to Φ just in case what favors his Φing is in some sense within his ken. Of the reasons there might be for an agent to Φ, I will assume that it is possible that a good many of them do not fall within his ken. Whether something can be a reason for a person without that person's being able to grasp it (given his present constitution) is a matter about which I will remain neutral, however.

Finally, I will assume that there is a distinction between what I'll call 'veridical' and 'nonveridical' reasons. Roughly put, an agent has a veridical reason to respond in a certain way only if she takes there to be a reason to respond in that way and things are as she takes them to be. By contrast, an agent has a nonveridical reason to respond in a certain manner only if she takes there to be a reason to respond in a certain way, but things are not as she takes them to be; nonetheless, that she takes things to be thus favors her responding in that way inasmuch as her taking things to be this way is well-founded.

---

[12] For more on this, see Murphy (2002), Ch. 1 and Dancy (2004).

To elaborate: While there is in principle any number of ways to flesh out the distinction between veridical and nonveridical reasons, a helpful way to do so is by appealing to a notion to which I have already appealed, namely, that of a state of affairs. According to the canonical understanding, states of affairs are entities that admit of both positive and negative polarities. When a state of affairs has a positive polarity, it obtains or is a fact. When it has a negative polarity, it exists, but fails to obtain or be a fact. So, the state of affairs of *Sam's being virtuous*, we can assume, exists. But it is not a fact, since Sam is not in actuality virtuous. That said, we can stipulate that S has a veridical reason to Φ only if (i) there is a state of affairs F that S takes to obtain and favor his Φing, and (ii) F obtains and favors his Φing. For example, I have a veridical reason to disapprove of Sam's having humiliated Margaret for mere pleasure only if there is a state of affairs of *Sam's having humiliated Margaret for mere pleasure* that I take to obtain and this state of affairs obtains, thereby favoring my disapproving of Sam's behavior. By contrast, S has a nonveridical reason to Φ only if (i) there is a state of affairs F that S takes to obtain and favor his Φing, and (ii) F either fails to obtain or its obtaining fails to favor his Φing, but (iii) the content of S's attitude favors his Φing because his taking F to obtain and to favor his Φing is well-founded.[13] For example, I have a nonveridical reason to disapprove of Sam's having humiliated Margaret for mere pleasure only if there is a state of affairs of *Sam's having humiliated Margaret for mere pleasure* that I take to obtain, but either this state of affairs fails to obtain or its obtaining fails to favor my disapproving of Sam. Nonetheless, my taking Sam's having acted in this way to favor my disapproval is well-founded. For it seems to me that Sam has acted in this way, and its seeming this way is not subject to defeaters of various kinds, such as being the product of my epistemically negligent behavior.

According to this way of thinking, reasons are a varied lot. Some are facts that obtain independently of an agent's mental states, while others are (or are comprised of) the content of an agent's representational states. (I assume that, generally, facts and the content of representational states are

---

[13] I assume here that it is the content of S's taking that favors his responding in a certain way. (Incidentally, 'taking' should be understood broadly here; it needn't refer merely to intentional takings.) Although I prefer this way of thinking of reasons, I don't intend to preclude a position according to which it is S's taking itself that favors his responding in that way. For more on the matter, see Dancy (2000), Chs. 5 and 6.

not identical, for the latter, but not the former, incorporates a particular way of thinking of an entity.) Moreover, thus described, reasons should be understood in a fairly fine-grained manner, as they confer different types of merit on the responses that agents have to them. For example, that something seems to me to be a certain way might yield the consequence that the resulting belief that things are that way is entitled insofar as it is not in any sense negligently formed. That things seem to me thus-and-so, however, might not yield the consequence that the belief in question is warranted, since my cognitive faculties might be ill-suited for the environment in which the belief was formed. If this is right, then we should think of reasons as being relativized to various merits: Among the reasons we have will be entitlement-conferring reasons, warrant-conferring reasons, justification-conferring reasons, and so on. At any rate, once we draw the distinction between veridical and nonveridical reasons, we can say that an agent's response displays a moral or epistemic merit if and only if it is an appropriate response to moral or epistemic reasons, respectively. (This is what I shall call in Chapter 7 'The Generation Thesis'.) Some such merits will be 'objective' in character insofar as they attach to a response to a veridical reason (or reasons). Other merits will be more 'subjective' in character insofar as they attach to a response to a nonveridical reason (or reasons).

The second similarity

Having now mapped some conceptual territory with respect to moral and epistemic facts, the second main similarity between moral and epistemic facts I wish to identify is more or less plainly in view. If what I have said earlier is correct, some moral and epistemic facts are, imply, or indicate categorical reasons. What this last section reveals is that not only are some such reasons categorical, but also the facts in which they are ingredients are structurally isomorphic. Facts of both kinds are either particular or general normative facts, on the one hand, or evaluative or deontic normative facts, on the other. Moreover, such facts are plausibly viewed as being constituted by reasons; in the case of (particular) deontic facts, the reasons favor responses of certain kinds, while in the case of (particular) evaluative facts, the reasons are accompanied by an appropriate or inappropriate mode of response. At any rate, it is a framework such as this that I will employ in subsequent chapters (especially Chapter 7).

III. Cut from the same cloth

In the last section, I drew attention to the structural isomorphism that
obtains between moral and epistemic facts. I want now to draw attention to
the nature of the responses that the reasons constitutive of such facts favor.

When one surveys a wide range of work in contemporary moral
philosophy and epistemology, it is difficult not to be struck by two
tendencies, both of which are relevant for our purposes. In the first place,
many moral philosophers write as if moral norms primarily govern actions
or intentions, the ascendant positions in the field being mostly concerned
with whether acts of certain kinds maximize goodness or intentions of
certain types are universalizable. In the second place, Anglo–American
epistemologists have almost single-mindedly focused on the application of
epistemic norms to beliefs—the central questions in the field regarding
that in which justification and knowledge consist. The impression one
can bring away from these discussions is that both moral and epistemic
norms apply to a rather small class of entities and, at that, entities of
different kinds. Moral norms apply primarily to intentions and actions
while epistemic ones apply primarily to beliefs. However, I think that such
an impression would be mistaken, as it fails to reveal the genuine character
of moral and epistemic norms. A better way to view the matter is this:
Both moral and epistemic norms apply to an extraordinarily wide array
of entities. Institutions, persons, intentions, actions, propositional attitudes
(e.g. beliefs, acceptances, inquiries, and hopes), character traits, emotions,
policies, ways of viewing things, ways of finding out things, and so forth,
are all plausibly thought to be subject to moral and epistemic norms. They
are, as we might say, morally and epistemically appraisable entities.

The thesis that a wide range of entities is amenable both to moral and
epistemic assessment has been defended recently by proponents of so–called
virtue ethics and virtue epistemology.[14] And while I do not wish to commit
myself to some of the more robust claims that advocates of such views
defend (for example, the claim that we should avoid moral terminology in
favor of that of 'admirability and the virtues'[15]), this claim regarding the

---

[14] I have found Zagzebski (1996) particularly helpful for thinking through these issues. The themes
I am developing here are indebted to what she says.
[15] See Slote (1997), 188.

scope of moral and epistemic appraisal seems to me correct and in keeping with our ordinary practices. Consider two examples to illustrate the point:

Sam finds himself on some occasion listening to a virtual stranger effusively explain to him the hard turns that life has given her. She is out of work and has no family, immediate or distant, to support her. Sam himself has no particular reason to disbelieve this woman's story. Nevertheless, he finds himself unmoved by the woman's testimony; he has a vague intuition that he should feel pity or compassion for her, but he feels nothing. Still, he forms an intention to promise her that he'll do his best to see if he can find her work and promises her as much.

If we are swimming along with strong currents in moral philosophy—wondering, perhaps, whether Sam's behavior maximizes value or whether his intentions are universalizable—we are likely to fix upon what Sam does, namely, promise the woman his aid. But consider how a more nuanced evaluation would go.

There is a reason here—viz., a woman's testimony about her needs—that counts in favor of Sam's responding with compassion and fellow feeling. His emotional aloofness is a moral demerit; he ought to have a different emotional response. Accordingly, we can morally appraise Sam's emotional state and—on the assumption that this state is an expression of a settled disposition—his character, on account of their coldness. Sam's vague intuition that he should feel compassion is also plausibly viewed as a moral demerit, for this conviction should be sharper and more pronounced than it is. But Sam also believes that he ought to help the woman who has expressed her misfortune to him. And he decides to help her. This belief and intention are morally meritorious, and we can evaluate them as such. (It is possible for Sam, out of cynicism, to have entirely dismissed this woman's testimony and not formed any such belief or intention.) Perhaps Sam's intention is not as good as it should be on account of its not being grounded in compassion, but it is morally good nevertheless. And so also is the promising that flows from his intention.

Now consider an epistemic analogue:

Shortly after his encounter with the stranger, Sam receives some critical feedback on a project in progress from his colleague Margaret. Margaret is astute and perceptive; however, she does tend to voice her views with verve, and the force of her comments is in keeping with this trait. Upon reading Margaret's comments, Sam finds himself believing that she doesn't really appreciate his work.

He thereupon finds himself annoyed and ultimately angry with her. Now, as it happens, his belief and his anger are poorly grounded; he has badly misinterpreted what Margaret has written—'read into things', as they say. Still, his anger with Margaret festers to the point where it colors the way in which he sees her comments and casts them, together with her abilities, in a less than charitable light. He finds himself thinking that she's not so astute after all and more intent on catapulting her own career than helping colleagues. In a fit of resentment, he forms the intention to ignore the generous criticism that Margaret has offered him and subsequently acts upon it.

If we are carried along by strong currents in contemporary epistemology—wondering perhaps what makes it the case that Sam's beliefs are unjustified—we will be tempted to appraise Sam's behavior in this case in such a way that we fix upon what is problematic with his beliefs. But there is more to assess epistemically regarding Sam's conduct than this, for in nearly all respects, it grades low from an epistemic point of view. To begin with, his interpretation of what Margaret has written is epistemically defective in various ways; it fails to get at what she really says. His beliefs that Margaret is not astute and doesn't appreciate his work are also epistemically deficient. They are the upshot of a poor diagnosis. And then there is his anger. It is, for one thing, intellectually obfuscating. His anger is not only evidentially unsupported, but it also inhibits him from clearly seeing the value of Margaret's comments and from pausing to rethink his interpretation of what she has said. It is, for another, the impetus for epistemically defective intention and action. Both Sam's intention to ignore and his action of ignoring Margaret's criticism are epistemic hindrances; they serve further to obfuscate a more accurate view of his work and the quality of Margaret's criticism. From an epistemic point of view, Sam ought not to believe, feel, intend, or do these things.[16]

If I am right, these two cases support a rather ecumenical approach to moral and epistemic assessment. According to this ecumenical approach, it

---

[16] By suggesting that we epistemically assess a wider array of entities than is sometimes assumed, I don't wish to suggest that *anything* that functions as an epistemic abettor or hindrance is thereby epistemically assessable. For example, that Sam has a severe headache may on some occasion prevent him from reasoning well. But it doesn't follow from this that his headache is thereby open to epistemic assessment. Is there a principled rationale that explains why we (appropriately) epistemically assess action plans and mental states such as beliefs, but not headaches? Allan Gibbard suggests that the difference lies in the fact that we can disagree with action plans and beliefs, but not headaches. I believe that this is along the right lines. See Gibbard (2003), Ch. 4.

would be incorrect to say that moral and epistemic facts are interestingly disanalogous because epistemic facts concern only 'theoretical' reasons, while moral ones concern only 'practical' reasons. If the cases I have described accurately capture how we assess agents and their behavior, some epistemic reasons are practical in nature, favoring the implementation of action plans of certain kinds. And some moral reasons are theoretical in character, favoring the formation, maintenance, and surrendering of propositional attitudes of certain types (and ways of forming, maintaining, and surrendering those attitudes). That said, I don't want to rest my case for the ecumenical approach simply on the scenarios I've described. For it seems to me that we can offer a deeper theoretical rationale for this type of approach, one that is a more or less natural upshot of the theoretical framework with which I've been working. The theoretical rationale to which I allude sheds light on why some moral facts concern 'theoretical' reasons and some epistemic facts concern 'practical' ones.

Return for the moment to what I have termed the 'content platitudes' with respect to moral facts. If platitudes of this sort hold, it is not surprising that intentions of various kinds are morally assessable. Intending to betray a friend for money, for example, is typically an expression of unwarranted disrespect for another. And when it is, it impairs the affected agent's participation in goods constitutive of human flourishing, such as sharing bonds of trust with others. However, if the content platitudes hold, it is also not surprising that various types of propositional attitudes are morally assessable. Believing that someone is a liar, for example, is sometimes an expression of unwarranted disrespect for another. And when it does evidence such disrespect, it is something that impairs the affected agent's participation in goods constitutive of human flourishing, such as being harmoniously related to others. Similarly, hoping that someone fails at a task is also sometimes the expression of unwarranted contempt for that agent. And when it does evidence such contempt, it is something that impairs the affected agent's participation in goods that comprise human flourishing, such as not being the object of others' derision. If the content platitudes be believed, it is precisely considerations such as these that make the holding of such attitudes morally appraisable, for propositional attitudes no less than intentions can contribute to or undercut an agent's well-being or the goods that comprise it. To which I add the observation that we appear morally to appraise propositional attitudes such as beliefs and hopes even when we think that an agent has little voluntary control over them. (Imagine, for example, that despite your best efforts you cannot but hope that a rival fails at some important task.) Indeed, in some cases, we morally evaluate the propositional attitudes for the same reasons we morally assess intentions and actions of certain kinds: We take them to express morally suspect character traits.

Now consider what I've called the 'content platitudes' with respect to epistemic facts. If platitudes of this type hold, it is not surprising that various types of propositional attitudes are epistemically assessable. Accepting a proposition on the basis of mere wishful thinking, for example, is almost invariably a case of epistemic impropriety. And when it is, it impairs an agent's ability to represent reality aright. Likewise, if the content platitudes hold, it is similarly unsurprising that various types of intentions and action plans are epistemically assessable. Intending to assess evidence of a certain kind at the cost of ignoring conflicting high-grade evidence, for instance, is sometimes the fruit of negligence. And when it is, a failure of this sort is often epistemically inappropriate because it lowers our chances of making cognitive contact with reality. Similarly, planning to employ an unreliable method of investigation when more reliable methods are readily available is sometimes the expression of being intellectually obtuse. And when it is, it is often epistemically defective, for it also impedes an agent's accurately registering the way the world is. If the content platitudes with regard to epistemic facts hold, then it is precisely features such as these that make intentions and action plans epistemically appraisable. Representing the world aright has a great deal to do with what we plan and what we do!

Considerations such as these, I believe, give us good grounds for maintaining that a wide range of entities are objects of moral and epistemic appraisal. They are not, perhaps, *equally central* objects of moral or epistemic appraisal. It is possible that one or another type of entity—say, character traits—are the central objects of moral or epistemic appraisal, other entities having only derivative moral or epistemic importance insofar as they help or hinder the formation and maintenance of morally or epistemically praiseworthy character traits (more on this in Chapter 5). Even so, they are morally and epistemically appraisable entities and, as such, plausibly viewed as modes of appropriate or inappropriate response to moral or epistemic reasons. As my comments will have indicated, there are some important differences between these modes of response: Cases of some types, such as intentions, are regularly under our voluntary control, while others, such as emotional states of certain kinds, are not (or are only minimally so). I shall have more to say about this shortly.

The third similarity

The second area of similarity between putative moral and epistemic facts to which I drew attention is that moral and epistemic facts are structurally isomorphic insofar as they can be divided into identical sub-categories of fact—particular and general, deontic and evaluative in the terminology I used. I now wish to draw attention to a further way in which facts of these kinds are isomorphic, which itself has two aspects.

Suppose we use the term 'normatively appraisable entity' to stand for any entity that is open to moral or epistemic assessment—any entity that can bear a moral or epistemic property. The first sense in which moral and epistemic facts are similar is that they are constituted by normatively appraisable entities of the same types. Now suppose we use the term 'mode of response' to refer to the types of response a reason can favor, such as the formation of propositional attitudes, the formation of motivational states, the implementation of action plans, and so on. And suppose we assume that moral and epistemic reasons are such that, for each type of reason, there is a class consisting in all and only the modes of response reasons of that type favor. Call the first class of responses 'the moral set' and the second 'the epistemic set'. Then we can say that the second sense in which moral and epistemic reasons are similar is that there is considerable overlap between the members of the moral and epistemic sets. Indeed, in light of the fact that it is difficult to identify some mode of response favored by moral and not epistemic reasons or vice versa, we are arguably entitled to a stronger conclusion than this: namely, that the members of the moral and epistemic set are identical. It follows that deontic and evaluative moral and epistemic facts consist in (or indicate) moral and epistemic reasons that favor identical modes of response.[17] These two claims constitute the third main area of similarity between moral and epistemic facts that I wish to highlight.

---

[17] A point of clarification: I do not assume that since moral and epistemic reasons favor the same types of modes of response, there cannot be situations in which moral and epistemic reasons favor incompatible responses. For example, it may be that there are cases according to which being a faithful friend morally requires giving the friend's testimony the benefit of the doubt, while being epistemically scrupulous requires otherwise.

A further connection

If there are relevant differences between moral and epistemic facts, I have suggested, it is not because moral and epistemic norms have different scopes of application, applying to entities of different kinds. I would now like to suggest that the second of the two scenarios involving Sam that we just considered indicates a further main area of similarity between moral and epistemic facts that underscores the extent to which the moral and epistemic domains are intermeshed.

In the second case we considered, Sam's behavior is not admirable in multiple respects. If we want to employ what is perhaps the thinnest term of epistemic assessment, we would rightly call him 'irrational'. While general terms of assessment such as this have their place, we can see that in this case the concept it expresses functions as a catch-all notion, telling us that Sam fails to exhibit qualities such as being intellectually open-minded, reliable, objective, and careful, among others. These are epistemic defects—intellectual vices, as the broadly Aristotelian tradition would label them. But at least some of these vices and others like them—such as intellectual sloppiness, inattentiveness, indiscretion, lack of autonomy (i.e. failing to think for oneself and not being unduly influenced by others), and so forth—have decidedly moral dimensions. In many cases, conforming or failing to conform to norms of intellectual open-mindedness, care, and autonomy is the occasion for moral blame or praise. (Think of how we disapprove of Sam on account of his inability to receive criticism.) On account of this, it is tempting to conclude that norms of these kinds just are moral norms, in which case it follows that an agent's failure to conform to them implies only that she suffers from a moral defect.[18] While such a position is consistent with the core argument I wish to develop, I suggest that it is more plausible to believe that norms of the kind I have mentioned are *hybrid* norms—norms that, as it were, have a foot in both the epistemic and moral realms. (That norms such as this have a foot in the epistemic realm is guaranteed by the fact that they direct us to represent or try to represent the world in certain ways.) Hybrid norms are such that, if any such norm applies to an agent, and that agent fails to conform to that norm, then (all else being equal) she exhibits both a moral and an epistemic

---

[18] Chisholm (1977a) and (1991), Wolterstorff (1997) and (unpublished), and Zagzebski (1996) all seem attracted to such a view.

failing. Correlatively, if any such norm applies to such an agent, and that agent appropriately conforms to that norm, then (all else being equal) she displays both a moral and an epistemic merit.

Let me expand upon this for a moment. Norms of fairness in evaluating the views of others are a vivid case of hybrid norms. Norms of this sort dictate that we do not allow improper sorts of bias to color our appraisal of others' views, that we take the appropriate time to evaluate their positions, that we not form snap judgments about their intentions, and so forth. Insofar as a person conforms to these norms, that person expresses respect for the person whose views he is evaluating. So, there is a moral dimension to these norms such that if an appropriately situated agent fails to conform to them, then (all else being equal) he thereby exhibits a moral demerit. Likewise, it is also true that insofar as a person conforms to these norms, that person does his best to represent reality aright. There is also, then, an epistemic dimension to these norms such that if an appropriately situated agent fails to conform to them, then (all else being equal) he thereby displays an epistemic demerit. The interesting feature of conforming to norms of fairness is that respecting the person whose views are being evaluated *consists* in doing one's best to interpret his views aright, and doing one's best to interpret his views aright *consists* in expressing respect of a kind. Here the moral and epistemic dimensions coalesce.[19]

As I said, there are different ways to think about the nature of hybrid norms, ranging from strict separationist views (positions that imply that

---

[19] David Enoch points out to me that there are cases in which the moral and epistemic dimensions of putative hybrid norms appear to come apart. For example, consider a case in which Sam is highly epistemically unreliable. As such, we can assume that Margaret has little epistemic reason to evaluate his testimony carefully. But suppose that Margaret's disregarding Sam's testimony would signal to him that she fails to respect him. If this is true, then it is arguable that Margaret has a moral reason to listen carefully to what he says nonetheless. It follows that, in this case, Margaret has a moral reason to evaluate carefully what Sam says, but not an epistemic one. And this—the suggestion runs—indicates that norms of conscientiousness and fairness are not hybrid norms at all, but simply amalgams of epistemic and moral norms.

My brief reply is this: At most what this case establishes is that, in the complex interplay of reasons, there may be moral, but not epistemic, reasons of certain kinds to attend to another's testimony. The case does not establish, however, that Margaret's conduct in this case is governed by moral, but not epistemic, norms of conscientiousness and fairness in evaluating the views of others. After all, it does not follow from the fact that Margaret does not have epistemic reason to listen attentively to Sam's testimony, that she is thereby free to indulge habits of sloppy or biased thinking when engaging with Sam. For had she done so, she would presumably have suffered from both epistemic and moral dis-excellences: Her behavior would have graded low from both the epistemic and moral points of view inasmuch as it failed to exhibit the appropriate care and attention that the views of others merit.

if something is an epistemic norm, then it is not a moral one, and vice versa), overlapping content views (some epistemic norms are moral norms), to identity views (moral and epistemic norms are identical). Since the argument I develop is compatible with any of these positions, I shall adopt a relatively neutral position, claiming only that some moral and epistemic facts are mutually implicative. (I assume that necessary coextensiveness is not identity.) According to this position, (particular) hybrid norms imply that there are moral reasons for agents to respond in certain ways. But, since such norms also concern the way we should represent reality, they also imply epistemic reasons for agents to respond in certain manners. My own preferred way to view moral and epistemic norms is as falling along a continuum. At the middle of the continuum are hybrid norms of intellectual fairmindedness, honesty, humility, and trust. Shading out from this are norms of conscientiousness, care, attention, and perseverance—norms such that, if they are not identical with, at least closely approximate, moral norms and, in many cases, have a moral dimension. Finally, there are decidedly moral norms such as norms of compassion at one far end of the spectrum and decidedly epistemic norms that concern reliably attending to evidential connections at the other far end.

It is a nice question as to why there are these types of intimate connections between the moral and epistemic realms—why, to employ the metaphor that figures in the title of this book, the normative domains form a web. I think that there is at least a partial answer to this question, one that, admittedly, is most congenial to a broadly Aristotelian view.[20] The suggestion is that it is the content platitudes concerning moral facts that explain (in part) why the similarities to which I have alluded hold. Recall that the content platitudes tell us that, in a wide range of cases, entities of certain kinds have one or another positive moral status in virtue of their being appropriately connected with the promoting, honoring, or sustaining of human flourishing or the participation in those states and activities that are components thereof. It is plausible to believe, however, that among the states and activities the participation in which comprises human flourishing are cognitive states such as knowledge, insight, and wisdom. If that is right, then we should expect to find noticeable similarities between the nature of

[20] Although, congenial not merely to a broadly Aristotelian view. Utilitarians such as James Griffin and Kantians such as Thomas Scanlon are also sympathetic with the idea that human flourishing has an epistemic component. See Griffin (1986) and Scanlon (1998), Ch. 3.

moral and epistemic facts. Both sorts of facts are, as it were, grounded in features that comprise the human good. Moreover, if it is their conceptual connections with the human good (and the participation in the states and activities that are components thereof) that account for the prescriptive nature of moral and epistemic facts, then it is unsurprising that such facts have a similar kind of authority. Their authority, to speak metaphorically, is reflective of the value of the states and activities that we are enjoined to protect, promote, honor, or the like. Consequently, I think there is a sense in which one can say that epistemology is a branch of ethics. But I submit that this is best understood as the claim that both disciplines are intimately intertwined with the constituents of the human good, and it is this that explains their deep similarities.

The fourth similarity

That moral and epistemic reasons are categorical, that such facts are structurally isomorphic, that they favor identical modes of response—these are the first three similarities between moral and epistemic facts I have identified. The fourth main area of similarity between moral and epistemic facts I wish to highlight is that some such facts are not only necessarily coextensive, but also that, in some cases, there is no obvious way to disentangle (ontologically, at least) their moral and epistemic dimensions: Some failings—think of failing to treat the testimony of another with sufficient care and attention—appear to be both moral and epistemic failings. And some excellences—think of treating the testimony of another with sufficient care and attention—appear to be both moral and epistemic excellences. As I shall argue in the next chapter, the similarities between putative moral and epistemic facts extend beyond these four. But having identified these similarities, this is a good place from which to build a case for the core argument's first premise.

IV. Two objections

The project I set for myself at the outset of this chapter was to identify four main areas of similarity between putative moral and epistemic facts so as to provide the conceptual groundwork for the argument of the next chapter. Having identified these four areas, I want in closing to consider two objections that purport to establish that moral and epistemic facts are sufficiently disanalogous that the core argument I am developing cannot be made to work. Before I do so, however, I want to emphasize two things.

First, there are in principle numerous differences between moral and epistemic facts, some of which hold considerable theoretical interest. But, second, the argument I am developing does not require that important dissimilarities between moral and epistemic facts fail to exist. All that it requires is that moral and epistemic facts are similar in this crucial respect: Were moral and epistemic facts to exist, then they would both display what I earlier called the 'objectionable' features—features such as *being intrinsically motivating, being categorically reason-giving, being causally idle*, and so forth. That said, the two objections I shall address are ones that, if sound, arguably render the acceptance of the core argument's first premise problematic. For they are objections that purport to show that there are ways in which the existence of moral facts is problematic, but the existence of epistemic facts is not.

The first objection

The first objection with which I am concerned is inspired by an influential article of William P. Alston's, 'The Deontological Conception of Justification'.[21] According to this objection, deontic norms—roughly, norms that require, forbid, or permit behavior of certain kinds—apply to only those entities that are under our direct or indirect voluntary control. But, the argument continues, a person's holding a particular level of confidence in the propositional content of a belief is not in the ordinary case under that person's voluntary control. A person cannot just decide, with respect to some proposition, to believe that proposition with a certain degree of firmness. For instance, I cannot just decide to believe with a high degree of confidence *that the antennae of red ants are more sensitive to movement than those of black ants*. Nor does it seem plausible to hold that I can with any sort of reliability 'over the long haul' carry out the intention to believe this proposition with a high degree of firmness. But if this is right, then deontic norms do not apply to a wide range of beliefs; beliefs are, for the most part, not the sort of thing that are under our voluntary control. And, thus, there

---

[21] Alston (1988), Ch. 5. Since the way in which I present the objection deviates in certain manners from Alston's presentation, I claim only that what I say is inspired by Alston's article.

is a serious disanalogy between ethics and epistemology. The entities that are the central objects of moral valuation, viz., intentions and actions, *are* ordinarily under our voluntary control. In the ordinary case, for example, I can volunteer to collect donations for famine relief.

This objection is potentially worrisome. As we'll see in the next chapter (categorical) deontic norms are frequently said to be 'queer' entities, ones that have no place in a plausible account of the world's inventory. But if central objects of epistemic appraisal such as beliefs are not subject to such norms, then one may rightly suspect that epistemology simply is not a normative discipline in the way that ethics is. And, thus, one might rightly suspect that whatever epistemic facts are, they are not themselves deontic norms or consist in the application thereof.

By way of response, let me introduce a distinction and then indicate why I think this objection is ultimately not persuasive.[22]

The distinction I wish to introduce is that between what I will call a 'responsibility norm', on the one hand, and a 'propriety norm', on the other. The 'oughts' distinctive of responsibility norms ordinarily apply only to voluntary intentions. For example, the general norm that enjoins us to give money to famine relief is plausibly viewed as a responsibility norm—intentions in the ordinary case being subject to voluntary control. The 'oughts' distinctive of propriety norms, by contrast, typically apply not only to our voluntary intentions, but also to entities ordinarily outside of our direct voluntary control. Take a case, for instance, in which Sarah believes that she is not loved by her family despite the fact that this is false and all her evidence indicates otherwise. There seems a clear sense in which Sarah ought not to believe this. The norm that tells us that Sarah ought not to believe this—ought not to believe this regardless of whether she can voluntarily control her belief—is plausibly viewed as a propriety norm. The norm, in effect, tells us that an epistemically virtuous agent—one whose cognitive faculties were working well in the appropriate circumstances—would not believe this. Depending on how one thinks of the nature of obligation, both responsibility and propriety norms of certain kinds can be seen as species of obligation (or as indicating them). If one

---

[22] A more intricate response to this objection can be found in Feldman (1988), (2000), (2001), and Wolterstorff (unpublished). Both Feldman and Wolterstorff question—rightly, in my view—Alston's assumption that ought implies can. The distinction between different types of norm to which I appeal is due to Wolterstorff.

adopts a virtue-based account of obligation, for example, according to which (roughly) one has an obligation to Φ just in case an epistemically virtuous agent acting in character would Φ, then both responsibility and propriety norms are plausibly viewed as being (or indicating) obligations.[23] Likewise, if one holds that Φing is obligatory for a person just in case not Φing would constitute an impairment of that person's epistemic excellence, then both responsibility and propriety norms are plausibly viewed as being (or indicating) epistemic obligations—from which, of course, it does not follow that if one fails to conform to a propriety norm one is thereby *blameworthy*.

This distinction having been made, the brief reply I wish to offer to the objection we're considering has two parts. First, the objection assumes that all norms are responsibility norms. But, if what I've suggested is correct, this is false. Some norms are propriety norms. And, whether or not one believes such norms are obligations, it is plausible to believe that they apply to a wide range of beliefs. For example, we regularly subject our beliefs to normative appraisal regardless of whether they are under our voluntary control. If, however, such norms apply to a wide range of beliefs—as I believe they do—then it is false that the realms of ethics and epistemology are disanalogous in the manner in which the objection says. The central objects of both moral and epistemic appraisal are subject to deontic norms. (In the next chapter, I will contend that some moral norms are not responsibility norms.[24])

---

[23] This kind of view is defended by Zagzebski (1996), Hursthouse (1999), and Swanton (2003), among others. Feldman (2000) and (2001) contends that propriety norms could not be obligations. He suggests instead that epistemic obligations be understood as 'role norms'—norms that describe the right way to play a certain role, i.e. the role of a believer. Role norms, says Feldman, can apply to an agent on a particular occasion even if she is unable to conform to them. For example, as a teacher, Jane may have an obligation to explain a concept clearly to her students even if she is unable to do so on a particular occasion.

It seems to me that there are role norms, and that Feldman has made a powerful case for the claim that not all obligations are a species of responsibility norm. However, it also seems to me that role norms are propriety norms of a certain kind. (Feldman, mistakenly I believe, takes all propriety norms to be norms that simply describe how a statistically normal thing of a certain kind would behave. See Feldman [2001], 87–88.) Such norms describe how someone would behave if she were functioning properly in the appropriate circumstances—where circumstances can include occupying roles of various sorts. If this is right, then there is no obstacle to seeing some propriety norms as being obligations of a certain kind. According to a broadly Feldmanian view, that subset of propriety norms that are role norms of a certain kind are obligations.

[24] Admittedly, the objection could be reformulated so as to assume only that moral, but not epistemic, norms are responsibility norms. But reformulated thus, I believe the objection misfires, as it

But, more importantly, even if the present objection were cogent, it would not establish that there are important dissimilarities between moral and epistemic facts. At most, what the objection establishes is that the moral and epistemic *domains* are disanalogous in the following sense: The central objects of epistemic appraisal (viz., beliefs) are not subject to deontic norms while the central objects of moral appraisal (viz., actions and intentions) are. (Of course if one held that character traits are the central objects of moral and epistemic appraisal, the objection would not even establish this.) It does not follow from the fact that the central objects of epistemic and moral appraisal are disanalogous in this sense, however, that moral and epistemic *facts* are disanalogous in any interesting sense. Indeed, as far as the objection is concerned, they look to be exactly analogous: If the objection is correct, both moral and epistemic norms govern entities that are under our voluntary control, including propositional attitudes such as acceptances and other entities such as intentions and character traits. (Here I follow L. Jonathan Cohen in taking acceptances to be distinct from beliefs. The former involve voluntarily 'taking a proposition on board', while the latter do not.[25]) Moreover, both sorts of norm appear not to govern entities and activities that fail to be under our voluntary control such as (if the argument is right) the formation of beliefs. In this respect, the parallel is exact.

The second objection

I turn now to a second attempt to show that moral and epistemic norms are interestingly disanalogous, found in John Pollock and Joseph Cruz's *Contemporary Theories of Knowledge*.[26] Pollock and Cruz write that epistemologists

have commonly supposed that epistemic norms are much like moral norms and that they are used in evaluating reasoning in the same way moral norms are used

rests on a highly restrictive account of the voluntary. For, as Alston himself points out, there are more capacious accounts of the voluntary according to which we can have indirect voluntary influence over our beliefs. For example, I can indirectly voluntarily influence the formation of the belief that Sam is trustworthy by first doing a background check on his character. Alston admits that an account of the voluntary of this sort seems capable of grounding epistemic obligations of various sorts. However, Alston finds this point uninteresting, since his main aim in the article I have cited is to offer an account of epistemic justification. And for reasons I won't go into here, Alston believes that obligations of this sort cannot underwrite an adequate account of epistemic justification. Be that as it may, Alston's concern is not relevant for our purposes, since I do not assume that the conformance or non-conformance to responsibility norms must underwrite an adequate conception of epistemic justification.

[25] See Cohen (1992).   [26] Pollock and Cruz (1999), Ch. 5.

in evaluating actions. One of the main contentions of this chapter will be that the parallel is not at all exact and that epistemologists have been misled in important ways by supposing the analogy to be better than it is.[27]

Pollock and Cruz make three main claims concerning epistemic norms.[28] First, they claim that epistemic norms are *procedural norms*—norms that are behavior-guiding and thereby guide and govern our behavior in a 'first-person' way. Second, they maintain that (i) knowledge of epistemic norms is not *declarative* knowledge, but *procedural* knowledge, and that (ii) conforming to an epistemic norm ordinarily does not consist in a person's explicitly consulting that norm. If Pollock and Cruz are right, then our knowledge of epistemic norms ordinarily consists in implicitly knowing how to do certain things in certain circumstances and does not consist in being able to 'give a general description of what we should do under those circumstances'.[29] Finally, Pollock and Cruz offer an account of the *origin* of epistemic norms. If I understand it correctly, their view is that epistemic norms are descriptions of what we do when we reason. Here is how they put the point:

We know how to reason, or more generally, how to cognize. That means that under various circumstances we know what to do in cognizing. This can be described equivalently by saying that we know what we should do. Our epistemic norms are just the norms that describe this procedural knowledge, and rational cognition is cognition in compliance with the norms…. [Epistemic norms] are descriptive of our procedural knowledge of how to cognize, articulating what we 'know to do' in cognizing.[30]

To which they add the point that their view has the benefits of being 'naturalistic' and not being 'mysterious'.[31]

Suppose epistemic norms have the three characteristics just canvassed. Where exactly is the disanalogy between epistemic and moral norms

[27] Pollock and Cruz (1999), 124.

[28] Pollock and Cruz characterize norms thus: 'Norms are general descriptions of the circumstances under which various kinds of normative judgments are correct. Epistemic norms are norms describing when it is epistemically permissible to hold various beliefs' (p. 123). The account of norms with which Pollock and Cruz work, then, is narrower than the one I have adopted. Norms, on my account, also encompass norms describing when it is epistemically obligatory and forbidden to hold various propositional attitudes, to form and maintain certain kinds of intentions, and so on.

[29] Ibid., 127. Pollock and Cruz actually claim that procedural knowledge *does* not (as opposed to *ordinarily* does not) involve being able to give a general description of what we should do in the appropriate circumstances. I take it that this claim is too strong for their purposes.

[30] Ibid., 129, 150.   [31] Ibid., 123, 130.

supposed to lie? According to Pollock and Cruz, in two places. There is an important disanalogy between the respective ways in which we know epistemic and moral norms and in their respective origin.[32] In response, I suggest that epistemic and moral norms are not disanalogous in the ways Pollock and Cruz claim.

Begin with the first putative disanalogy. As far as I can tell, there is no very interesting difference between the ways in which we know epistemic and moral norms.

In the first place, Pollock and Cruz probably underestimate how frequently we explicitly consult epistemic norms and our ability to state explicitly in a general fashion the epistemic norms to which we take ourselves to conform. When some of us attempt to arbitrate marital disputes, for example, we often consciously and explicitly remind ourselves that we ought to keep certain pieces of evidence before our minds, aspire to a level of objectivity by listening to both sides of the story, and so on. But, more importantly, I doubt that moral knowledge ordinarily consists in a person's explicitly consulting one or another moral rule and then deducing from that rule what she ought to do, believe, or feel. Furthermore, I cannot see that we are significantly better able to state explicitly the various moral norms to which we take ourselves to conform than we are able to articulate the various epistemic norms to which we take ourselves to conform. Rather, as the proponents of virtue ethics have emphasized, it is very plausible to hold that moral knowledge is often procedural in nature and consists in implicitly *knowing how* to go about doing, believing, feeling, or perceiving the morally appropriate thing. To use one of Alasdair MacIntyre's examples, knowing how much time to take when making a point in conversation is usually a matter of implicitly knowing how to negotiate the give and take of social interactions.[33] Accordingly, I submit that Pollock and Cruz haven't given us sufficient reason to believe the first putative disanalogy between moral and epistemic norms is genuine.

The second putative disanalogy is more telling, however. If what Pollock and Cruz say is true, we can explain the origin of epistemic norms by adverting to ways in which we reason, but we cannot explain moral norms

---

[32] 'Norms are general descriptions of the circumstances under which various kinds of normative judgments are correct. Epistemic norms are norms describing when it is epistemically permissible to hold various beliefs.' Pollock and Cruz. (1999), 228.

[33] See MacIntyre (1999), 110–11.

in such a way, for moral norms are not mere descriptions of how we cognize. And this difference, arguably, is one that does make a difference for our purposes. If we have a straightforward 'naturalistic' explanation of the origin of epistemic norms, but not moral ones, we may have good reason to accept the existence of norms of the former but not the latter sort. In short, if a story such as Pollock and Cruz's can be vindicated, it may be that epistemic norms do not possess the objectionable features that moral norms would were they to exist.

It seems to me that what Pollock and Cruz say is right about this much: Moral norms are not mere descriptions of how we reason. Nevertheless, even if we grant that epistemic norms concern only how we reason (and not, say, how we conduct inquiries by way of implementing action plans), I doubt that the source of epistemic norms can be explained in the way Pollock and Cruz claim. For consider the claim that epistemic norms are mere descriptions of how we reason. If the 'we' to which this account refers remains unspecified, then we do not have a sufficiently determinate explanation of the source of epistemic norms. The problem is that, if we take some arbitrary range of propositions, not all of us reason in the same way with respect to those propositions or, for that matter, reason well with regard to them. Now if Pollock and Cruz were to claim that the source of epistemic norms lies in how *ideal* or *epistemically virtuous* agents reason, then, I think, we would have a sufficiently determinate proposal that merits serious consideration.[34] In that case, Pollock and Cruz would be defending a version of proper function or virtue epistemology, a type of view that has been articulated with some care by contemporary epistemologists.

Suppose, then, that the position that Pollock and Cruz wish to defend is best characterized as a type of proper function or virtue epistemology. Do we then have an interesting disanalogy between the origin of epistemic and moral norms? It seems to me not, as there are plausible positions in moral theory that tell us that moral norms supervene on the way that properly

---

[34] Another way to put the point is this: Pollock and Cruz sometimes say that epistemic norms are descriptions of how we reason when we do so *correctly*. But if this is to be sufficiently informative, we need an account of what it is to reason correctly. On pain of vicious circularity, we cannot say that it consists in reasoning in conformance with epistemic norms. Nor can we say that it consists in reasoning in a truth-conducive manner. For as Pollock and Cruz themselves point out in their criticism of reliablism, there is much more to reasoning correctly than reliably getting at the truth.

For examples of virtue epistemology, see Zagzebski (1996), Plantinga (1993a), and Greco (2000).

functioning or morally virtuous agents behave.[35] If any such view were true, and Pollock and Cruz were right about the origin of epistemic norms, then there would not be any very interesting sense in which the origins of epistemic and moral norms differ. I myself have reservations about whether this type of approach can be satisfactorily developed in either the epistemic or the moral realm. But *if* such a virtue-based view could be made to work, then there would be a rather exact parallel between the origin of both epistemic and moral norms.

I conclude there is no reason to believe that the origin of epistemic and moral norms is interestingly different: If the reservations regarding a virtue-based account of moral and epistemic values to which I have alluded turn out to be vindicated, then it is doubtful that norms of either sort are virtue-based. But if these reservations do not indicate problems with virtue-based views, then we haven't been provided with a reason to believe that epistemic but not moral norms are virtue-based.

V. Conclusion

My aim in this chapter has been to lay out the structure of paradigmatic epistemic realism, emphasizing the importance of the content platitudes for understanding the view. I have highlighted four respects in which moral and epistemic facts are relevantly similar and responded to a pair of objections that purport to establish that facts of these kinds are relevantly disanalogous. I do not suppose to have identified all or even most of the ways in which moral and epistemic facts are or are not similar. Some of these ways will emerge in subsequent discussion. But for the time being, my overall assessment is that there are close parallels between moral and epistemic facts—so close in fact, that the moral and epistemic domains are helpfully viewed as overlapping and interpenetrating in various ways. My project in the next chapter will be to build upon these findings by providing an argument for the core argument's first premise.

---

[35] See, for example, Hursthouse (1991) and Zagzebski (2004). For an example of a non-virtue theory that relies on the notion of proper function, see Donagan (1977), 53.

3

The Parity Premise

The task in which I am presently engaged is to defend the first premise of the core argument or the claim that:

(1) If moral facts do not exist, then epistemic facts do not exist.

In the last chapter, I claimed that the argument for this claim comes in two stages. The first stage of the argument, which was the project of the last chapter, is to identify several respects in which moral and epistemic facts are similar and to allay concerns that any attempt to argue for (1) would founder on some rather deep differences between the nature of moral and epistemic facts. As I glossed it, the aim of the first stage of the argument is preparatory in nature, its purpose being to lay some conceptual footing for the argument to come. The second and principal stage of the argument, which is my concern in this chapter, is to offer a direct argument in favor of the core argument's first premise. The argument I offer has two parts.

In the first part, I argue that there is a class of objections standardly employed to argue against moral realism such that, were they to establish that moral facts do not exist, they would also, when suitably modified, establish that epistemic facts do not exist. In the second part, I draw the consequence that, if the standard objections are sound, there is a class of features—what I call 'the objectionable features'—such that were moral and epistemic facts to exist, they would both display them. According to the standard objections, the objectionable features are what render moral facts 'queer': If moral facts do not exist, then this is wholly because they would display these features. But presumably there is nothing unique to moral facts that makes their having these features objectionable; it is the *features themselves* that render moral facts philosophically unacceptable. If this is right, then we can agree that:

If moral facts do not exist, then nothing has the objectionable features.

However, on the assumption that the argument to this point is on target, we also know that if epistemic facts exist, then there is something that has the objectionable features. Put differently, we know that:

If nothing has the objectionable features, then epistemic facts do not exist.

And from these two claims it follows that the core argument's first premise is true: If moral facts do not exist, then epistemic facts do not exist.

I. The standard objections

There are, by my counting, six major types of argument that are typically pressed against moral realism.[1] In what follows, I shall sketch a representative version of each type of argument and contend that, if sound, each version proves more than moral realists and antirealists alike have typically acknowledged. The sketch I provide will be in some respects rough, but it should suffice to bring out the fundamental contours of the arguments in question.

The first argument

Lying at the heart of moral realism is the thesis that moral facts are determined by, or strongly supervene on, what we might call 'mere descriptive facts'. (We can think of such facts as those that are neither deontic nor evaluative facts.[2]) It is in virtue of having various sorts of mere descriptive properties (e.g. causing gratuitous pain), says the realist, that actions have moral properties such as *being cruel* or *being wrong*. It is the putative supervenience of the moral on the merely descriptive that some philosophers claim presents a serious problem for the moral realist.[3] In

---

[1] In what follows, I am not going to consider the so-called moral twin earth argument developed by Horgan and Timmons (1992) and elsewhere. My reason for not doing so is that the argument is directed against not moral realist views as such, but only a certain type of naturalist view in ethics. That said, I take it to be clear that an argument similar to that developed by Horgan and Timmons could be developed against analogous views in epistemology.

[2] The term 'descriptive fact' is, in a certain way, infelicitous, as the facts in question don't describe anything, but rather are the semantic values of what we might call 'merely descriptive expressions' of certain kinds. Nevertheless, in deference to widespread philosophical usage, I will persist in using the term.

[3] Variants of the present argument can be found in Mackie (1977), Horgan and Timmons (1992), Blackburn (1993), Chs. 6 and 7, Schiffer (1987), and others. Schiffer writes, for example, 'invoking a special primitive metaphysical relation of supervenience to explain how non-natural moral properties

short, the problem is that, although realists freely speak of mere descriptive facts 'determining' moral facts, they offer no plausible account of what this determination relation is. The relation cannot be a causal one, for that would be too weak. According to the realist's view, it is supposed to be conceptually impossible for an entity to have a certain range of mere descriptive features and not have the requisite moral features. But if mere descriptive facts determine moral facts by simply causing them, there would be no way to account for this conceptual impossibility. Nor could the relation in question be one of identity, for that would be too strong. It would leave out the normative or prescriptive dimension of moral facts by identifying them with merely descriptive ones.[4] At best, the relation appears to consist in moral facts being bound to mere descriptive facts, in Hilary Putnam's phrase, by some sort of mysterious 'metaphysical glue'.[5] But, on the plausible assumption that there are no such mysterious determination relations, it follows that there are no moral facts.

Supervenience claims are, of course, not limited to the moral domain. They are the stock and trade of philosophers of mind and philosophers of language, among others. So, won't the present argument yield the unacceptable consequence that we should not admit putatively supervenient entities such as propositional attitudes, qualia, and meanings into our ontology? Perhaps not. Simon Blackburn, for instance, has argued that the sort of determination relation that is supposed to obtain between mere descriptive and moral facts is quite different from the type that obtains between non-mental and mental facts.[6] In so arguing, Blackburn's aim is to show that there really is something odd about the case of the supervenience of the moral that is not present in the case of the supervenience of the mental.

---

were related to physical properties was just to add mystery to mystery, to cover one obscurantist move with another' (p. 153). Incidentally, I assume here that the supervenience relation is an asymmetrical determination relation. I am aware that the relation is often viewed as a purely modal one, with no implications about determination or identity. Difficulties about specifying the nature of the relevant 'in virtue of' relation notwithstanding, it seems to me that the more robust account of supervenience holds a central place in discussions of moral ontology. Accordingly, it is the notion with which I will work. (In fact, if Hare [2001], Ch. 2, Sect. 5 is correct, when the concept was first introduced by Duns Scotus, it was used in something like this sense.)

[4] Let me emphasize that some philosophers call their views 'realist' and defend such an identity (see Jackson [1998], Chs. 5 and 6, for example). These positions are not, however, paradigmatic realist views, which is what I am interested to defend.

[5] Putnam (1983), 18. In this piece, Putnam is talking not about the relation between mere descriptive and moral facts, but about the reference relation.

[6] Blackburn (1993), Ch. 7.

For my purposes here, it doesn't matter whether Blackburn is right about this. What I want to emphasize is that there is nothing *uniquely* odd about the nature of moral supervenience. For take any claim to the effect that some entity bears some epistemic property such as *being justified* or *being rational*. It is widely agreed upon by philosophers that, if an entity has some such epistemic property, then it does so in virtue of its having certain merely descriptive, non-epistemic features.[7] The dependence relation in question, however, does not seem to be causal. In this case, too, it also seems to be conceptually impossible for a thing to have a certain range of merely descriptive properties and not have the requisite epistemic property. Furthermore, the relation does not appear to be one of identity. To identify the epistemic with the merely descriptive would be to omit the normative or prescriptive dimension of epistemic facts. But if this is right, then it appears as if epistemic facts are bound to the natural world by the same type of mysterious metaphysical glue that putatively binds moral facts to merely descriptive ones. Far from being 'utterly different from anything else in the universe',[8] as J. L. Mackie thought, moral and epistemic facts are exactly alike in this putatively objectionable respect. It follows that, on the assumption that there are no supervenience relations of this kind, there are no epistemic facts.

The second argument

The second argument I want to consider accuses the moral realist of propagating a different sort of mystery. According to this argument, were moral facts to exist, they would have—to use Mackie's phrase—an inexplicable 'to-be-pursuedness' built into them.[9] According to one way of understanding this 'to-be-pursuedness', the argument runs as follows.[10]

Consider a putative moral fact that directs a particular agent to conduct himself in a certain manner (or an evaluative moral fact that implies this). Consider, for example, the fact *that Sam ought to apologize to Margaret* or *that not apologizing to Margaret is wrong*. A moral fact of this sort, so the

---

[7] See, e.g. Sosa (1991), Chs. 5, 9, and 10, Goldman (1986), Ch. 1, Kim (1993), Ch. 12, and Van Cleve (1999a). Lehrer (1997) is a dissenter here. But if Lehrer is right, then it will also be true that moral facts do not supervene on non-moral facts.

[8] Mackie (1977), 38.   [9] The phrase comes from Mackie (1977), 40.

[10] Strains of the argument can be found in Mackie (1977), Ch. 1, Blackburn (1984), Ch. 6 and (1998), Ch. 3, Gibbard (1990), Parts I and II, and others.

argument goes, would have to be the type of thing that, when grasped by Sam in the appropriate kinds of circumstance, necessarily motivates Sam to some degree to act appropriately. As it is sometimes said, moral facts of this kind would have to be 'intrinsically motivating'. But this yields two problems. In the first place, it is hard to see how a fact could be intrinsically motivating or have this 'to-be-pursuedness' built into it; this seems to be a highly mysterious feature of the world. Second, the claim that moral facts are intrinsically motivating is at odds with our best account of motivational psychology, viz., the Humean one. The Humean account tells us that whether an agent is motivated to act at some time depends on the contingent fact that she already has desires of the appropriate kind; merely grasping a fact of a certain sort won't do. So, according to the Humean story, whether an agent were to be motivated to act upon grasping some moral fact would depend on that agent's already having contingent desires of the appropriate kind.[11] It follows from this that moral facts could not be intrinsically motivating. And, so, moral facts do not exist.

Let's suppose for the moment that moral realists really are committed to the claim that moral facts are intrinsically motivating. Do we have any reason to think that epistemic facts are different in this respect? I doubt it. Consider epistemic facts that direct an agent to conduct himself in a particular manner (or evaluative epistemic facts that imply this). Consider, for instance, the fact *that Sam rationally ought to engage in a certain plan of inquiry* because it is by far more reliable than rival plans of inquiry. Or take the fact *that Sam's maintaining a high level of confidence in a proposition is unwarranted* because his doing so is bullheaded, intellectually foolish, or indicates that he is oblivious to the evidence. If facts such as these were to exist, then they would seem to have a motivational magnetism similar to that of moral facts. Indeed, it is difficult to discern any reason why epistemic facts of these sorts would not be intrinsically motivating while the fact *that not apologizing to Margaret is wrong* is. If this is right, we have excellent reason to believe that, were epistemic facts to exist, they would also have to be intrinsically motivating. If we concede this, however, then we have this additional conclusion: If the present argument is sound, epistemic realism is also at odds with the Humean theory of motivation.

---

[11] At least this is true of the position according to a rough-and-ready characterization of it. I offer a more exact formulation of the view in Cuneo (2002).

Contingent desires are superfluous for being motivated by the grasp of epistemic facts of certain kinds. And from this it follows that epistemic facts are not intrinsically motivating and, accordingly, do not exist. (Of course, if the Humean theory were true and moral facts were not intrinsically motivating, then we should expect that epistemic facts would also not be intrinsically motivating.)

I suspect that some philosophers will find themselves unsatisfied with this attempt to establish that, if moral facts are intrinsically motivating, then so also are epistemic facts. The reason being—to put things somewhat vaguely—that moral facts have a more intimate connection with the will than do epistemic ones. Since this seems to me a natural worry to harbor, let me introduce some terminology, identify a manner in which this concern should not be understood, and then suggest a more promising way to understand it. Having done this, I will contend that this concern can be allayed.

First, the terminology: Suppose we understand a motivational state to be a mental state of a person that consists in that person's being inclined to try to bring about some state of affairs that that person believes she can bring about. And let's say that a 'directive' is any particular normative fact F that directs an agent S to Φ insofar as it implies that S ought to Φ.[12] For our purposes, we can divide directives into two sorts. What I shall call 'volitional directives' are particular normative facts that direct an agent S to try to Φ, while 'non-volitional' directives are ones that direct S to Φ, but needn't direct her to try to Φ.[13] (I will furnish examples of each type of directive in a moment.) Finally, let's say that a directive F is intrinsically motivating if and only if, necessarily, for any agent S in some range of circumstances C, S's grasping F in C itself inclines S to try to bring about some state of affairs that F directs S to try to bring about and that S believes she can bring about.

The objection to moral realism we're considering tells us that moral facts are intrinsically motivating. However, if this claim is to have any plausibility, it needs to be understood in a fairly circumscribed sense. The

[12] I borrow the term 'directive' from Wiggins (1991), 95.

[13] The distinction I am making here closely corresponds to that made in the last chapter between responsibility and propriety norms. The difference between the two types of distinction is that (according to certain views) volitional and non-volitional directives, but not responsibility and propriety norms, can be either deontic or evaluative facts.

thesis cannot be that all putative moral facts are intrinsically motivating; my grasping a moral fact such as *that Lee Marvin was a man of moral integrity* by reading a thirty-year-old *T.V. Guide* may, after all, have little connection with any of my motivational states. (Marvin's goodness, in my case, is too removed from me, both in time and in person, to be 'motivationally charged'.) Rather, the claim has to be that only a certain class of putative moral facts, viz., a subset of the class of facts that I've called 'volitional directives', is intrinsically motivating, for these are facts that direct us to try to bring about states of affairs of certain kinds. On the assumption that this is correct, we can identify one way *not* to argue for the claim that moral facts have a more intimate connection with the will than epistemic ones. The argument cannot be:

(1) The only sorts of fact that are likely to be intrinsically motivating are directives.

(2) Since epistemic directives primarily govern the formation of beliefs, and since the formation of belief is largely outside of our (direct or indirect) voluntary control, they are (for the most part) non-volitional directives.

(3) However, since moral directives primarily govern the formation of intentions, and intentions are largely within our (direct or indirect) voluntary control, they are (for the most part) volitional directives.

(4) So, on the assumptions that (i) non-volitional directives are not intrinsically motivating, and (ii) epistemic directives are but moral directives are not (for the most part) non-volitional directives, it follows that epistemic directives are not (for the most part) intrinsically motivating, while moral directives are.

As I stressed in the last chapter, this line of argument cannot be right because both the second and third premises are false. If moral and epistemic facts exist, then they apply to a whole range of entities. Some moral directives are volitional; however, others direct us to do such things as form, hold, or surrender beliefs, desires, and other attitudes at certain times.

To pick two examples among many, a person may be morally required (or at any rate, have a strong moral reason) at a certain time not to believe that the Holocaust was a fraud propagated by Jewish sympathizers even if the surrendering of this belief is largely outside his voluntary control at that time.[14] The problem in this case is that the content of his belief is

---

[14] The norm in question is plausibly viewed as being what I called in the last chapter a 'propriety norm'.

morally objectionable, and it is so regardless of how he acquired the belief. Likewise, an agent may be morally required (or at any rate, have a strong moral reason) not to feel pleasure on account of the suffering of others at some time, even if the forming or the having of such an affective state is largely outside his voluntary control at that time. In this case, the agent manifests bad affective states—such states being bad, in part, because they often contribute to morally bad action in which an agent manifests them. These are cases of moral malformation—the malformation being such that it reflects negatively on the moral character of the agent, signaling that something has gone wrong there (rather than, say, with his sensory make-up). In any event, if cases such as these are numerous—and I believe they are—then a good many moral directives are non-volitional.[15] Likewise, while many epistemic directives are non-volitional, we've seen that others direct us to do such things as engage in lines of inquiry of certain types, maintain particular levels of confidence in our beliefs, keep certain bits of evidence before the mind, and so on. But these are all activities over which we have a good measure of control and, thus, the directives in question are naturally understood to be volitional.

Moral directives, then, do not have a more intimate connection with the will than epistemic ones insofar as it is of their nature primarily to be volitional, while it is not of the nature of epistemic directives to be volitional. But if this is right, how should we formulate the concern that moral facts in some sense have a more intimate relation to the will than epistemic ones?

One way to do so is by observing a distinction between the *authority* of obligations and their *normative force*. The authority of obligations, as I've already indicated, consists in the fact that they are, imply, or indicate

---

[15] For a defense of the position that non-volitional moral directives apply to moral beliefs, see Adams (1987), Ch. 1 and (1985). I also borrow here from Wolterstorff (1997). An anonymous referee has raised the worry that it is much more intuitive to say that, in the first example I furnish, the agent is morally required not to hate Jews, but merely epistemically required to believe that the Holocaust occurred. While I agree that the agent has this moral obligation, I do not find this the more intuitive rendering of the case. Suppose, on the one hand, that the holding of this belief is an expression of deep-seated hatred toward Jews. If so, it seems natural to assess it morally, much in the same way we assess intentions when they express morally vicious character traits. Suppose, on the other hand, the holding of the belief is not an expression of hate. For example, suppose that the agent has been apprised of the evidence, but still finds herself believing that the Holocaust is a fraud. In this case, one would think that the agent had missed something; her belief is the product of not being fair-minded, being intellectually 'muleish', or the like. If my discussion of hybrid-norms in the last chapter is correct, however, this would also be a case in which this agent's belief is open to moral assessment.

reasons that are categorical. The normative force of obligations is different, however, for it concerns how important an obligation is. The importance in question is typically captured by the idea that obligations of some kinds are such that failure to conform to them warrants feeling guilt. When we distinguish these two features of obligation, an important disanalogy between epistemic and moral obligations appears to surface.

The apparent disanalogy is this: While moral obligations are plausibly viewed as having both authority and normative force, epistemic obligations are not. We do not typically claim that epistemic obligations are overriding, for example. Nor do we claim that failing to conform to them warrants guilt. It may be true, for instance, that a logic student has an epistemic obligation to conduct his reasonings in a careful and accurate fashion. But, at best, his culpably failing to conform to this obligation warrants his feeling silly or inadequate, not his feeling guilty. In any case, it is natural to suppose that this difference between putative moral and epistemic obligations (or reasons) has implications for motivation. Avoidance of guilt is a major impetus for conforming to our moral obligations. It is also a motivational impetus that is apparently lacking in the epistemic realm. If this is right, we should expect there to be a marked difference between those cases in which we are putatively motivated by the grasp of moral obligations and those cases in which we are putatively motivated by the grasp of epistemic obligations (or reasons).

To this line of thought, let me say two things in response. First, according to the antirealist's argument, the realist is supposed to be saddled with the claim that it is the apprehension of moral facts of certain kinds *itself* that motivates agents to act. Notice, however, that if the realist were committed to this claim, then feelings of guilt could play (at least in a wide range of cases) only a limited role in generating moral motivation in which such apprehension is an ingredient. For if the apprehension of a moral fact is itself sufficient to motivate a person to action, then feelings of guilt could at best overdetermine such motivation or strengthen motivation that is already present. Suppose, then, that feelings of guilt play this subsidiary motivational role in the moral case and not in the epistemic one. Nothing interesting for our purposes follows. The fact that guilt plays a subsidiary role in the moral case does not show that epistemic facts are not intrinsically motivating in the very same sense that moral facts are.

Second, even if the realist can account for the fact that guilt can play a major role in the genesis of moral motivation, it does not follow that the apprehension of epistemic facts of certain kinds motivates us in a way very different from that in which the apprehension of moral facts does. We should remember, first of all, that some epistemic facts are very close cousins to some moral facts; in some cases, no clear line separates the epistemic from the moral. If this is true, then the grasp of some epistemic facts may also have intimate connections with feelings of guilt. More importantly, we should beware of oversimplifying the structure of motivation. Guilt is one spring of motivation, but there are other potent springs of motivation as well. Take shame, for example. The received view has it that shame is best described as the internalization of the contempt, disapproval, or negative evaluation of others.[16] Could shame play a role in those cases in which we are motivated by the grasp of some epistemic fact? It would seem so. Upon seeing that engaging in a plan of inquiry A would be manifestly irrational, while engaging in plan of inquiry B would not, I find myself motivated to engage in B and not A. A plausible (if partial) explanation of why I am thus motivated is that I would be ashamed to engage in a second-rate epistemic activity such as B.

In summary, the claim that moral facts are intrinsically motivating is best understood as the thesis that moral facts of certain kinds in a certain range of circumstances are intrinsically motivating. Since epistemic facts would be intrinsically motivating in only this sense, facts of both kinds appear to be exactly on par in this respect. Moreover, while moral motivation may be more intimately connected with feelings of guilt than epistemic ones, these feelings could (in a wide range of cases) at best play a subsidiary role in moral motivation if moral facts were intrinsically motivating. In the epistemic case, a subsidiary motivational role of this sort, furthermore, may be played by feelings of shame. The conclusion to which we're drawn is that, if we assume that nothing could be intrinsically motivating in the manner described, then we have excellent reason to believe neither moral nor epistemic facts exist.

The third argument

The argument we just considered trades on the claim that putative moral facts are objectionably odd insofar as they have 'to-be-pursuedness' built

---

[16] See Blackburn (1998), 14–21.

into them. It is fairly clear, however, that when Mackie made this accusation against moral realism, he had not one but two things in mind. 'To-be-pursuedness', as it is predicated of putative moral facts, implies not only that putative moral facts are intrinsically motivating, but also that they are (to use the terminology of Chapter 1) *authoritative*. And by claiming that such facts are authoritative, Mackie meant to say that they would have to be the sort of thing that implies, first, that there are moral reasons to conduct ourselves in certain ways and, second, that these reasons inescapably govern our conduct or are categorical. So, according to Mackie's understanding of ordinary moral views, whether I have a moral reason to attempt to stop the occurrence of a wicked deed doesn't depend on whether I have certain cares that would be satisfied by attempting this, or whether so attempting would further my interests, or whether I enjoy a certain type of social standing. But nothing—so the argument goes—answers to this description of a moral fact. If there are any reasons, then they are hypothetical in character; they apply to agents only insofar as they have cares, interests, projects, or social standings of certain kinds. It follows that moral facts don't exist.[17]

The proponent of this argument and the moral realist of a paradigmatic sort agree on this much: If there are moral reasons, then some are authoritative or categorical in nature. And, as I emphasized in Chapter 2, the epistemic realist of a paradigmatic sort is committed to an analogous claim: If there are epistemic reasons, then some of these are also authoritative or categorical in nature. The epistemic realist, moreover, espouses this second conditional for reasons structurally identical with the reasons that the moral realist offers in favor of the first. In the epistemic case, commitment to such a proposition seems deeply embedded in our commonsensical conception of the epistemic realm. To return to an example used in the last chapter, if I were to reproach you for having ignored considerable and easily available evidence in favor of believing a proposition p, it would not suffice to reply that this evidence failed to furnish a reason to believe p because you don't care about believing whether p is true. But given the common rationale offered by both moral and epistemic realists for thinking that moral and epistemic reasons are authoritative, it follows that we have good reason to believe that, if moral reasons are authoritative, then so also are epistemic reasons.

---

[17] This is the general form of argument developed in Joyce (2001).

Now it doesn't immediately follow from this that we also have good reasons to believe that nothing answers to the realist's concept of an epistemic reason and, hence, that epistemic antirealism is true. It might be said, after all, that the chief reason why we must assume that moral reasons are hypothetical is that, if they weren't, they could not explain why agents act, which is unacceptable. And, it might be continued, since epistemic reasons are not generally in the business of explaining why we act (on the assumption that beliefs themselves are not acts), their authority is not nearly so objectionable.

I will have more to say about this line of argument toward the end of Chapter 7. For present purposes, let me suggest that, if the earlier discussion of the second type of moral antirealist argument is on the mark, then we should find the authority of epistemic reasons no less puzzling than that of moral ones. Two points are worth re-emphasizing in this regard: First, it would be mistaken to assume that moral reasons as such are connected with motivation. Rather, as I suggested earlier, it seems that there are moral reasons of various sorts, including those that enjoin us to form attitudes of various types with certain degrees of confidence toward propositions of certain kinds. And, on the assumption that the formation of these attitudes is largely not under our voluntary control, then there are moral reasons that are not tied (at least directly) to motivation. Second, it would be mistaken to assume that a large class of epistemic reasons is not intimately tied to motivation. Epistemic reasons to pursue lines of inquiry, alter one's confidence in a proposition, keep certain pieces of evidence in mind, and so forth, are all tied in one or another way to the will. However, if both these points are right, it appears as if any differences regarding the type of authority that attaches to putatively moral and epistemic reasons is negligible; some reasons from each category are not tied closely to the will, and some are. It follows that, if the authority of putative moral reasons yields the conclusion that moral facts do not exist, then the authority of putative epistemic reasons yields the conclusion that epistemic facts do not exist.

The fourth argument

The fourth argument in the antirealist repertoire can be stated briefly. This argument starts with the observation that we don't have any explanatorily informative story about how we could gain epistemic access to moral facts.[18] That is, we do not have any informative account of how facts about what morally ought to be the case impinge on our cognitive faculties so as to produce the corresponding states of knowledge. And it is difficult to imagine what type of story could be told. In light of this failure, it is best to conclude that there is no explanation available. But on the assumption that, if moral facts were to exist, then some such explanation would be available, it follows that moral facts do not exist.

I think it should be admitted that this argument poses a serious challenge to moral realism. But I take it to be fairly plain that the argument poses an equally serious challenge to epistemic realism. For if it is the normative nature of moral facts that is supposed to debar us from an informative story about how we grasp them, then the same holds for epistemic facts. And if it is the lack of an informative story of how we grasp moral facts that implies that we ought not to admit them into our ontology, then the same holds for epistemic facts. Considerations of the same sort counsel against the acceptance of the existence of both moral and epistemic facts.[19]

An interlude on naturalism

To this point I've traversed some fairly familiar territory in contemporary metaethics—four variants of Mackie's celebrated 'argument from queerness'.[20] I want now to interrupt the flow of the discussion for a moment to make a general comment about what is going on in these antirealist arguments and to draw out a further implication of my argument.

The four lines of argument we've considered hinge on the claim that, were moral facts to exist, they would be objectionably 'mysterious' and, hence, we have excellent reason to believe they do not exist. While it is fairly commonplace to hear philosophers say such things, it is not always so obvious what is meant when they do so. Imagine an outsider listening in on this discussion between moral realists and antirealists—one who, say, is used to wondering about whether there are four-dimensional space-time worms,

---

[18] Mackie (1977), Ch. 1, Horgan and Timmons (1992), Sayre-McCord (1996), McGinn (1993), Ch. 6, and Oddie (2005), Ch. 1, formulate versions of the argument. My formulation of the argument owes something to McGinn's way of putting things, though I should emphasize that McGinn is a moral realist.

[19] Sometimes this argument hinges on the assumption that, since normative facts are not causally efficacious, there is no plausible story to tell about how we could gain epistemic access to them. I shall have something to say about the explanatory role of putative moral facts shortly.

[20] Mackie's argument is found in Mackie (1977), 38–42.

closed space-times, event-horizons, or universals. She might find herself deeply puzzled by the discussion thus far. What, after all, renders moral facts more objectionably mysterious than these other kinds of putative entities? And why should this oddness count against the existence of moral facts?

I take the answer to be that the antirealist thinks that moral facts are mysterious in two ways. They are mysterious, first, in the sense of being *anomalous*; moral facts don't fit into our best picture of what the world is like. Moral facts are mysterious, second, in the sense that they are *impenetrable*. We have no illuminating account of their nature or behavior. Of these two senses of mystery, I judge that it is the first that is doing the most work in the antirealist's arguments.[21] So, let's focus on it for a moment.

That nothing is brutely anomalous I take to be a truism. Entities are always anomalous relative to some set of assumptions or background picture of what the world is like. And it is no secret that the background picture against which moral facts are supposed to be anomalous in the arguments we've considered thus far is a naturalist picture of the world.[22] Almost without fail, antirealists object to moral facts because they appear to fit so poorly into the world picture science is supposed to give us. Simon Blackburn puts the point particularly vividly in his essay 'How to Be an Ethical Anti-Realist', when he writes that moral antirealism is 'demanded' by a naturalistic worldview and claims that, according to moral antirealists, 'moral properties ... are not in this world at all, and it is only because of this that naturalism remains true'.[23] If Blackburn is right, a necessary condition of naturalism's being true is moral realism's being false. Now my own conviction is that this is not the sort of thing a naturalist ought to say. According to a popular and broadly Quinean understanding of naturalism, the naturalist's creed is that we ought to follow science wherever it goes.

---

[21]   Thus Mackie: 'If there were objective values, then they would be entities or qualities or relations of a very strange sort, utterly different from anything else in the universe' ([1977], 38). Some philosophers seem to believe that the mere fact that an entity's nature is impenetrable can itself support antirealism about entities of that kind. I myself find no reason to believe this. See McGinn (1993) for a probing discussion of this matter.

[22]   Blackburn (1993), Ch. 9 and (1998), Ch. 3, Gibbard (1990), Part II, Horgan and Timmons (1990/91), Mackie (1977), Ch. 1, and Timmons (1999), Ch. 1, are explicit about this. In my estimation, the term 'naturalism' is a philosopher's weasel-word, which admits of a great variety of incompatible meanings. In some senses of the term, I believe that moral and epistemic realism are compatible with naturalism. My use of the term borrows from Rea (2002), Ch. 3.

[23]   Blackburn (1993), 168 and 174.

Arguably, however, accepting this creed is incompatible with claiming that naturalism implies that moral realism is false, for we cannot rule out a priori that science may reveal that there are moral facts and, hence, that moral realism is compatible with naturalism.[24]

Be that as it may, what I would like to point out is that, if naturalism implies that there are no moral facts and if this claim implies that there are no epistemic facts, then naturalism gives us strong reason to believe that there are no epistemic facts. If, however, my overarching argument is correct and there are epistemic facts, then we have good reason to believe that naturalism—at least of the kind that is driving the arguments we've considered—is false. The apparent price of tying naturalism so closely to moral antirealism is, I suggest, to increase the vulnerability of the naturalist project.

The fifth argument

The four arguments that comprise Mackie's argument from queerness have two common features. First, they lean heavily on the idea that moral facts are (to use a phrase of Terry Horgan and Mark Timmons)—'oddball entities'—entities distinctively out of place in a naturalistic worldview.[25] Second, their aim is to establish that there are no moral facts at all. The next two arguments I will discuss differ from the ones we've considered along both of these dimensions.[26] They neither rest upon a version of naturalism nor aim to establish that moral facts do not exist in any sense.

The fifth antirealist argument is driven by a commitment to what we can call 'The Explanatory Principle'.[27] According to this principle,

Moral facts exist only if such facts play explanatory roles R.

[24] Rea (2002), Chs. 2 and 3, develops a similar line of argument and discusses the substantive positions to which naturalists can be committed.

[25] See Horgan and Timmons (1990/91), 449.

[26] At least this is true of the versions of the arguments that I will consider. As Hampton (1998), Ch. 1, points out, Gilbert Harman's version of the fifth argument implicitly leans on the idea that moral facts are queer.

[27] Versions of this argument are developed by Harman (1977), Ch. 1, Gibbard (1990), Ch. 6, Leiter (2001), Williams (1985), Ch. 8, and Wright (1992) and (1995). Two points are worth noting about The Explanatory Principle: First, the principle is read in different ways. For example, some philosophers such as Wiggins (1990/91) maintain that the relevant explanatory role is *being indispensable for theorizing*. (I will have more to say about this suggestion in Chapter 8.) Others maintain that the role must be explicitly causal in nature. In the interest of brevity, I have fixed upon only one such reading. Second, in contrast to the way I have formulated it, The Explanatory Principle is often formulated not as an ontological claim about the conditions under which moral facts exist, but as an epistemic principle regarding the conditions under which we have reason to believe they exist. For my purposes, this distinction needn't matter much. The principle can easily be reformulated as an epistemic principle,

And what explanatory roles might these be? Although antirealists have offered nothing like a developed account of what the requisite explanatory roles are that moral facts must satisfy, philosophers such as Crispin Wright have suggested that, were moral facts to exist, at least the following must be true: Such facts would have to explain the existence of non-moral facts of a sufficiently wide array of types.[28] According to Wright, an ordinary descriptive fact such as *that the rocks are wet* can explain the existence of facts of many different sorts, including the facts *that I perceive the rocks to be wet, that I've slipped and fallen, that a small (pre-linguistic) child is interested in his hands after touching the rocks, that there is an abundance of lichen growing on the rocks,* and so forth. By contrast, if a putative moral fact such as *that an act is wrong* explains anything, it does so only by dint of its being 'mediated' (that is, represented in some sense) by propositional attitudes of various sorts. The putative fact *that an act is wrong* might, for example, explain why you believe that a given act is wrong and, thus, why you have acted to prevent it. But a putative fact of this sort does not directly explain any states of affairs in the world that do not involve propositional attitudes; arguably, it doesn't *do* anything at all. If this is right, however, then the putative moral fact *that an act is wrong*—and presumably any other putative moral fact—fails to satisfy The Explanatory Principle. From which it follows that moral facts do not exist.

This is so far forth to trace the argument under consideration along the lines suggested by Wright. Let me now add a qualification that Wright himself highlights. Although one might take the failure of putative moral facts to satisfy The Explanatory Principle to imply that there is no sense in which moral facts exist, there is a less severe and, arguably, more attractive verdict to draw. For suppose we distinguish between facts robustly construed and mere 'facts'. Something counts as a fact robustly construed, we can say, if it is such that it can be 'seriously' represented (this is Wright's expression) by our propositional attitudes and plays a wide range of explanatory roles. An ordinary descriptive fact such as *that the*

---

in which case what I am calling the 'fifth' argument purports to establish that we do not have reason to believe that moral (or epistemic) facts exist. Of course if the principle were reformulated thus, the argument would not be one that aims to establish moral (or epistemic) antirealism. Presumably, its role for the antirealist would be ancillary in character, aiming, with the aid of other arguments, to undercut the claim that moral (or epistemic) facts exist.

[28] See Wright (1992), Ch. 5.

rocks are wet is a robust fact thus understood. Something counts as a mere 'fact', by contrast, if it cannot be 'seriously' represented and fails to play a wide range of explanatory roles. A putative fact such as *that an act is wrong* is, according to some, a good candidate for being a mere 'fact'.[29] While Wright suggests there is a sense in which we can say mere 'facts' exist, he also suggests that they are nonetheless best thought of as being mere 'shadows' cast by the assertoric form of the sentences we utter, entities that come for 'free' given the assertoric form of moral discourse. Now what exactly 'serious' representation and this metaphor of a 'shadow' amount to is something I'll discuss later in Chapter 6. For present purposes, there are two points to emphasize.

First, moral facts as the realist understands them are not mere 'facts'. For, if they were, they would not play the role of truth-makers, as they would not be what is represented (in a non-deflationary sense) by the content of moral claims.[30] It follows that the argument under consideration, if sound, implies that moral facts as the realist understands them do not exist. But, second, the argument we're considering is perfectly compatible with the claim that our use of the term 'moral fact' stands for, not moral facts realistically understood, but mere moral 'facts'.

So, there is a sense in which the present argument is less ambitious than the other objections to moral realism we've considered (at least as they are often developed). That said, it is plausible to believe that, when suitably modified, the argument we're now considering (if sound) yields a similar conclusion regarding epistemic facts. For consider a putative epistemic fact such as *that engaging in a plan of inquiry is irrational*. A fact of this sort appears not to have a wide explanatory role; it appears no more to explain phenomena in nature such as that which biologists and physicists study than does the putative fact *that an act is wrong*. If this putative epistemic fact explains why certain states of affairs obtain, then it too does not do so 'directly', but only by way of being mediated by our propositional attitudes. If this is true, however, putative epistemic facts such as *that engaging in a plan of inquiry is irrational*—and presumably any other epistemic fact—fail a suitably modified version of The Explanatory Principle. And, thus, it follows that facts of this kind do not exist. To which it is worth adding

---

[29] See Blackburn (1998) and (1999), for example.

[30] Wright himself suggests that moral 'facts' could not be identical with moral facts, since he believes that the former cannot be categorical reasons. See Wright (1992), 200–1.

that this implication also appears to be compatible with a view according to which epistemic facts are 'mere' facts—facts that are 'shadows' cast by the assertoric form of epistemic discourse and are not (or fail to generate) categorical epistemic reasons.

Let me add to this an additional point. The type of argument under consideration is one that concerns the explanatory role of moral and epistemic facts. It does not, however, deny that there may be interesting differences between the explanatory roles of moral *concepts*, on the one hand, and epistemic concepts, on the other. It might be, for example, that epistemic concepts are more entrenched in our best science and metaphysics than moral ones. And, as I'll suggest in Chapter 6, it might be true that there is no coherent way of doing metaphysics and science without employing various kinds of epistemic notions. But it is worth emphasizing that the fact that epistemic concepts are more deeply entrenched in the practice of metaphysics and science does not itself imply that we should understand such concepts to pick out epistemic facts. Indeed, if Wright's argument (or something like it) is sound, even if such concepts did (in some sense) pick out epistemic facts, this would at best yield the consequence that those entities are mere 'facts', since they fail to play a wide explanatory role.

In fact, I think we can say something even stronger than this. Moral antirealists such as Timmons, Horgan, and Richard Joyce agree that a moral antirealist position should not be so revisionary as to recommend that we cease to engage in moral discourse. According to these philosophers, such a recommendation would be fruitless, for moral concepts are so deeply entrenched in ordinary discourse that we couldn't jettison them even if we tried. But, contrary to what we might suppose, the entrenchment of moral concepts in ordinary discourse is offered not as a reason to embrace moral realism, but rather to *reject* it.[31] The claim is that, since moral discourse plays such an indispensable role in human life, it would survive rejection of the idea that there are objective moral facts. If we assume, however, that human concepts are not likely to have application conditions more opulent than is required by the purposes they serve, then the fact that moral discourse would survive our rejecting the existence of robust moral facts is reason to believe that ordinary moral discourse is at most committed to there being moral 'facts'. And, thus, according to these philosophers,

---

[31] See Timmons (1999), 174, Horgan and Timmons (2000), 143–44, and Joyce (2001), Ch. 6.

there is reason to believe that there is a sense in which moral antirealism is not nearly so revisionist as some philosophers have made it seem. It is—so the suggestion goes—the realist who lards our ordinary views with controversial ontological theses.

Once again, I don't intend to weigh in on whether this argument is sound. (One naturally wonders about its implications for realism regarding the external world.) I simply wish to note that if it is, then it is equally powerful against epistemic realism. If the argument is cogent, the entrenchment of epistemic concepts is no reason to believe that our ordinary and scientific practices are committed to the existence of epistemic facts; rather, it is a reason to believe they are not.

The sixth argument

Width of explanatory role, then, seems not to be a feature that divides putatively moral facts from epistemic ones. Still, there might appear to be a feature of moral *judgments* that divides them from epistemic ones and thereby supports the claim that epistemic but not moral facts exist. In particular, it might be said that there is a significant amount of convergence in opinion on epistemic matters, but not on moral ones, and that this gives us reason to embrace epistemic but not moral realism.

Here we touch upon issues that lie at the heart of the so-called argument from disagreement.[32] In its paradigmatic form, the argument starts by pointing out that there is massive and seemingly ineradicable disagreement among otherwise competent parties concerning certain kinds of moral issues. There is, for example, widespread, deep, and seemingly ineradicable disagreement about whether abortion is permissible or whether animals have moral rights. Note that the argument doesn't start with the observation that there is massive and intractable disagreement about whether there *are* such things as morally permissible or impermissible actions or whether there are moral virtues and vices. That is, the argument doesn't start with the claim that there is massive and seemingly interminable disagreement about 'second-order' metaethical issues that concern whether moral features of certain kinds exist. Rather, the claim is that there is massive and seemingly ineradicable disagreement about certain kinds of 'first-order'

[32] The argument is developed by Harman (1975) and (1996), Loeb (1998), Mackie (1977), Stevenson (1963), Williams (1985), Ch. 8, Wong (1984), and others. For a helpful survey, see Gowans (2000).

moral issues—massive and seemingly ineradicable disagreement about whether actions of various sorts *display* moral features of certain kinds. Nevertheless, the proponent of the argument maintains that this first-order moral disagreement is really symptomatic of deeper differences in moral outlook. The reason people disagree about the permissibility of abortion, for example, is not merely that they are misapplying moral concepts, or being tripped up by the complexity of these issues, or that some of the parties are suffering from a type of cognitive shortcoming. It is rather that they have different views about what justice, kindness, and the like require. They have different views about the *nature* of these putative moral features.

From here the argument is typically run in either of two directions. According to some philosophers, the best explanation of these differences in moral outlook is that moral features such as justice, kindness, and the like have no common nature about which we are disagreeing. This view has it that there is no such thing as justice *simpliciter*, kindness *simpliciter*, or moral reasons *simpliciter*. There is only justice-relative-to-one-group, justice-relative-to-another-group, moral reasons-relative-to-one-group, moral reasons-relative-to-another-group, and so forth. The conclusion drawn by proponents of this way of developing the argument is that there are moral facts of a sort. They are facts determined by the conventions that obtain at one or another group. But, says the advocate of the argument, there are no moral facts as the realist thinks of them, for the realist believes that some moral reasons are authoritative. That is, the realist believes that some such reasons are categorical, inescapably governing persons regardless of their desires, projects, or social allegiances. And she holds that the decisiveness of some such reasons is not a function of an agent's desires, projects, social allegiances, or the like. At least one of these claims is incompatible with moral relativism, however. According to some understandings of the relativist position, moral reasons-relative-to-a-group govern an agent only if that agent is a member of the group to which such reasons are indexed. According to other versions of the view, some moral reasons-relative-to-a-group govern all agents, but whether any such reason is decisive for an agent is determined by whether that agent is a member of the group to which such reasons are indexed—no such reasons being stronger or better than others *tout court*.

According to other philosophers, however, the pervasive differences in moral outlook evident in ordinary moral practice are evidence not for relativism, but for the view that there are no moral facts at all. As these philosophers see things, just as the best explanation of religious disagreement is not religious relativism, but atheism, so also the best explanation of moral disagreement is moral nihilism.[33]

If there is any argument that would appear to damage moral but not epistemic realism, it is probably this one. But here we need to proceed with care. As I have stated it, the argument from disagreement does not say that mere disagreement about first-order moral issues is evidence against the existence of moral facts. Rather, it says that disagreement between 'otherwise competent parties' about first-order moral issues is evidence against the existence of moral facts. The first thing to get clear on, then, is who the 'otherwise competent parties' engaged in moral disagreement are.

One option is to claim that they are the experts concerning moral matters—where the 'experts' are not sages and wise persons, but expert *theoreticians* about moral matters. (I assume that as a matter of empirical fact, the two classes of persons do not significantly overlap.) If this is what the advocate of the argument is assuming, however, then there is a rather exact parallel between disagreement about moral and about epistemic issues. Granted, there is ample disagreement among, say, bioethicists and moral philosophers about the nature of moral features. But the philosophical literature attests that there is also massive and seemingly intractable disagreement among epistemic 'experts' such as epistemologists and cognitive scientists about the nature of various epistemic features such as justification, rationality, knowledge, and the like. William Alston, for example, contends that there is so much disagreement among philosophers about the nature of justification that we have reason to believe there is no common concept about which they are disagreeing.[34] The desired contrast between moral and epistemic disagreement, apparently, does not lie here.

Better, then, to say that the otherwise competent parties in question are some subset of ordinary folk. If we assume this, then there does seem to be a disanalogy between the nature of moral and epistemic disagreement. Disagreement about first-order moral matters among the folk seems to be deeper and more extensive than disagreement about first-order epistemic ones. We seem to disagree more about what is just than about what is rational.

---

[33] See Mackie (1977) and Sturgeon (1994). Sturgeon himself is not a moral nihilist, but a realist.
[34] See Alston (1993).

I myself think we should hesitate to embrace this line of thought, though. First, as I've already emphasized, the moral and epistemic domains interlace with and interpenetrate each other in various fashions. Our discussion in the last chapter indicated that some norms are hybrid in nature and, as such, it is impossible to pull apart (ontologically, at least) their moral and epistemic dimensions. But if hybrid norms such as intellectual honesty, intellectual humility, and fairness in evaluating the views of others are such that their epistemic and moral dimensions intertwine in this fashion, then it would seem incredible that the present argument should yield the result that we should be relativists or nihilists about their moral dimensions and not their epistemic ones. There is not sufficient conceptual space between moral and epistemic features for this type of division.

Second, I doubt that we should accept the claim that first-order disagreement among the folk about moral features is considerably more systematic and pronounced than first-order disagreement about epistemic ones. Consider, in this regard, an especially contentious subject matter such as the rationality of religious belief. We know, on the one hand, that many people believe that it is rationally acceptable to accept ancient texts such as the Bible, the Koran, or the Bhagavad Gita as authoritative guides for life. Among these folk, many also believe that it is rationally permissible (and even obligatory) to cling to religious beliefs and the pronouncements of religious authorities in the face of contrary evidence—even when this contrary evidence appears to be generated by our best science. Moreover, many of these people hold that believing these things is perfectly sensible, since reason has a very limited domain and that, on many issues of importance, faith in the mysteries of religion takes precedence.

We also know, on the other hand, that many non-religious persons think that these sorts of religious views, attitudes, and practices are simpleminded, foolish, or backward. Between these two parties there is, then, a first-order debate about what sorts of things are epistemically rational to accept, believe, intend, or do. More exactly, since the predicate 'epistemic rationality' in this context is probably best understood as one that stands for a constellation of thicker epistemic concepts such as wisdom, understanding, judiciousness, epistemic humility, epistemic honesty, and objectivity, the disagreement in question is plausibly viewed as being concerned with whether religious beliefs exhibit these thicker epistemic merits.

Disagreement about religious issues of this sort is deep and pervasive and, from what the sociologists tell us, shows no sign of abating.[35] Now it will be remembered that in the moral case the antirealist encouraged us to see first-order moral disagreement as symptomatic of second-order disagreement about the nature of justice, kindness, and so forth. Is disagreement about first-order issues regarding the rationality of religious belief also symptomatic of second-order disagreement about the nature of rationality? Well, there seems no more reason to believe that in the religious domain disagreement of the type at issue is simply a function of our misapplying epistemic concepts or being tripped up by the complexity of religious issues. Rather, it seems as if the various parties to the debate are expressing very different views about what rationality is—expressing, as it were, very different epistemological *pieties*.[36] At the heart of the epistemological pieties of (at least a wide range of) the theistic religions is the conviction that epistemic rationality fundamentally consists in obedience to God and religious authorities, the cultivation of certain ascetical practices, recognition of our cognitive limitations as the manifestation of human sinfulness, and so on. By contrast, non-theistic epistemological pieties reject all this. According to these views, obedience or disobedience to God plays no role in explaining why we succeed or fail to understand the world aright.

I've said that, if the structure of the argument from disagreement is correct, first-order disagreement about the rationality of religious belief is sufficiently widespread and deep that it is indicative of second-order disagreement about the nature of putative epistemic features such as rationality. It follows that, if the argument from disagreement supports antirealism with respect to moral facts, then it also supports antirealism with regard to epistemic facts. There is not, then, the sort of disanalogy between the moral and epistemic domains that our initial formulation of the argument from disagreement might have led us to expect. Indeed, upon reflection, it seems that what we should have expected is that we would find deep disagreement as endemic to both domains. A great deal of moral disagreement is, after all, the result of our having deep differences in opinion about broadly metaphysical issues such as the nature of persons, whether God exists, what counts as human flourishing, and so forth. Ordinary

---

[35] See Smith (1998).

[36] The term is taken from Wolterstorff (1994). Chapter 10 of Wolterstorff (2001) notes that, even among theists, there are rather different epistemological pieties expressed.

persons disagree about issues such as the permissibility of abortion, in part, because they disagree about what counts as a person, whether God has forbidden abortion, and so forth. But if these different and very general metaphysical views are driving disagreement in the moral domain, there is little reason to believe that they would not have similar effects elsewhere, such as in the domain of epistemology. And it appears that they do. A great deal of first-order epistemic disagreement is also plausibly viewed as the upshot of deep metaphysical differences about the nature of persons, whether there is a God, the nature of the human good, and so forth. Ordinary persons disagree about whether it is rational to trust in divine providence in the midst of severe trials, for example, because they don't agree about whether there is a God who could allow creatures to be tried in this way.[37]

II. The argument's second stage and three types of antirealist view

At the outset of our discussion, I said that the argument of this chapter divides into two parts. The first part of the argument is now complete. Its aim has been to argue that there is a range of objections to moral realism—what I've called the 'standard objections'—that aim to establish that moral facts (as they are understood by the paradigmatic moral realist) do not exist. On the assumption that these arguments exhaust the objections to moral realism, I have contended that, were these objections to establish that there are no moral facts, then they would also establish (when suitably

[37] Don Loeb has suggested to me that a different version of the argument from disagreement trades on the claim that, even if we were to agree on all the merely descriptive facts, we would continue to disagree about the moral ones. He has further suggested that this may mark a difference between disagreement concerning moral issues and disagreement concerning epistemic ones: After all, it seems plausible to believe that, were all the merely descriptive facts to be settled, epistemic disagreement—at least of the sort I have just considered—would disappear. It seems to me, however, that if first-order moral disagreement were to persist in the face of agreement about the merely descriptive facts, then so also would first-order epistemic disagreement. Presumably, if clashes regarding how to weigh, say, the values of justice and mercy would continue in the moral realm, then so also would disagreement about how to weigh the theoretical values of explanatory power and simplicity in the epistemic one. (Indeed, there is a sense in which first-order epistemic disagreement would simply piggy-back on moral disagreement. Disagreement about how to weigh moral values would, perforce, imply that we also disagree about whether we have sufficient epistemic reason to weigh one moral value more than another.)

modified) that epistemic facts do not exist. The second part of the argument offers an explanation of why this is so and can be stated briefly. According to this part of the argument, what the standard objections establish, if sound, is that there is a cluster of features that moral and epistemic facts of certain kinds would display were they to exist—features such as *being supervenient on merely descriptive facts, being intrinsically motivating, being (or implying) categorical reasons, failing to play a wide range of explanatory roles*, and so on. Call these features the 'objectionable features'. As I understand the standard objections to moral realism, the assumption is that if moral facts do not exist, then this is simply because they would display these features. But presumably there is nothing unique to moral facts themselves that makes them objectionable on this score. The objectionable features are sufficiently problematic that, if moral facts do not exist, then nothing has them. However, on the assumption that the argument developed thus far is sound, we know that if epistemic facts exist, then there is something that has the objectionable features. Or, equivalently, we know that if nothing has the objectionable features, then epistemic facts do not exist. These two claims, however, imply the core argument's first premise: If moral facts do not exist, then epistemic facts do not exist. This premise I will call the 'parity premise'.

Three types of antirealist position

As it happens, I believe that the parity premise requires a further round of defense, for the discussion in subsequent chapters may raise the suspicion that there are reasons to admit the existence of epistemic facts even if they display the objectionable features. However, I am going to defer discussion of this issue until the last chapter, after the relevant issues have emerged. In the meanwhile, I am going to assume that we have assembled at least a prima facie case for accepting the parity premise. What I should now like to emphasize is that antirealists generally agree that some combination of the standard objections implies or makes it likely that moral realism is false—although, let it be added that the agreement among antirealists ordinarily extends no further than this. Having ostensibly established that moral realism is indefensible, moral antirealists typically divide into three factions. Some claim that we ought to adopt a nihilist 'error-theory' according to which predicative moral discourse purports to represent moral reality, but fails to do so because there are no moral facts. Others defend an expressivist view according to which there are no moral facts, but moral discourse does not purport to represent moral reality. Still others maintain that we ought to embrace one or another reductionist view according to which moral discourse is genuinely assertoric, but functions to represent moral facts reductively construed. And, I might add, within these groups we find a flowering of different emphases and proposals.

In the next four chapters, I will explore the epistemic analogues to moral nihilism, expressivism, and reductionism. It is instructive to notice at the outset that epistemic nihilist and expressivist views are virtually absent from the philosophical literature. In my judgment, this is testimony to the fact that philosophers have frequently overlooked the implications that these various antirealist arguments have for epistemology. In any event, my general strategy in the subsequent chapters will be as follows: Take the relevant moral antirealist position and then construct its epistemic analogue. When we draw out the implications of accepting these views, I shall argue that we will discover that epistemic antirealism comes at a heavy price.

4

Epistemic Nihilism

My purpose in the preceding two chapters has been to defend the parity premise, which tells us that, if moral facts do not exist, then epistemic facts also do not exist. In this chapter and those that follow, I wish to lay the conceptual groundwork for a defense of the claim that epistemic facts exist. As I indicated in the Introduction, the case I shall make for this claim is largely negative in character, as it consists in teasing out the implausible implications of its denial.

The view with which I shall concern myself in this chapter is the epistemic counterpart to J. L. Mackie's error-theoretic account of morality.[1] This position—which I will call 'epistemic nihilism'—is comprised of three claims.

In the first place, epistemic nihilists agree with epistemic realists in adopting:

The Epistemic Realist's Speech Act Thesis: Some epistemic discourse is assertoric.

Epistemic nihilists, then, reject the attempt to offer any sort of expressivist or deflationary reinterpretation of epistemic discourse. Epistemic discourse is generally as it seems, viz., robustly assertoric.[2] Furthermore, epistemic nihilists agree with epistemic realists insofar as they hold that deflationary and epistemic theories of truth should be rejected in favor of the realist

---

[1] See Mackie (1977), Ch. 1. Joyce (2001) develops a position with affinities to Mackie's.
[2] I assume that so-called fictive discourse—roughly, discourse wherein an agent assents in certain circumstances to propositions without believing them—is not a mode of robustly assertoric discourse. I will have more to say about discourse of this type in Ch. 6.

conception of truth. But unlike their realist rivals, epistemic nihilists defend:

The Epistemic Realist's Alethic Thesis: The contents of some predicative epistemic claims are true and, if the contents of such claims are true, then they are true in the realist sense.[3]

The nihilist has an explanation for adopting the alethic thesis. It is:

The Epistemic Nihilist's Ontic Thesis: If there are any particular epistemic facts, then they are as the realist says, and there are no such facts.

It is worth stressing that this last claim needs to be understood aright. The nihilist's ontic claim is not: It doesn't *seem* as if there are (particular) epistemic facts. (Henceforth, I shall omit the qualifier 'particular', assuming it to be understood.) To the contrary, epistemic nihilists readily admit that it pre-reflectively seems as if there are epistemic facts. They merely claim that there are no such facts. Nor, I should emphasize, is the claim merely: There are no epistemic facts as the realist understands them. That would leave open the possibility that there are epistemic facts in some other less robust, minimalist sense. (For example, it would leave open the possibility that epistemic reasons are all hypothetical in nature.) Rather, epistemic nihilists hold that, if there are any epistemic facts, then they are as realists say; but, there are no such facts. The epistemic nihilist is a disenchanted realist.

Thus understood, epistemic nihilism is an unpopular position in contemporary philosophy. One is, in fact, hard pressed to find a philosopher who explicitly embraces the view.[4] That said, I don't think that this itself gives us reason to dismiss the position. We are, after all, familiar with philosophical positions, such as positions that claim that we cannot know anything, whose theoretical importance is wildly disproportionate to the number of persons who actually hold them. These positions are of interest not because of their popularity, but because they promise to teach us something very

---

[3] It is worth emphasizing that this claim does not imply that any or all the content of epistemic discourse is false. First, as Joyce (2001), Ch. 1 points out, nihilism with respect to the subject matter of assertoric discourse of some kind is compatible with that discourse's being non-referring and, hence, neither true nor false. Second, the nihilist's alethic thesis is compatible with the thesis that some general epistemic claims are true. For example, it is open to the nihilist to claim that a conditional such as *if God exists, then there are epistemic facts* is true on account of its antecedent's being necessarily false.

[4] Quine, in certain places, appears to endorse the view. See Quine (1969). Cf. also Jaegwon Kim's discussion of Quine in Kim (1993), Ch. 12.

important about a given domain. I want to suggest that epistemic nihilism is a position such as this. Identifying the objections to which epistemic nihilism is vulnerable proves to be instructive primarily because other epistemic antirealist positions—ones that are explicitly formulated so as to avoid the pitfalls of epistemic nihilism—are (so I will argue) vulnerable to the same objections. My primary task in this chapter is to identify these objections. The thesis I will develop is that epistemic nihilism is deeply unattractive because it implies what I call 'the three undesirable results'.

I. The three undesirable results

The first undesirable result

Suppose we take the locution 'reason to believe' to mean epistemic reason to believe—reason to believe from the perspective of representing reality aright, gaining true belief, knowledge, understanding, or the like. And suppose we use the term 'rational' to mean epistemic rationality.[5] We can identify The First Undesirable Result by formulating the following dilemma for epistemic nihilism: Either epistemic nihilists hold that we have reasons to believe epistemic nihilism or that we do not. If epistemic nihilists hold that we do have reasons to believe their position, then their position is self-defeating in the sense that it presupposes the existence of the very sorts of entity that it claims not to exist. After all, if we have reasons to believe epistemic nihilism, then it follows by conceptual necessity that we rationally ought, all other things being equal, to believe it. But there are no rational oughts according to epistemic nihilists; there are no facts that imply that certain propositions are belief-worthy or that failing to believe something on good available evidence renders one (all other things being equal) irrational.

If, by contrast, epistemic nihilists hold that we do not have epistemic reasons to believe their position, then their position is polemically toothless in the following sense: No one would make a rational mistake in rejecting it and no one would be epistemically praiseworthy in accepting it. Thus we have:

---

[5] I realize that many views are labeled 'epistemic' accounts of rationality. The plurality of views shouldn't matter for my purposes since my aim is to distinguish epistemic rationality from prudential rationality and 'rationality all things considered' (i.e. being appropriately responsive to the best reasons).

The First Undesirable Result: Either epistemic nihilism is self-defeating and, hence, we have no (sufficient) reason to believe it, or, it implies that there are no epistemic reasons and, *a fortiori*, that we have no reason to believe it.

The second undesirable result

In what follows, I will assume that The First Undesirable Result is sufficiently unattractive that any minimally adequate philosophical position will be at pains to avoid being committed to it.[6] Still, there remains an interesting question about what exactly the foregoing argument shows and whether it might yield further undesirable consequences.

Let's grant that grasping the first horn of the dilemma commits epistemic nihilists to a position that is incoherent. Grasping the second horn of the dilemma, however, appears to have less severe consequences. At worst, it might seem to imply that epistemic nihilists are only committed to accepting a Moorean paradox of the following sort:

(1) Epistemic nihilism is true, but there is no reason to believe it.

As I pointed out in Chapter 1, propositions such as this appear to be absurd because the person who accepts it is committed to accepting both its conjuncts. However, the acceptance of the proposition expressed in its second conjunct undercuts the justification or warrant we might have for accepting the proposition expressed in its first conjunct. And the type of justification or warrant in question seems to be *epistemic* in character—justification or warrant from the perspective of gaining truth. So, if epistemic nihilists grasp the second horn of the dilemma, they appear committed to accepting a proposition, the mere acceptance of which guarantees that it is unjustified or unwarranted.

---

[6] Admittedly, there are so-called eliminativists about the mental who deny that there are propositional attitudes in the manner that philosophers typically think of them (see Churchland [1989]). These philosophers are committed to the nihilist-sounding claim that nothing could count in favor of believing a proposition, for they deny that there are believings.

It doesn't follow from this, however, that eliminativism implies The Epistemic Nihilist's Ontic Thesis. It is possible, for example, that the eliminativist surrogates for propositional attitudes are subject to epistemic evaluation. In that case, we could reformulate epistemic nihilism so that it is a thesis regarding the computational surrogates for belief.

In any event, eliminativism is not a position that I propose to discuss. This is largely because I consider it a highly radical position for which there must be very good reasons to accept. And I do not understand how any of the considerations proffered in its favor could be reasons to accept it. If the only way to circumvent the present argument against epistemic nihilism were to accept eliminativism, I think that would be good evidence in favor of epistemic realism. For critiques of eliminativism, see Hasker (1999), Ch. 1, Baker (1987), and Haack (1993), Ch. 8.

However, if this is the correct diagnosis of why accepting a claim such as (1) is absurd, we should not attribute to nihilists a paradoxical position, for nihilists who grasp the second horn of the dilemma deny that anything could have the property of being epistemically justified or warranted. Consequently, according to the nihilist view, a person's accepting the claim that there is no reason to believe epistemic nihilism cannot undercut her justification for accepting epistemic nihilism. If nihilism is true, a claim such as (1) cannot even rise to the level of paradox.

It does not follow from this that (1) is not an instance of a Moorean paradox. Epistemic nihilism may be false in which case the position would have the unenviable status of both being false and committing those who accept it to accepting Moorean paradoxical propositions. In a moment, I am going to explore whether the second horn of the dilemma stated earlier—viz., the claim that there are no epistemic reasons—implies that epistemic nihilism is false. For now, let me point out what the second horn of the dilemma clearly does imply, viz., that a sweeping form of epistemological skepticism is true. For if there are no epistemic facts or reasons, then none of our propositional attitudes can exhibit epistemic merits or demerits; none of our propositional attitudes can be justified, warranted, entitled, irrational, a case of knowledge, based on reasons, or the like. Accordingly, epistemic nihilism is committed to:

The Second Undesirable Result: Either epistemic nihilism is self-defeating or it implies a radical version of epistemological skepticism according to which no entity can display an epistemic merit or demerit.

The third undesirable result

The Second Undesirable Result, I will assume, is also sufficiently unattractive that any minimally adequate philosophical theory will be at pains to avoid being committed to it. One wonders, though, whether the screws can be turned a little tighter yet. Assuming that nihilists adopt the second horn of the dilemma posed earlier—viz., the claim that there are no epistemic reasons—might we now have the material for an argument to the effect that epistemic nihilism is false?

I believe not; there is no plausible non-question-begging argument to establish that epistemic nihilism is false. I want further to suggest that this is an interesting result, for it implies that the denial of the second horn of the dilemma stated in The First Undesirable Result is not something that can or should be argued for. Rather, its denial is part of what we can call, harkening back to terminology introduced in Chapter 1, our 'commonsensical conception of the world'; its denial is what ordinary mature adults must and do take for granted in their lives in the everyday. Of course to say that the denial of this type of epistemic nihilism is part of our commonsensical conception of the world is not to claim that epistemic *realism* itself is part of our commonsensical conception of the world. Still, the more limited claim under consideration is of interest for our purposes. For suppose a position were touted as being consistent with our ordinary understanding of the epistemic domain, but implied the three undesirable results (the third of which I'll state in a moment). If there were such a view, then we could conclude that, contrary to what its advocates claim, it would not be consistent with the content of our commonsensical conception of the epistemic realm. In the next chapter, I will contend that this is exactly what we should conclude about epistemic expressivism. If my contention is correct, epistemic expressivism is also incompatible with the content of our commonsensical conception of the epistemic realm, as (inasmuch as it offers an account of epistemic judgment) it also implies the three undesirable results.

As I say, the details of this argument will come later. For present purposes, let me attend to the immediate task of arguing that the position expressed in the second horn of the dilemma posed earlier is not one that we could have non-question-begging reasons to reject.

The position captured in the second horn of this dilemma says that there are no epistemic reasons. Let's call this position 'nihilism' (for short). Now consider as a representative argument against nihilism the following simple piece of reasoning, what I shall call 'the short argument':

(2)   If nihilism is true, then radical skepticism is true.
(3)   Radical skepticism is false.
(4)   So, nihilism is false.

While I deem this a sound argument, it fails as a non-question-begging argument against nihilism in several respects. Let me highlight what I take to be its most glaring problem.

The short argument purports to establish that nihilism is false and, thus, that there are epistemic reasons. But we might rightly ask how we could *argue* in a non-question-begging fashion for these claims. For suppose we accept the plausible view that, in the paradigmatic case, the premises of an argument are offered in support of its conclusion in the sense of providing evidential support for its conclusion. (In what follows, unless the context indicates otherwise, I will use the term 'argument' to stand for an argument in its paradigmatic use.[7]) A statement's being offered as evidential support for a conclusion, however, is just a matter of its being offered as a *reason* for accepting that conclusion. And, when all goes well, premises *are* reasons to accept a conclusion. This has two implications.

The first is that there are no non-question-begging arguments that could establish that nihilism is false. Were a person to press such an argument against nihilism, she would endeavor to establish that there are reasons by tacitly assuming that some statements provide evidential support to believe others. But—and this is the second implication—if nihilism were true, it would be impossible that there were premises of an argument that provide evidential support for its conclusion. And thus we have:

The Third Undesirable Result: Either epistemic nihilism is self-defeating or it implies that there could be no arguments for anything.

The third undesirable result, I will also assume, is sufficiently unattractive that any minimally adequate philosophical theory will be at pains to avoid being committed to it.[8] And, in combination, I will assume that the three undesirable results render epistemic nihilism a very unattractive position.

Now, by claiming that the three undesirable results render epistemic nihilism unattractive I don't mean to suggest that nihilism does not imply other undesirable results. It may well do so. For example, some philosophers hold that belief attributions are normative in character. According to these philosophers, to say of a person that she believes a proposition p is to imply

---

[7] I realize that this is not the only way to think about the nature of arguments. Harman (1986), for example, distinguishes argument from inference, maintaining that the rules of argument are simply principles of implication. If one were attracted to a view such as this, then one could state The Third Undesirable Result as the following thesis about inference: Either epistemic nihilism is true or it implies that there could be no good inferences.

[8] Of course The Third Undesirable Result is consistent with there being activities that are non-paradigmatic uses of arguments—ones in which we do not endeavor to offer premises as evidential support for a conclusion. It may be that some such activities establish in a non-question-begging fashion that epistemic nihilism is false, say, by establishing that premise (3) of the short argument—or the claim that radical skepticism is false—is at least probably true. Still, even if this were the case, the short argument (or any argument for that matter) would not give us any reason to reject nihilism or any reason to believe that its premises imply its conclusion.

(analytically) that insofar as she believes p, then she ought to surrender p if she sees that p is incompatible with some obvious truth, or that she ought to hold p with greater confidence if it receives confirming evidence, and so on. Now if the 'oughts' in question are epistemic (as it would seem), and persons believe propositions, then epistemic nihilism is a position that would be literally unbelievable.[9] Likewise, some philosophers have held that meaning attributions are normative in character. According to these philosophers, to say that a claim has a certain meaning is to imply (analytically) that insofar as that claim has that meaning, then one ought to infer certain further claims, or not believe certain further claims, and so forth. If the normativity in question is epistemic (as some have suggested) and some claims are meaningful, then epistemic nihilism is a meaningless position.[10] While I have sympathy with the claims that belief attribution and meaning are normative in character, my strategy in this chapter has not been to defend these more controversial claims and thereby charge epistemic nihilism with still more undesirable results. Rather, it has been simply to indicate some of the more obvious and unattractive implications of epistemic nihilism—implications sufficiently unattractive that we should not want to embrace the view.

II. Conclusion

J. L. Mackie was a moral nihilist. He thought that there are no moral facts and that moral discourse is systematically mistaken. But he expressed no sympathy for epistemic nihilism. As far as I can tell, he never seriously entertained the position as worthy of acceptance. Were he to have considered the position, however, I doubt that he would've had much sympathy with it. For Mackie believed in the power of reason and argument.[11] So, while I do not take the argument of this chapter to strike fear into the heart of unregenerate epistemic nihilists—they, no doubt, would see it simply

---

[9] For more on the normativity of belief attribution and its consequences for metaethics, see Dreier (2002a) and Shafer-Landau (2003), 33–7.

[10] See Kripke (1982) and Boghossian (2003) for a discussion of the normativity of meaning attributions.

[11] When addressing the issue of the existence of God, for example, Mackie (1982) writes: 'It is my view that the question whether there is or is not a god can and should be discussed rationally and reasonably, and that such discussion can be rewarding, in that it can yield definite results' (p. 1).

as drawing out the implications of their view!—I think that philosophers such as Mackie, who championed the cause of rationality, should take it more seriously. For fundamental to our commonsensical conception of the world, I've suggested, is the assumption that radical epistemological skepticism is false. In their everyday doings and believings, ordinary agents implicitly assume that any position according to which there are no epistemic reasons, no beliefs that display epistemic merits and demerits, and no arguments should be rejected. Suppose we call an agent who assumes that radical epistemological skepticism is false a 'minimally rational agent'. (A minimally rational agent at least *takes* himself to have reasons for believing what he does.) If what I've argued in this chapter is correct, accepting epistemic nihilism is incompatible with being a minimally rational agent, for epistemic nihilism implies radical epistemological skepticism. On the further assumption that ordinary agents have strong reason to be at least minimally rational, it follows that such agents have strong reason to reject epistemic nihilism.

5

Epistemic Expressivism: Traditional Views

I suggested in the last chapter that we examine epistemic nihilism not because it is a popular position among philosophers, but because its failure would help us to see where the difficulties with other epistemic antirealist views lie. I am going to argue in this chapter and the next that the failures of epistemic nihilism are especially helpful for identifying the difficulties with so-called expressivist views in epistemology. Put in an overly simple fashion, my central thesis is that since expressivist views adopt an ontology that is either identical with or very similar to that of epistemic nihilism, they are vulnerable to objections of the type raised against epistemic nihilism in the last chapter. However, arguing for this thesis will take some doing, as expressivist views come in a variety of families and ordinarily exhibit a high degree of sophistication. My strategy for handling this complexity is to divide the subsequent discussion into two parts. In this chapter, I will explore what I shall call 'traditional' members of the expressivist family, while in the next I shall consider 'nontraditional' ones. (In a moment, I will explain what I mean by these labels.) I should emphasize at the outset of our discussion that, with the exception of Allan Gibbard's 'norm-expressivism', expressivism regarding the epistemic domain is not a view that has been explicitly developed by philosophers. With the exception of Gibbard's view, then, the views I shall consider are ones that are *modeled* on expressivist views concerning the moral domain and not elaborations of positions explicitly defended by moral expressivists themselves.

Before we take a closer look at these views themselves, let me begin with an admission: Expressivism is a difficult position with which to engage. As I've indicated, the position is both diverse and resourceful, taking rather different forms in response to different lines of criticism. This presents a challenge to anyone wishing to engage with the view. One wonders: Which of its various forms should one take as paradigmatic? While the subsequent discussion would gain in elegance if it were to focus on one representative version of the view, I have opted instead for an approach that traces the view through a series of permutations. In short, I trace a series of expressivist positions that move from those views that are least concerned to accommodate the realist appearances of ordinary epistemic thought and discourse to those that are most concerned to do so. In this chapter, I consider expressivist positions of the former sort. These views deny either that epistemic claims are truth-apt or that they aim to represent epistemic reality. Views such as Gibbard's norm-expressivism fall into this category. In the next chapter, I consider expressivist views of the latter type. These positions maintain that epistemic discourse is both truth-apt and functions to represent epistemic reality in some sufficiently deflationary sense of 'true' and 'represent'. Positions such as Simon Blackburn's quasi-realism belong to this category. There are, then, two main types of expressivist positions that I am concerned to explore. Positions that fall into the first category I will call 'traditional' versions of expressivism. Positions that fall into the second category I call 'nontraditional' versions of expressivism.[1]

A final point: It might be wondered why it is advantageous to trace the evolution of expressivist views in the way that I propose. Why not engage with only the most sophisticated versions of the view? I believe that there are several advantages to proceeding in the fashion I propose, principal among which is this: There is a persistent worry among philosophers that, given the considerable similarities between realism and sophisticated forms of expressivism, there really is no difference between these two types of view—or at least, that we don't know how to say what it is.[2] Consequently, some philosophers believe that traditional expressivist views may in fact be the best type of position to embrace for those suspicious of realism, as they represent a clear and viable alternative to realism. (At the very least, these philosophers believe that traditional expressivist

---

[1] Given the fact that there have been hardly any epistemic expressivists—let alone 'traditional' epistemic expressivists—I realize that these labels can be misleading. As I think of it, traditional expressivism is traditional only in the sense that it is modeled on views in the moral arena that are aptly labeled 'traditional'.

[2] See, for example, Dreier (2002) and (2004), Gibbard (2003), Ch. 9, and Zangwill (1992).

views represent the best fallback position were what I call 'nontraditional' forms of expressivism to collapse into realism.) Since both traditional and nontraditional expressivist views are very much 'live' positions, it is, in my judgment, best to give these more traditional views a hearing by beginning our discussion with them.

I. Common commitments

To frame our discussion, let me begin with the general project of identifying four commitments that form the core of that family of views I am calling 'expressivist'.

Suppose we restrict our use of the term 'epistemic fact' so that it stands for those entities that are represented by epistemic claims or make such claims true. (Recall that I am thinking of representation as a genuine relation between entities of various kinds. I'll have more to say about this in the next chapter.) First among expressivism's commitments is:

The Expressivist's Ontic Thesis: There are no epistemic facts.

As I will emphasize in what follows, expressivists themselves divide on what exactly this claim implies; some maintain that there are no epistemic facts whatsoever, while others claim that there are epistemic 'facts' in some more minimal sense of this term. At any rate, on the assumption that a realist conception of truth implies that true predicative epistemic claims require facts or states of affairs that make them true, The Expressivist's Ontic Thesis implies:

The Expressivist's Alethic Thesis: The contents of none of our epistemic claims are true in the realist sense.

Now the expressivist's ontic and alethic theses are not unique to expressivism; epistemic nihilists, for example, also accept them both. (Somewhat more exactly, they accept claims that imply the ontic and alethic theses, but are not implied by them.) However, what *is* distinctive of expressivism is the following thesis about the character of epistemic discourse:

The Expressivist's Speech Act Thesis: When an agent sincerely utters a predicative epistemic sentence, that agent does not thereby assert an epistemic proposition, but rather (at least) performs some other speech act such as expressing an attitude of endorsement, approval, condemnation, disapproval, or the like toward a non-epistemic state of affairs.[3]

Expressivists do not take the speech act thesis to imply that ordinary epistemic discourse *looks* as if it were not discourse wherein agents assert epistemic propositions. To the contrary, common to expressivism and its cognitivist rivals is the conviction that ordinary epistemic discourse looks as if it were assertoric epistemic discourse. Expressivists, for example, readily admit that much of ordinary epistemic discourse appears truth-apt (e.g. 'It is true that you ought to believe x') and embeds in both conditionals (e.g. 'If you ought to x, then you ought to y') and propositional attitude ascriptions (e.g. 'I believe that I ought to x'). Fundamental to expressivism, however, is this denial: Expressivists deny that the surface form of epistemic discourse gives us very good reason to believe that it is genuinely assertoric epistemic discourse. We cannot, say expressivists, read off the linguistic function of some area of discourse simply by gazing at its surface syntax.[4]

Thus described, expressivism is a very general position that includes among its members such diverse views as emotivism, prescriptivism, norm-expressivism, quasi-realism, and assertoric nondescriptivism with respect to the epistemic domain.[5] At this point in our discussion, however, I want to focus primarily not on what divides, but on what unites these expressivist positions. And what unites these positions, I suggest, is not simply the three theses that I have just identified, but a common rationale for accepting them. Simon Blackburn states this rationale when he writes that the very 'essence' of expressivism is 'to protect ... against the descent into error

---

[3] I understand a 'sincere' utterance of an epistemic sentence to be an utterance that is not intended for the purpose of dissembling. I understand an epistemic state of affairs to be either an epistemic fact or a possible epistemic fact (e.g. *that S is justified in believing p*). Furthermore, I assume that epistemic propositions are as I described them in Chapter 2—entities that purport to represent (or are) epistemic facts. Finally, in what follows, I mean by 'epistemic discourse' speech that consists only in the sincere utterance of what I called in Chapter 2 'predicative epistemic sentences'.

[4] See Blackburn (1993), 57, (1998), 50, and Gibbard (1990), 8.

[5] See Ayer (1936), Stevenson (1963), Hare (1981), Gibbard (1990), Blackburn (1984), (1993), (1998), and Timmons (1999). Gibbard calls the view he develops in Gibbard (2003) an expressivist position. Strictly speaking, however, his view is not a version of expressivism in the sense that I am using the term, for Gibbard takes his position not to be a description of how normative discourse functions, but merely a hypothesis about how it might work (see Gibbard [2003], x). I shall not assume, then, that the argument I develop in this chapter and the next applies to it. That said, Gibbard does claim that he believes his hypothesis to capture the way in which 'important parts of our actual [normative] language' work (p. 8). If Gibbard is right about this, then what I argue does bear upon his position—albeit indirectly.

theory'.[6] Central to epistemic expressivism, then, is the conviction that any view that implies that ordinary folk are massively in error about epistemic matters is unacceptable.[7] Accordingly, the expressivist urges that any acceptable view regarding the epistemic realm should satisfy the following injunction:

The Expressivist's Guiding Rationale: Avoid an error-theoretic account of ordinary epistemic discourse (while also avoiding a commitment to epistemic realism).

The Expressivist's Guiding Rationale is crucial in three respects for understanding epistemic expressivism.

In the first place, it explains why expressivists reject cognitivist views of epistemic discourse in favor of The Expressivist's Speech Act Thesis. For suppose we were to accept The Expressivist's Ontic Thesis or the claim that there are no epistemic facts. And suppose also we were to accept epistemic cognitivism or the view that epistemic discourse expresses epistemic propositions. Having accepted these two views, we would find it impossible to satisfy the guiding rationale, for then we would be committed to a view according to which epistemic discourse purports to represent epistemic reality, but fails to do so because there is no such reality to represent. If expressivists are right, the only plausible way by which we can at once accept The Expressivist's Ontic Thesis and satisfy the guiding rationale is by embracing the claim that epistemic discourse does not even purport to represent epistemic reality. Then (and perhaps only then) there is—to use Blackburn's words—'no real *mismatch* between the truth about the nature of [epistemic] ... claims, and their content'.[8]

---

[6] Blackburn (2002), 167. Blackburn (2006), 154, writes that his 'quasi-realist' expressivist position 'is well seen as the attempt to save expressivism from error theory. It attempts to show that ordinary moral thought is not infected root and branch with philosophical myth'. See also Gibbard (2003), 37.

[7] See, for example, Blackburn (1993), Ch. 8, and (1984), 171. Like Blackburn, Gibbard claims that his account does not leave 'normative language defective or second-rate' ([1990], 8). Timmons says something similar when he writes that, in his view, assertoric non-descriptivism is not at odds with our ordinary moral practice because 'I just do not think that ordinary moral discourse presupposes that ethics is objective *in the sense that realism and some versions of constructivism attempt to capture*' ([1999], 175). See also Hare (1981), 81–3.

[8] Blackburn (1993), 56. In a somewhat different context when speaking of moral truth, Blackburn writes that for the expressivist there 'is no problem of relativism because there is no problem of moral truth. Since moral opinion is not in the business of *representing* the world, but of assessing choices and actions and attitudes in the world ...' ([1999], 214).

The second respect in which the guiding rationale is crucial for understanding expressivism is that it helps us to see that we have good reason to understand The Expressivist's Speech Act Thesis not as a proposal for how we ought to use ordinary epistemic discourse, but as a descriptive claim about how we actually use it. For notice, if the speech act thesis were simply a proposal for how we ought to engage in epistemic discourse, it would be compatible with the view that ordinary epistemic discourse is massively in error and, thus, incompatible with satisfying The Expressivist's Guiding Rationale. In saying this, I don't mean to claim that expressivists have been entirely clear about the way in which the speech act thesis should be understood. They haven't.⁹ I do claim, however, that interpreting the speech act thesis as a descriptive claim fits best with a major rationale offered in favor of their view. In the interest of thoroughness, however, I will, at the end of the next chapter, raise the question of whether the speech act thesis might plausibly be taken to be a recommendation for how we should revise ordinary epistemic discourse.

The third respect in which the guiding rationale is important for understanding expressivism is closely related to the second. Expressivism, I've suggested, is best understood as offering a descriptive account of the character of ordinary epistemic discourse. As expressivists make clear, however, this description is not supposed to be revisionary; rather, its aim is to save the appearances of ordinary moral thought and discourse as best possible.¹⁰ When I say that the speech act thesis is best interpreted as a descriptive thesis, then, this should be understood to mean the

---

⁹ Timmons apparently takes the moral analogue to the speech act thesis to be a descriptive claim: 'Moral statements, in their primary use, do not purport to make such ontological claims; rather, their primary function is to evaluate, not to describe' ([1999], 154). Joyce (2001), 201, n. 38, interprets Blackburn's quasi-realism as a project that seeks to protect ordinary moral discourse, as does Dreier (1999). R. M. Hare, moreover, writes that 'ordinary people when they use these [moral] words are not intending to ascribe objective prescriptive properties to actions' ([1981], 86). Allan Gibbard's view in *Wise Choices, Apt Feelings* is more elusive. In this book, Gibbard claims, on the one hand, that 'norm-expressivism is meant to capture whatever there is to ordinary notions of rationality if Platonism is excluded' ([1990], 154). On the other hand, Gibbard makes it clear that his account of rationality is not so much intended to capture what people ordinarily mean by the term 'rational', but is a proposal about how we can plausibly reconstruct normative language (see ibid. 30–4). In light of The Expressivist's Guiding Rationale, I shall take the former strain of Gibbard's thought as more nearly approximating his considered view (in Gibbard [1990] at least). For a different interpretation of Gibbard, see Sturgeon (1995).

¹⁰ For example, Horgan and Timmons (2006) defend the '*Moral phenomenology criterion*: A metaethical theory ought, if possible, to account for and vindicate as many of the deeply embedded aspects of moral thought and moral discourse—the phenomena of morality—as possible' (p. 223).

following: The speech act thesis is intended to furnish an account of ordinary epistemic discourse that not only avoids the implication that such discourse is systematically mistaken, but also captures the meaning of such discourse.

II. The central thesis

We've seen that on matters of ontology expressivism is a close cousin to epistemic nihilism, as both these positions imply that there are no epistemic facts and, thus, that none of our (predicative) epistemic judgments are true in the realist sense. I spent the last chapter arguing that accepting this combination of claims has undesirable consequences. Let go of epistemic reasons, I claimed, and either we are saddled with an incoherent or a radically skeptical position according to which we cannot rationally believe anything—including epistemic nihilism itself. (Epistemic reasons, recall, I assume are either a species of epistemic fact or the components thereof.) Now expressivism is typically not nearly so lacking in nuance as is epistemic nihilism. It won't do, then, simply to rehearse this type of objection against it. And while expressivists such as Gibbard, Blackburn, and Jonathan Bennett do not consider the type of objection developed in the last chapter, I take it that teasing out their line of response to it is not very difficult: Concede that epistemic realists are correct to say that, if expressivism were true, then there would be no proposition that there is a reason to believe in the sense that realists think of reasons. Deny, however, that this has any untoward results on the grounds that expressivism captures everything we could plausibly mean when we say that a belief is rational, or that we have a reason to accept a proposition, or that a normative judgment is correct.

This is a familiar type of strategy of response in philosophy; it is commonly employed in debates about the existence of universals, for example. And while it may be promising when applied to some domains, I shall argue in this chapter and the next that it is not in the case we are considering. My response to this strategy can be stated succinctly: Epistemic expressivism implies that there are no epistemic reasons in the sense I have specified. (As I shall argue in the next chapter, strictly speaking, it implies that there are no epistemic reasons in any sense.) To avoid implying a version of radical skepticism that is no less objectionable than that implied by epistemic nihilism, I suggest the view must satisfy the following challenge—what I will call 'The Expressivist's Challenge': Offer a construal of epistemic discourse consistent with expressivism that captures (or that we have sufficient reason to believe captures) everything that we could plausibly mean by the standard and sincere use of epistemic locutions, but does not imply that ordinary epistemic discourse is systematically in error. (I realize that the phrase 'everything that we could plausibly mean' is vague. I think this cannot be helped. But, as will become evident, I shall assume that 'everything that we could plausibly mean' should at least include being consistent with platitudes regarding the competent use of epistemic concepts.[11]) Since, however, expressivism fails to offer such a construal, the view implies a version of epistemological skepticism that is no less objectionable than that implied by epistemic nihilism. It is this last claim that is the central thesis I wish to defend.

In this chapter, the argument I will develop for this central thesis runs as follows. I will present a version of traditional expressivism, contending that this view falls afoul of two very plausible claims about epistemic concept-application. In particular, I am going to argue that traditional expressivism has a difficult time handling the phenomenon of second-order epistemic judgments. If this is right, traditional expressivism will have to go. If expressivism is to satisfy its twin goals of both avoiding an error-theoretic account of epistemic discourse and adequately capturing what we mean when we engage in such discourse, it must take a nontraditional form.

III. Traditional expressivism

As I understand them, traditional expressivist views stand apart from other expressivist positions for the following reason: Views of this kind follow

---

[11] It is also vague in this further sense: Some philosophers believe that there is a sharp distinction between the meaning of a locution and the ways in which we use it. I will not observe this distinction. Rather, when I use phrases of the form 'x captures everything that we could plausibly mean by y', I assume that the occurrence of the term 'mean' in locutions such as this can refer to either how we use language or to the sense of the linguistic items that we use in language. (Granted, if meaning is in some sense a function of use, then the looseness with which I talk about meaning won't matter much.) That expressivism is best characterized not as a position regarding the sense of normative terms, but as a thesis concerning how we use normative discourse is defended in Joyce (2001), Ch. 1.2.

their emotivist forebearers by understanding The Expressivist's Ontic Thesis and The Expressivist's Alethic Thesis in a robust fashion. According to traditional expressivist views, there are no epistemic facts of *any* sort, and the content of our epistemic discourse neither purports to represent epistemic reality nor is truth-apt in any sense.[12] The objection I want to raise against views of this kind, I believe, emerges most clearly if we probe what is arguably the most sophisticated version of traditional expressivism, viz., the norm-expressivist view developed by Gibbard in his *Wise Choices, Apt Feelings*.[13] Let me, then, develop Gibbard's position in enough detail so as to introduce the problem I wish to identify.

Norm-expressivism

What makes Gibbard's norm-expressivist position a version of traditional expressivism, I have suggested, is that it accepts a robust interpretation of the expressivist's ontic and alethic theses while also championing the claim that epistemic discourse is not assertoric but expressive in character. Earlier I claimed that a central rationale for embracing this account of epistemic discourse is that it allows expressivists to avoid an error-theoretic account of epistemic discourse. Gibbard, however, also offers an independent rationale in favor of the speech act thesis that goes as follows: Suppose, says Gibbard, we begin by taking rationality as our fundamental normative concept. Then suppose we ask: What is it to call something 'rational'? According to Gibbard, any answer to this question must take into account the fact that to 'call something rational is to endorse it in some way'.[14] Thus, when we call an action rational, we mean to say that it 'makes sense' or is 'the best thing to do'.[15] The fundamental problem with assertoric accounts of normative language, suggests Gibbard, is that they fail to capture this endorsing role. Gibbard puts the point as follows:

---

[12] Thus Gibbard writes: 'The [norm-expressivist] analysis is non-cognitivistic in the narrow sense that, according to it, to call a thing rational is not to state a matter of fact, either truly or falsely' and that according to his view 'apparent normative facts will come out, strictly, as no real facts at all' (Gibbard [1990], 8 and 23; see also 34, 92, 107, and Ch. 5 as well as Gibbard [2003], x, 62). Jonathan Bennett, who defends a view close to Gibbard's, writes that: 'What we most centrally care about in statements that have truth values is their truth. When someone affirms a moral judgment, on the other hand, our focus of concern is not on *whether he has the attitude* that he represents himself as having, but rather *the attitude* (whether or not he has it). ... So it is a deep feature of expressivism, not a superficial add-on, that it implies that moral judgments do not have truth values' (Bennett [1993], 459).

[13] Gibbard's own views, I should note, have shifted; see Gibbard (2003) for his latest views.

[14] Gibbard (1990), 6.   [15] Ibid. 6–7.

What, though, of the special element that makes normative thought and language normative? There is such an element, I am claiming, and it involves a kind of endorsement—an endorsement that any descriptivistic analysis treats inadequately. The problem is not merely that every time one loophole in the analysis is closed, others remain. It is that a single loophole remains unpluggable by descriptivistic analysis.[16]

But what is it to endorse something as that which 'makes sense' to do? Gibbard says it is to accept a system of norms that permit that we do that thing.[17] To accept a system of norms of this kind is for an agent to make a rational 'judgment'. What, though, does Gibbard mean by a 'norm'? And what does he mean when he says that to make a normative judgment is to 'accept' a system of norms?

Gibbard spends relatively little time explaining what a norm is according to his view. What he says is that a norm is an imperative or a 'linguistically encoded precept' that a sophisticated observer could formulate.[18] More exactly, Gibbard says that a norm is an imperative or rule whose primary function is to help coordinate our actions in mutually beneficial, fitness-enhancing ways. This relative lack of concern about the nature of a norm is explained by Gibbard's contention that the 'main thing to be explained is not what a norm is, but what "accepting a norm" is ...'.[19] And Gibbard says a great deal about what it is to accept a norm. Indeed, Gibbard says so much, and his discussion is so rich and subtle, that I cannot hope to do full justice to it here. So, the following will have to suffice. For a person to accept a norm, in Gibbard's view, is for that person to *avow* that norm and be *governed* by it.[20] When a person accepts a norm, that acceptance plays a psychological role of a certain kind: That person is reliably motivated in certain ways in certain situations, tends to take particular stances in

---

[16] Gibbard (1990), 33. In Ch. 1, I noted that some realists, such as Copp (2001), have taken Gibbard's challenge to heart. They defend a view according to which normative discourse is both assertoric and expressive.

[17] For ease of explication, I will often speak of an agent's endorsing a norm rather than his endorsing a system of norms. On a different note, Gibbard recognizes that there is a fair amount of slack in his account of the concept of rationality. As I understand it, his official account says that to 'call something rational is to express one's acceptance of norms that permit it' (p. 7). Elsewhere, however, he says that the 'rational alternative is the one supported by a preponderance of reasons' (p. 160). These are arguably not identical accounts of the rational. It is plausible to believe that, say, a course of action could be permissible without being what is supported by a preponderance of reasons.

[18] See Gibbard (1990), 46, 57, and 70.   [19] Ibid., 46.

[20] Ibid., 75. Gibbard uses the term 'avowal' to stand for 'a wide range of expressions we might count as taking a position in normative discussion' (p. 73).

discussions of certain kinds, feels emotions of various sorts in certain kinds of circumstance, and so forth.

As it stands, Gibbard acknowledges that his account of norm acceptance does not account for the 'objective pretensions' of normative discourse. What is missing, according to Gibbard, is a richer account of the rational authority that a person claims for the norms she accepts.[21] We have already seen one sense in which accepting a norm is authoritative. Accepting a norm is authoritative for a person insofar as that acceptance plays a particular role in that person's psychological economy; to accept a norm is to be *psychologically governed* by that norm. Gibbard adds to this three additional points. First, accepting a norm is *attitude-independent* in the following sense: 'Anyone who takes a norm to constitute a requirement of rationality takes a norm to apply independently of his own accepting it.'[22] Second, norm acceptance is a *multi-leveled* phenomenon. 'To accept a norm as a requirement of rationality ... is to accept it along with higher order norms that require its acceptance.'[23] And, finally, accepting a norm is to make *conversational demands* of others. When a person accepts a norm, he 'is demanding that the audience accept what he says, that I share the state of mind he expresses'.[24] Put these additional features in place, suggests Gibbard, and we have a much richer account of the ways in which accepting a norm captures the objective aspirations of normative discourse and thought and can mimic 'the search for truth'.[25]

Of the various features of Gibbard's position, let's focus our attention for the moment on Gibbard's contention that we should take rationality as our primitive normative concept. We've seen that, in Gibbard's view, 'to call something rational is to endorse it' and to say that it 'makes sense' or is 'the best thing to do'. Gibbard suggests, however, that there is more to the concept of rationality than this and proposes that we think of it in two ways. For an agent to think that a judgment is 'subjectively rational' is for her to think its formation or maintenance makes sense in light of her limited information—in light of 'what she knows, what she has reason to believe, and the degrees of plausibility she should ascribe to various eventualities given her information'.[26] By contrast, for an agent to think

---

[21] See Gibbard (1990), 171.   [22] Ibid., 155.   [23] Ibid., 169.
[24] Ibid., 172.   [25] Ibid., 218.
[26] Ibid., 89. Gibbard indicates that for an agent S to judge that someone else's judgment is rational is for S to accept norms that permit the formation or maintenance of that person's judgment. See, ibid., 46.

that a judgment is 'objectively rational' is for her to think that it is *advisable*; it is what makes sense to believe in light of all the facts, whether or not she has any way of knowing them.[27] And let's note, finally, that Gibbard himself indicates that, thus understood, rationality is not a prudential, but an *epistemic* concept.[28]

Understood thus, norm-expressivism is supposed to furnish an adequate analysis of those states that we express when we engage in ordinary epistemic thought and discourse. I want now to argue that this analysis either yields the conclusion that ordinary epistemic thought and discourse is fraught with error or does not capture everything we could plausibly mean when we engage in ordinary epistemic discourse. In short, I want to suggest this view does not satisfy The Expressivist's Challenge.

The problem of second-order epistemic judgments

In Chapter 2, I introduced what I called the 'content platitudes with respect to epistemic facts'. The content platitudes, recall, tell us (roughly) that a mental state exhibits an epistemic merit such as *being rational, warranted, a case of knowledge*, or the like, only if it is representative. (An entity x is representative, I claimed, only insofar as it is representational—that is, purports to represent some entity—and represents that which it purports to represent, or is likely to do so, or is the product of an agent's having done a sufficiently adequate job of trying to ensure that it represents reality aright.) Thus understood (and modulo a refinement I shall make in a moment), the platitudes imply a thesis about concept-application, viz., that epistemic merit concepts can be properly applied to a mental state only if it is representative. I also indicated that among the class of epistemic merits are so-called alethic merits—roughly, merits whose presence in a propositional attitude indicates that the content of that attitude is truth-relevant. And an attitude is truth relevant, let's say, only if its content is true, likely to be true, or is such that it is accepted by an agent because that agent has done an adequate job of trying to ensure that that attitude's content is true.

---

[27] Gibbard (1990), 90.

[28] See ibid., 181. In their article 'Expressivism, Morality, and the Emotions', Justin D'Arms and Daniel Jacobson write of Gibbard's view that the 'state of accepting a norm is difficult to characterize, and Gibbard seeks to point to its place in human life more than to describe it. Perhaps the most illuminating thing to be said is that to accept a norm is to judge something *warranted*. The notion of warrant in place here is the familiar, epistemic one. ... To accept a norm, say for a belief, is to bestow on it a kind of endorsement, one of rational justification' (D'Arms and Jacobson [1994], 740–1).

Thus understood (and modulo a refinement I shall make in a moment), the content platitudes with respect to alethic merits also imply a thesis about concept-application, viz., that alethic merit concepts properly apply to a mental state only if it is truth-relevant.

Now for the refinement alluded to above: Consider a case in which an agent formulates a question regarding a proposal and does so because she has thought hard and well about whether certain claims the proposal makes are true. Reflection on ordinary practice suggests that we frequently call questions such as these 'astute', 'penetrating', or 'reasonable'. And presumably the reason we do so is because we believe that a question thus formulated is evidence that an agent has astutely perceived one or another feature of her environment that is relevant to the truth of the claim under consideration. (Perhaps she has seen that the proposal in question traffics in a subtle confusion.) Ordinary practice suggests, then, that we predicate epistemic merits of states that are not themselves representative or truth-apt, but do so because the state in question is evidence that there is some other entity that displays an epistemic merit. Merits that apply to non-representative, non-truth-apt entities, we might say, apply *derivatively* to such entities. Put more formally, we can say that a mental state

x displays an epistemic merit F *non-derivatively* if and only if x is F, but not simply because x's being F is evidence that there is some other entity y that displays an epistemic merit (or x's being F is otherwise conducive to y's displaying an epistemic merit).

And, conversely, we can say that:

x displays an epistemic merit F *derivatively* if and only if x is F, but not non-derivatively.

On the assumption that evidential relations must terminate somewhere, the fact that an entity exhibits an epistemic merit derivatively is itself evidence that there is some other entity that possesses an epistemic merit non-derivatively.

Given this distinction between non-derivative and derivative epistemic merits, we can formulate two platitudes about the competent deployment of epistemic merits concepts—concepts such as 'being a case of knowledge', 'being justified', 'being rationally entitled', and so forth. These platitudes about concept application, I will assume, are such that any position interested in capturing the deeply embedded features of ordinary epistemic thought and discourse should honor them.

Suppose we say that representational content is content that purports to represent the world as being a certain way. The first such platitude to which I draw attention is:

The Prime Epistemic Platitude: Epistemic merit concepts properly apply to a mental state non-derivatively only if it expresses representational content.

The second platitude is:

The Prime Alethic Platitude: Alethic merit concepts properly apply to a mental state non-derivatively only if it is truth-apt.

For both of these claims to be genuinely platitudinous, they need to be understood in such a way that they are neutral between different views regarding the nature of representation and truth-aptitude, including so-called robust and deflationary views about representation and truth-aptitude. In what follows, I will assume that these claims are so understood. (In this case, then, I relax the stipulation that my use of the term 'representation' stands for robust representation.) The thesis that I wish now to defend is that, so understood, these platitudes are incompatible with a traditional expressivist account of second-order epistemic judgments or claims of certain kinds.

Let me develop this point as follows: Suppose we take a judgment concerning a general epistemic norm—for example, a judgment that one ought to form one's beliefs on the basis of adequate evidence. Suppose we call any judgment of this type a 'first-order E-judgment' ('E' for epistemic). Now take a second-order epistemic judgment of the following form:

S* judges of S's first-order E-judgment,

> that it is a case of knowledge,
> that it is warranted,
> that it is justified,
> that it is rational,
> that it is entitled,
> that it (epistemically) ought to be accepted,
> etc.

Call any such judgment a 'second-order E-judgment'. According to the norm-expressivist analysis we're considering, first-order E-judgments are mental states that simply consist in the acceptance of norms of certain kinds (in the sense of 'acceptance' explained earlier). To judge that one ought to form one's beliefs on the basis of adequate evidence is, according to the norm-expressivist, to avow in a certain way an imperative of a certain kind, make conversational demands of others, and so forth.[29] But what about second-order E-judgments to the effect that a first-order E-judgment is itself rational, entitled, or justified? How ought we to understand judgments such as these? The analysis of such claims that I take to be consistent with the norm-expressivist's official account of the character of epistemic thought and discourse is that such judgments consist in higher-order endorsements

---

[29] This is a point at which exegesis of Gibbard becomes problematic. Gibbard's official view of epistemic discourse is that to 'call something rational is not to attribute some particular property to that thing—not even the property of being permitted by accepted norms' and that 'to call a thing rational is not to state a matter of fact, either truly of falsely' (Gibbard [1990], 7–8). What we find in Gibbard's development of his position, however, is that judging that a particular claim p is, say, justified has at least these two components: It is, first, to endorse a general norm—for example, an imperative that instructs us to believe only those propositions based on good evidence. And, second, it is to believe that p is 'endorsed' by the norm in question or that the norm applies to it (see ibid., 181, 91.) But (apart from being a nihilist about properties and their instances altogether) it is hard to see how one could coherently believe that a norm applies to a claim and also deny that this claim has the property of *falling under the accepted norms* or *being permitted by the accepted norms*. Consequently, it is hard to see how one could at once believe that an epistemic norm applies to a claim and also fail either to state or presuppose this when one expresses an epistemic judgment.

Two things follow: First, Gibbard's official account of epistemic judgment does not fit well with his developed account of such judgment. For, if the developed account were true, when an agent expresses the judgment that p is justified, she would thereby either presuppose or believe that p is permitted by the accepted norms, which is what the official account denies. More importantly, it is difficult to see that Gibbard's developed account of the nature of epistemic judgments is really a version of traditional expressivism at all. Traditional expressivism, I assume, is committed not only to the thesis that epistemic judgments do not *express* propositions to the effect that p is permitted by the accepted norms, but also to the thesis that such propositions are not *presupposed* or *taken for granted* when rendering such judgments. But since Gibbard's developed view implies that at least one of these claims is false, it is not a version of traditional expressivism.

For a similar conclusion that Gibbard's view is not genuinely expressivist, albeit reached via different routes, see Dreier (1999) and Wedgwood (1997). Gibbard's reply in *Thinking How to Live* (Gibbard [2003]) to the worry that his view collapses into cognitivism is that, even if this line of objection were correct, it is not fatal. For what is distinctive of expressivism is its methodology: At the outset of constructing a normative theory, the expressivist begins by not assuming that there are normative facts or judgments that purport to represent them. At the end of developing such a theory, however, the expressivist may end up maintaining that there are epistemic facts and epistemic judgments that purport to represent them. For reasons that will be apparent in the next chapter, my response is that this methodology cannot be employed in the domain of epistemology. Be that as it may, if what I've called Gibbard's 'developed' view is correct, the type of reply offered in Gibbard (2003) will not be one to which a norm-expressivist can appeal. For it will not be true that norm-expressivism is genuinely expressivist at the outset of inquiry.

of a certain kind. For example, to judge of S's first-order E-judgment that it is rational is to endorse higher-order norms that permit the holding or formation of the first-order E-judgment in question. If we glide over the nuances of Gibbard's formal semantics of normative judgment and offer a traditional expressivist account of second-order E-judgments, then we should say something like the following: If norm-expressivism is true, the content (or object) of this second-order judgment is not a proposition, but is itself the (state of) acceptance or endorsement of a system of norms, which dictate that one ought to base one's beliefs on adequate evidence.[30]

Now we can identify a problem. Both of the prime platitudes tell us that central epistemic concepts such as knowledge, justification, warrant, rationality, and the like apply non-derivatively to only those sorts of mental state whose content is either representative or truth-apt. However, if the content of a first-order E-judgment is an endorsement of a kind (or is even a cluster of imperatives), then the content of first-order E-judgments is neither representative nor truth-apt. So, if traditional expressivism is true, epistemic merit concepts do not properly apply non-derivatively to first-order E-judgments. But, as a matter of fact, in the course of ordinary epistemic thought and discourse, we make second-order E-judgments. And, many of them appear to involve the application of epistemic merit concepts non-derivatively to first-order E-judgments.

Suppose we confine our attention, for simplicity's sake, to that class of judgments whose only members are second-order E-judgments that appear to apply alethic merit concepts non-derivatively to first-order E-judgments. Now either second-order E-judgments are such that they involve the application of alethic merit concepts non-derivatively to first-order E-judgments or they do not. Suppose they do. And suppose, also, that we accept the plausible premise that, if a judgment implies the improper application of a concept, then that judgment exhibits conceptual

---

[30] Two points: First, as the context indicates, I use the term 'content' in a fairly liberal fashion. Content includes anything that a speaker seeks to communicate or that a hearer must grasp to understand what the speaker is saying (*see* Alston [2000], 15). According to norm-expressivism, what a person who endorses a norm seeks to communicate when engaging in epistemic discourse is the endorsement of that norm (see Gibbard [1990], 84–6 and (2003), 47). Accordingly, I will assume that endorsements can function as the content of E-judgments. Second, by supposing this, I assume that second-order epistemic judgments are amenable to a de re-style analysis in which we apply epistemic concepts to mental states themselves. (I do not deny that we can also offer a de dicto-style account of these judgments, however.)

confusion of a certain kind; in the case at hand, the confusion is a type of category mistake—a mistake similar to that of predicating truth of a question or a request.[31] It follows that, insofar as second-order E-judgments are such that they imply the application of alethic merit concepts non-derivatively to first-order E-judgments, these second-order E-judgments exhibit conceptual confusion. And, on the assumption that we do apply these concepts, traditional expressivism implies that ordinary epistemic thought and discourse exhibit systematic conceptual confusion of the sort just specified.

Now, admittedly, the mistake in question does not imply that epistemic discourse is systematically *false*. So, my claim is not that traditional expressivism of this type collapses into error theory traditionally conceived. The point is, rather, that there are lots of ways in which a domain of discourse can be in error—being systematically false and involving the systematic misapplication of concepts being two such ways. However, if a theory aims to protect ordinary epistemic discourse from error, then attributing either of these two sorts of mistake to such discourse should be avoided, as neither type of mistake is more palatable than the other. To which it is worth adding the following observation: What distinguishes traditional expressivism from its nontraditional cousins is (in part) that the former view (but not the latter) understands The Expressivist's Speech Act Thesis in such a way that it implies that epistemic discourse is not truth-apt. Nonetheless, traditional expressivism understands this same thesis in such a way that epistemic discourse *looks* and *behaves* as if it were truth-apt. But given this combination of claims, were traditional expressivism true, falling into conceptual confusion of the sort just illustrated would appear inevitable. Given the broadly realist appearances of epistemic discourse, it is difficult to see how a mistake could fail to be made.[32]

---

[31] Granted, the intentional misapplication of concepts is also the stuff of good humor! However, I assume that for present purposes we can bracket such considerations.

[32] There is a response to this line of argument worth noting. Suppose the first-order E-judgment to which we apply an epistemic merit concept is a so-called thick epistemic judgment comprised of a descriptive and evaluative component. Might it be said that we can properly apply epistemic merit concepts to these judgments because such concepts apply only to the descriptive component of such judgments?

I don't think so. First, this reply assumes that we can satisfactorily isolate the merely descriptive and normative components of a thick epistemic judgment. This, however, is controversial, for in many cases it seems that these components are so conceptually enmeshed that putatively mere descriptive features have an evaluative component. (See Little [2000] for more on this.) Second, not all first-order

In light of this consequence, let's consider the second option, viz., that second-order E-judgments are such that they do not imply the application of alethic merit concepts non-derivatively to first-order E-judgments. That is, let's consider the claim that, appearances to the contrary, when a person judges of a first-order E-judgment p that she, say, justifiably believes it, she does not thereby purport to judge that p is likely to be true, but rather simply endorses p in a certain way.[33] This option has at least this much to recommend it: It does not imply that participants in ordinary epistemic discourse systematically fall into the confusion of systematically misapplying alethic merit concepts. But on the plausible assumption that epistemic judgments of the type under consideration necessarily involve the application of alethic merit concepts, the view under consideration has the consequence of implying that so-called second-order E-judgments are not epistemic judgments at all. And this is not a welcome result. For if the view we are considering has this consequence, it is difficult to see how it could come close to capturing what we mean to say when we express judgments that have the form of second-order E-judgments. But capturing what we mean by the use of such discourse is exactly what we wanted norm-expressivism to accomplish![34]

Let me move the dialectic forward one more step. It might be suggested that, even if the foregoing argument were correct, there is a third option for expressivists. This option is to supply surrogates of alethic merit concepts that capture enough of our commonsensical understanding of

E-judgments are thick, so even if this strategy were to work, it is not clear that it resolves the general problem under consideration. Third, if the discussion of Chapter 2 is correct, thick judgments such as *that pursuing a line of inquiry is conscientious* or *that a belief is the product of being intellectually scrupulous* are naturally thought of as expressing the thought that an agent has responded to reasons appropriately. Translated into the norm-expressivist's vernacular, this is naturally glossed as expressing the thought that an agent's behavior satisfies certain norms that one endorses. But if this is the thought that is expressed, then norm-expressivism collapses into a form of cognitivism. See n. 29.

[33] I realize that some expressivists think of truth-ascriptions as mere endorsements. In the next chapter, I will address views such as this. Let me note that, strictly speaking, there is another option that is open to norm-expressivists, which is to claim that all second-order E-judgments involve the derivative application of alethic merit concepts. Since I cannot think of a story in which this option could plausibly be developed, I am going to pass over it.

[34] There is a further problem, which I develop in Cuneo (2006a). It is plausible to hold that ordinary agents believe or take it for granted that when they express claims that have the form of second-order E-judgments they thereby apply alethic merit concepts. (Of course they needn't think of these concepts in such a way that employs this terminology.) If so, then these beliefs or presuppositions are systematically mistaken. And, thus, this position implies an error theory of a kind—one according to which the beliefs or presuppositions of ordinary folk about ordinary epistemic discourse are systematically mistaken.

the epistemic domain, but do not make essential use of the notions of truth or representation. Gibbard himself, for example, appears to furnish an expressivist surrogate for epistemic merit concepts in *Wise Choices, Apt Feelings* when he develops the concept of 'rational objectivity'.[35] According to Gibbard, a judgment is rationally objective for a fully coherent person only insofar as that person accepts a set of norms and takes herself to have a 'coherent epistemic story' about why she is in a better position to judge this issue than others. When we press Gibbard's view, however, it turns out that the sense of 'better' in question means more *reliable*: It is because a person has a better memory, or more extensive experience, or superior training in the relevant subject matter that she is better suited to judge of the subject matter at hand. Now perhaps there is a conception of epistemic reliability that does not trade on the notion of accurate representation or truth. But the conception of reliability to which Gibbard's account appeals, I take it, is not such an account. It is not a surrogate for our ordinary concept of epistemic reliability; rather, as best I can tell, it looks to be straightforwardly alethic in character. To say that one has a better memory than one's sibling, for example, is to say that one's memory is (on the whole) more powerful and accurate than one's sibling.

In summary: I have argued that traditional expressivist views have difficulty accounting for how alethic merit concepts could properly apply to second-order E-judgments. (I assume that we could construct a parallel argument that employs the notion of epistemic merits more generally.) My claim has been that if second-order E-judgments involve the application of these concepts, then ordinary epistemic discourse is systematically mistaken. Alternatively, if such judgments do not involve the application of these concepts, then they are not themselves epistemic judgments. Neither option is attractive, since neither option allows traditional expressivism satisfactorily to address what I earlier called 'The Expressivist's Challenge'. I want now to suggest that the problem I have raised generalizes. Provided that the norm-expressivist's account of rationality is true, the problem I have raised also affects the norm-expressivist account of first-order E-judgments.

Consider again the norm-expressivist analysis of what it is for a person to judge that something is rational in the subjective sense of this term: For an agent to judge that something is rational is for her to endorse something

---

[35] See Gibbard (1990), 181, 192–3.

'in the light of what she knows, what she has reason to believe, and the degrees of plausibility she should ascribe to various eventualities given her information'. So, for any content p, for an agent to judge that it is rational to accept p involves doing so in the light of what she knows, what she has reason to believe, the degrees of plausibility she should ascribe to various eventualities given her information, and so forth. Following Gibbard, let's call this constellation of so-called reasons, knowledge, degrees of plausibility, and the like, an agent's 'subjective circumstances'.[36] Now presumably among an agent's subjective circumstances are second-order E-judgments of various kinds—judgments to the effect that it is rational to judge that one ought to form one's beliefs on the basis of adequate evidence, that one is rationally entitled to bring one's knowledge to bear on the formation of judgments, and so on. If we assume this, however, it is plausible to believe that the norm-expressivist analysis of first-order E-judgments depends on its analysis of second-order E-judgments: To explain the character of first-order E-judgments, one would also need to appeal to second-order E-judgments of various sorts. If this is right, however, then there is a further worry concerning norm-expressivism. For, if what I've argued is sound, there are considerable problems with the norm-expressivist analysis of second-order E-judgments. But if we explain the character of first-order E-judgments in terms of second-order E-judgments, then whatever problems that afflict the norm-expressivist analysis of second-order E-judgments transfer to the norm-expressivist analysis of first-order E-judgments in which an agent judges that something is rational. The problem with the norm-expressivist account of epistemic judgment, then, is not local to second-order E-judgments; it seeps into the texture of epistemic judgment itself.

IV. Summary

The central thesis I wish to defend in this chapter is that expressivist views are subject to problems similar to those that affect epistemic nihilism, viz., that such views imply the type of epistemological skepticism enshrined in the three undesirable results. I've argued for this thesis by claiming that there

---

[36] Gibbard (1990), 89.

is a challenge that any adequate expressivist position needs to meet: Furnish an expressivist construal of epistemic discourse that sufficiently captures everything that we could plausibly mean when we engage in the standard and sincere use of such discourse, but does not imply that ordinary epistemic discourse is systematically in error. My argument in the last section was that traditional expressivist views fail to meet this challenge. For, given a plausible claim about the application of epistemic concepts, this view implies that either ordinary epistemic discourse is systematically mistaken or that traditional expressivism fails to capture adequately what we are doing when we engage in ordinary epistemic discourse. The consequence is that traditional expressivism implies that there are no reasons in the realist sense or in any other sense acceptable to traditional expressivists themselves.

This, I believe, gives us good reason to believe that traditional expressivism is no more attractive than epistemic nihilism. Indeed, it seems to me that there is good reason to believe that, on the whole, traditional expressivism is *less* attractive than epistemic nihilism. After all, if what I have argued is correct, both epistemic nihilism and traditional expressivism are on par in this respect: Both positions imply the three undesirable results inasmuch as they imply that there are no epistemic facts. However, epistemic nihilism, but not traditional expressivism, appears to more nearly capture what we could plausibly mean when we engage in ordinary epistemic thought and discourse, as it maintains that epistemic discourse is (at least) straightforwardly assertoric. As such, it has the virtue of accounting for significant characteristics of ordinary epistemic thought and discourse that expressivism does not.

Let me now acknowledge that while I believe that traditional expressivism is no more plausible than epistemic nihilism, I doubt that the argument of this chapter provides adequate reason to reject expressivist views as such. As I indicated at the outset of our discussion, expressivism proves to be a highly resourceful position capable of very closely mimicking realist views of epistemic thought and discourse. My aim in the next chapter is to contend that even expressivist views of this more sophisticated variety fail to offer a satisfactory account of ordinary epistemic thought and discourse. That is, I want to contend that views such as this also do not satisfactorily discharge what I've called 'The Expressivist's Challenge.'

6

Epistemic Expressivism:
Nontraditional Views

My overarching aim in the last two chapters has been to argue for the claim that epistemic facts exist by way of teasing out the implausible implications of its negation. At the heart of the argument I've offered is the thesis that insofar as views such as epistemic nihilism and traditional epistemic expressivism reject the existence of epistemic facts, they imply a radical form of epistemological skepticism that we do well not to embrace. I indicated at the end of the last chapter, however, that it would be overly hasty to reject epistemic expressivism simply on the basis of the considerations we advanced against traditional versions of the position. This is because epistemic expressivism proves to be a resourceful view capable of incorporating realist-seeming elements that allow it to respond to objections—in some cases, convincingly so—that are commonly leveled against it. Accordingly, I want in this chapter to take the argument developed in the last chapter a step further. In particular, I wish to explore the issue of whether what I call 'nontraditional' versions of expressivism have the resources to meet the challenge articulated in the last chapter: Offer an expressivist account of epistemic discourse that at once captures what we ordinarily mean when we engage in such discourse without implying that such discourse is in systematic error.

My argument in this chapter is that nontraditional expressivist views do not possess these resources. But before we dive into the argument, it may prove helpful to get our bearings by returning to the distinction between traditional and nontraditional versions of expressivism that I introduced in the last chapter.

According to the characterization offered earlier, traditional expressivist views make relatively few concessions to realism, as they deny either that epistemic thought and discourse is truth-apt or that it is representative in character. Nontraditional views, by contrast, concede significant stretches of conceptual territory to realism, maintaining (among other things) that epistemic thought and discourse are both truth-apt and representative. How do they manage to say such things? In large measure, by embracing what I call 'the deflationary package'. The deflationary package is a set of claims about the character of epistemic discourse, truth, representation, and facthood, which offers a deflationary account of these notions. Non-traditional expressivists accept this package, while traditional expressivists do not.

As I understand it, the deflationary package can itself take a variety of forms. This is mostly because deflationism with respect to some domain of entities is a *degreed* phenomenon; such positions are always more or less deflationary regarding the nature of assertion, truth, representation, facthood, and the like. In what follows, we'll need a way to talk about the different forms the deflationary package can take. I propose to do this by dividing nontraditional expressivist views into two types. The first type I will call 'minimalist' versions of expressivism. As the title suggests, expressivists of this type stay rather close to their traditional roots, preferring a fairly minimalist interpretation of the deflationary package. The second type I will call 'maximalist' versions of expressivism. In contrast to minimalist views, positions of this type come rather close to affirming a type of realism. Quasi-realist views—defended by Simon Blackburn among others—I am going to suggest, can be read as embracing either sort of position. My discussion in this chapter is dedicated to exploring both these types of nontraditional expressivism.

The discussion unfolds as follows. I begin by identifying the commitments common to all versions of nontraditional expressivism. Having done this, I turn first to minimalist expressivism, setting forth their particular way of understanding the four components of the deflationary package. Against minimalism, I press two objections—what I call the 'modal' and 'perspective' objections, respectively. Both of these objections charge that, despite its considerable sophistication, minimalism fails to meet The Expressivist's Challenge. Since minimalism is not the expressivist's best option, I then turn to consider maximalist expressivism. While this view is not vulnerable to the objections I raise against minimalism, I maintain that it is nonetheless incoherent. The overall conclusion at which I arrive is that epistemic expressivism in both its traditional and nontraditional forms should be rejected.

I. Common commitments

All members of the expressivist family, I claimed in the last chapter, embrace three commitments—three commitments that concern the ontological status of epistemic facts, the character of epistemic truth, and the nature of epistemic discourse. Distinctive to nontraditional versions of expressivism is that they qualify these claims in the following ways.

The first qualified claim is:

The Expressivist's Modified Ontic Thesis: There are no epistemic facts, only epistemic quasi-facts.

The second claim concerns the sense in which epistemic convictions are true. It is:

The Expressivist's Modified Alethic Thesis: The contents of some epistemic claims are true, but only in a deflationary sense.

The third thesis concerns the character of epistemic discourse. I state it as:

The Expressivist's Modified Speech Act Thesis: When an agent sincerely utters a predicative epistemic sentence, that agent does not thereby assert an epistemic proposition, but rather 'asserts' an epistemic quasi-proposition.

In what follows, a good deal of my attention will be focused on discerning what these claims mean. But however we understand them, it is instructive to see that each claim is stated in such a way so as to allow expressivists to satisfy what I called in the last chapter:

The Expressivist's Guiding Rationale: Avoid an error-theoretic account of ordinary epistemic discourse (while also avoiding a commitment to epistemic realism).

My immediate task is to present the minimalist's understanding of these commitments. I do this by exploring their account of what I've termed the 'the deflationary package'.

II. Minimalism stated

The deflationary package, I've said, is a set of claims about epistemic discourse, truth, representation, and facthood that offers a deflationary account of these notions. I am now going to present each of the four components of this package as they are understood by minimalist expressivists, beginning with the minimalist's account of epistemic discourse and then moving finally to their view of epistemic facts. As it turns out, it is somewhat misleading to say that I will 'present' the four components of the deflationary package. For this suggests that I will simply present what expressivists themselves say when explicating the deflationary package. But, as a matter of fact, expressivists themselves typically offer rather little by way of detailed presentations of the deflationary package. So, it will be necessary for me to fill out their view somewhat. In effect, this will involve offering a 'rational reconstruction' of their view, expanding upon lines of thought not fully developed by minimalists themselves. While filling out the details of the deflationary package will require some space, it will allow us to fashion a position that makes best sense of the various things that minimalists say.

The first component: epistemic discourse

In his *Morality without Foundations*, Mark Timmons notes that at the heart of the realist polemic against moral expressivism lies a simple but attractive argument that rests on three assumptions. The first assumption—what Timmons calls the 'semantic assumption'—tells us that moral assertions and beliefs (if any there be) are such that their content aims to represent moral reality. The second assumption—what Timmons dubs the 'thesis of semantic unity'—tells us that the grammatical and logical trappings that constitute a discourse are indicative of the real semantics of that discourse. The third assumption—call it 'the empirical thesis'—says that moral discourse does in fact manifest the grammatical and logical trappings of assertoric discourse.[1] Since these three assumptions are jointly incompatible with traditional expressivism, expressivists have been forced to reject at least one of them. And almost without exception, expressivists have opted to reject the second assumption, thereby committing

---

[1] See Timmons (1999), 130.

themselves to the view that the grammatical and logical trappings of moral discourse function not to reveal, but to *mask* its deep expressive structure. Distinctive to Timmons's own position is the claim that expressivists needn't take this route. Rather, Timmons proposes that expressivists can plausibly reject the semantic assumption, but retain both the thesis of semantic unity and the empirical thesis. That is, Timmons proposes that expressivists can plausibly maintain that moral discourse is assertoric but does not function to represent moral reality. (Timmons is thinking of representation as a genuine, substantive relation.) In so doing, Timmons contends, expressivists can handily address a host of puzzles, such as the problem of 'embedded contexts', which has long bedeviled expressivist views.[2]

The proposal is at once bracing and strange: How could one plausibly reject the claim that the content of assertions (or beliefs) aims to represent reality? Timmons's suggestion is that we can do so if we distinguish between two types of cognitive content that assertions can express: descriptive and non-descriptive content.[3] Descriptive content aims to represent reality; for an agent to assertively express some descriptive content p is for her to purport to represent the fact *that p*. Thus understood, descriptive content is propositional content as it is ordinarily understood. Non-descriptive content, by contrast, resembles descriptive content insofar as it manifests certain features characteristic of such content. For example, non-descriptive content embeds in propositional attitude ascriptions and conditionals, is truth-apt (in a deflationary sense), is irreducible to what is expressed in non-declarative sentences such as imperatives and questions, and so forth. However, non-descriptive content neither purports to represent nor represents what the world is like. To perform a speech act that expresses some non-descriptive content p, then, is not thereby to purport to represent the fact *that p*; it is rather to do something different such as 'evaluate' a state of affairs.[4] Nondescriptive content, as we might put it, is quasi-propositional content—where quasi-propositions are entities whose job description includes mimicking propositions in

---

[2] See Geach (1960) and (1965). For an overview of the issue, see Section II.7 of Shafer-Landau and Cuneo (2007).

[3] See Horgan and Timmons (2000).

[4] Timmons puts the matter thus regarding moral judgments: 'moral judgments are not aimed at representing or describing a world of facts. Their content is not representational but evaluative—aimed at choice and guidance of action' (Timmons [1999], 139).

certain important respects, but which do not purport to represent the world.[5]

There is much more to say about the character of quasi-propositions. But for present purposes, we should have a sufficient understanding of their nature to state the first component of the deflationary package. The first component of this package is one concerning the character of epistemic thought and discourse. It tells us that epistemic discourse is assertoric only in the sense that it consists in an agent's performing speech acts that express epistemic quasi-propositions—epistemic quasi-propositions being the non-descriptive content of these acts.

The second component: truth

For those operating with a traditional realist conception of truth, the expressivist's view thus far described is perplexing. The expressivist wants, in one breath, to claim both that epistemic claims do not purport to represent epistemic reality and that some of these claims are true. How can expressivists say both these things?

In a phrase, by 'going deflationary' about truth. What, however, do expressivists mean when they say that epistemic claims are true, but only in a deflationary sense?

This, it turns out, is an extraordinarily vexed question for several reasons. In the first place, while deflationists tell us a great deal about what it is to *say* that a claim is true, they have typically said comparatively little about what it *is* for a claim to be true. Otherwise put, as they are usually presented, deflationary views are not primarily views about the property of *being true* and the conditions under which this property is displayed, but positions about the role of the truth *term*. And what deflationists say about the role of the truth term bears a striking resemblance to what epistemic expressivists say about the role of epistemic terms: According to deflationists, ordinary language shouldn't lull us into thinking that the function of the truth term is such that it purports to pick out some property or relation whose

---

[5] Somewhat differently, Gibbard (2003) contends that the content of quasi-propositions (at least with respect to the all-things-considered-ought) consists in planning states or decisions. I think this cannot be correct, for at least the following reason. According to this view, were I to claim that you ought to believe a proposition would be for me to express the thought that, were I in your shoes, I would decide to believe that proposition. But if a large range of our beliefs is simply not the sort of things we can decide to form—which seems correct—then it is very implausible to hold that claims of this sort express hypothetical planning states.

underlying structure will be revealed by philosophical or scientific analysis. Rather, the suggestion is, the truth term simply plays an expressive or logical role. For example, according to the so-called performative theory of truth championed by P. F. Strawson and others, to say that the content of a claim is true is simply to endorse or commend it in some way.[6] According to others, the term functions mainly as a device for generalization—a device that plays an important and perhaps indispensable role in ordinary discourse. To illustrate: Suppose a committed Roman Catholic doesn't recall all the pronouncements made on morals and dogma by the various Bishops of Rome over the last two thousand years. She can, nevertheless, express her commitment to what the various Popes have said by claiming, 'Everything the Popes have said about morals and dogma is true'. Without the truth term, the claim is, she would be without the conceptual resources to express this commitment. And, let's add, the term allows her to do this with great economy of expression.[7]

Connected with this first point is a second reason why it is difficult to know exactly what epistemic expressivists mean when they say that epistemic claims are true: Deflationists may agree that the truth term simply functions as a logical device or a term of commendation, but there is a wide range of disagreement about exactly how to understand its logical or expressive roles.[8] Moreover, some of these views about the function of the truth term are poorly suited for the epistemic expressivist's purposes. Consider in this respect the so-called performative theory of truth mentioned above. We saw in the last chapter that any adequate account of the epistemic realm must recognize that epistemic merits such as knowledge and warrant are alethic merits; they are merits that attach to claims (non-derivatively) only insofar as the content of these claims is

---

[6] See Strawson (1950) and Rorty (1985). Blackburn (1993) appears to express sympathy with this view when he writes that 'to think that a moral proposition is true is to concur in an attitude to its subject' (p. 129); cf. also Blackburn (2002a), 128.

[7] The thesis that the truth term is primarily a device for generalizing was first developed by Quine (1970) and Leeds (1978). It has since been developed by Horwich (1998), Grover (1992), and Brandom (1987), among others. Horwich writes that 'the deflationist's contention (which is founded on a survey of linguistic usage) is that whenever we deploy the concept of truth non-trivially ... it is playing this role: a device of generalization' (Horwich [1998a], 106). Unless one is prepared to say that each case in which we predicate truth of a singular proposition is a 'trivial' use of the truth predicate, this strikes me as an inaccurate assessment of how we actually use the truth predicate.

[8] For a survey of the different ways in which deflationists think of the role of the truth term, see Soames (1997) and O'Leary-Hawthorne and Oppy (1997).

truth-relevant. But now consider a schema for an epistemic merit such as *being reliably formed*. According to such a schema:

S's belief p is reliably formed if and only if it is produced by a belief-forming faculty that produces mostly true beliefs.

If the performative theory were correct, however, it is difficult to see how one could understand this schema, for it makes no sense to say that:

S's belief p is reliably formed if and only if it is produced by a belief-forming faculty that produces mostly yes! beliefs.[9]

It won't do, then, simply to say that expressivists are committed to one or another deflationary account of truth. We need to say something more about the type of deflationary view that can best be fit with their position.[10]

I suggest that the way forward on this issue is twofold: first, identify a minimal core regarding the nature of truth that fits well with expressivism and, second, assume that expressivism is committed only to this minimal core. To have this minimal core before us, it will be helpful to introduce some terminology.

Let's say that a *robust truth predicate* is one that designates a robust truth property. Let's say, further, that something is a *robust truth property* if and

---

[9] Here I echo Sosa (1993). There is a related problem lurking here, even if we opt for a different version of deflationism. According to standard deflationary views, the truth term is simply a logical device for making generalizations. Accordingly, the schema regarding reliable belief gets translated something like this:

S's belief is reliably formed if and only if it is produced by a belief-forming faculty F such that for all beliefs p, if p is produced by F, then mostly p.

For a paraphrase such as this to be adequate, however, we have to know how the quantifier phrase 'for all beliefs p' interacts with the occurrences of the schematic letter 'p' in the rest of this schema. One thing to say is that the schematic letter stands for beliefs. This would yield nonsense, though: It wouldn't be intelligible to say that for all beliefs p, if p is produced by F, then mostly the belief that p. So, the last occurrence of the variable must stand for something other than a belief such as the fact or truth that p. In this case, we get something like:

S's belief is reliably formed if and only if it is produced by a belief-forming faculty F such that for all beliefs p, if p is produced by F, then it is likely that p is true.

But this way of putting things presupposes the notion of truth, in which case we haven't been given an adequate deflationary paraphrase of the schema in question. See David (2004), 380–1.

[10] The type of view I am about to describe is not the only conception of truth that expressivists have employed. Blackburn (1984), for example, develops a broadly coherentist position. Given the difficulties with this type of view (see Hale [1986])—and Blackburn's apparent sympathy with deflationism in his later writings—I am not going to consider it.

only if it is a 'substantial property', that is, a property that is amenable to a certain kind of conceptual analysis—what I'll call an 'accounting for analysis'.[11] And let's say that a truth property is *amenable to an accounting for analysis* if and only if it can be analyzed by the following schema:

For all p, if p is true, then p is true simply in virtue of C

—where 'p' ranges over the content of either mental states or sentences. An accounting for analysis is a statement of illuminating necessary and sufficient conditions for the presence of the truth property. So, for example, assuming that 'p' stands for the content of an atomic claim, 'C' might be something such as *its being a fact that p, p's obtaining in the actual world, p's being ideally justifiable, p's being pragmatically useful,* and so forth. As such, the 'in virtue' locution as it is used in this schema designates the *truth-making* relation. Unfortunately, I have no detailed account to offer of the nature of this relation, so the following rough-and-ready gloss will have to do: The 'in virtue' relation is an asymmetrical dependence relation—a supervenience or 'accounting for' relation, as I've called it—that in this case obtains between the content of claims, on the one hand, and states of affairs, facts, situations, or propositions, on the other.[12] To take just two examples: In the case of the correspondence theory of truth, what accounts for p's being true is *its being a fact that p* (and not vice versa). In the case of a prominent version of the identity theory of truth, what accounts for p's being true is *p's being a state of affairs that obtains* (and not vice versa). In any case, let's say, finally, that something is a *non-robust truth property* if and only if it is a truth property, but not a robust one.

Deflationists commonly claim that 'truth has no nature'.[13] I am suggesting that we can understand this slogan in terms of an accounting for analysis. Truth has no nature, according to the deflationary view, not only because

---

[11] In putting matters thus, I am taking my cues from Horwich (1998), Ch. 1 and McGrath (2003). Two further points: First, in what follows, I do not assume that the analysis must be non-circular. Second, I am not assuming that the schema stated above is accepted because it is an implication of so-called truth-maker views, which state that, for each claim that is true, there is some entity that, by its mere existence, makes that claim true.

[12] Some deflationists, such as McGrath (2003), maintain that their view can satisfy an accounting for analysis, for they can say that what accounts for p's being true is the truth that p. My own view, as I've already made evident, is that we should recognize that views with regard to truth can be more or less deflationary in character. Since McGrath's view implies that truth consists in a thought's being related to the world in a certain way, it seems to me a position that is not particularly deflationist in character.

[13] See David (2004).

there is no one feature that all true propositions have in common, but also because there is nothing informative to say about that in virtue of which true propositions are true.[14]

With the aforementioned terminology in hand, we can state the minimal core of deflationary views of the requisite kind thus:

The Minimal Core Regarding Truth: (i) The truth term is not a robust truth predicate, and (ii) there is a property of being true, but it is non-robust.

Let me offer two comments on the minimal core.

First, while clause (i) tells us that the truth term is not a robust truth predicate, it is neutral on the issue of whether the truth term is a predicate of *some* sort. In what follows, I will assume that at the very least the truth term is what we can call a 'quasi-predicate'. That is, I will assume that although the truth term may not function to designate some (substantial) property or relation, it at least plays many of the types of logical and grammatical role played by standard predicates. To draw an analogy: Expressivists about morality deny that terms such as 'wrong', 'right', 'compassionate', and so forth are standard predicates that designate moral properties. But they do not deny that these terms act like standard predicates. And, according to expressivists such as Blackburn, the fact that moral terms act like standard predicates implies that they are predicates of some kind.[15] However, if a term's acting like a predicate implies that it is a predicate of some type, it follows that the truth term is a predicate too, if only what I've called a 'quasi-predicate'.

Second, at this point in the discussion, I assume that expressivists are committed to there being a truth property. My reason for assuming this is that expressivists such as Blackburn claim that the conditions for property-hood are met easily: 'where we have predicates', says Blackburn, 'we ascend

---

[14] By saying this, I don't intend to offer a sufficient condition for being a deflationist about truth. There are also 'primitivist' views about truth that maintain that truth is a genuine, substantive property, but that is not amenable to an accounting for analysis. See Moore (1953) as well as Cartwright (1987) and Sosa (2001). As Sosa notes, it is difficult to tell what distinguishes minimalists from deflationists (at least of the sort I am concerned with) about truth. Briefly, the basic difference seems to be that deflationists believe that truth is not amenable to an accounting for analysis because it is too thin: The truth property is simply a 'semantic shadow' of a predicate that functions as a syntactic device. Primitivists, by contrast, hold that the truth property is not amenable to such an analysis not because it is too thin a property, but because it is too basic to our conceptual scheme to admit of any such analysis. See Dodd (2000), 129–30, n. 14.

[15] Blackburn (1996), 92.

to properties'.[16] And I take what Blackburn says to mean not simply that when we have predicate-*talk* we can ascend to property-*talk*, but that, if a term functions logically as a predicate, then it (in some sense) stands for a property. But, since the truth term does function as a predicate (in some sense), it follows that expressivists are also committed to there being a property of *being true*, if only in some deflationary sense.

Let me now bring the various strands of our discussion about truth together. The second component of the deflationary package maintains that the contents of some epistemic claims are true, albeit only in a deflationary sense. I have suggested that we understand this to mean that the contents of some epistemic claims are true, but their being true consists simply in their having a non-robust truth property.[17] Moreover, to predicate truth of the content of an epistemic claim is not to say that it has some robust truth property, but to do something else such as commend that claim, repeat it, predicate of it a non-robust truth property, or the like.

The third component: representation

What goes for truth, suggests Simon Blackburn, also goes for representation. For, according to Blackburn, ' "represents the facts" means no more than "is true".'[18] Now I doubt very much that Blackburn is right about this; there is no equivalency in meaning here. Nonetheless, the deeper point is that once we have a deflationary account of truth in hand, we can extend that account to elucidate the character of representation.[19] If what we said in the last section is on the mark, the counterpart deflationary view regarding representation runs something like this.

Begin with the notion of a *representation-term*. Examples of such expressions are 'refers', 'represents', 'denotes', 'designates', 'is true of', 'corresponds to', and the like. A *robust representation predicate*, let's say, is a representation-term that designates a robust representation relation. And

---

[16] Blackburn (1996). See also Blackburn (1993), 8, 206 and Horwich (1998), 141–4. I ignore here various complications regarding this strategy, for example, that the predicates in question not fail the unrestricted comprehension axioms of naïve set theory.

[17] One wonders: What, according to the deflationists, are the conditions necessary and sufficient for the presence of the truth property? If what I have said is right, deflationists are debarred from saying anything informative on this score. See, for example, Timmons (1999), 133–4, 169 and Horgan and Timmons (2006a), 88, n. 17.

[18] Blackburn (1998), 78.

[19] The primary proponents of deflationary accounts of representation are Brandom (1994), Field (2001), and Horwich (1998a). What I say borrows most heavily from Horwich.

let's say that something is a *robust representation relation* if and only if it is a substantial relation—a relation that is amenable to what I called earlier an 'accounting for analysis'. Taking our cues from what we said earlier about such an analysis, let's say that a representation relation is *amenable to an accounting for analysis* if and only if it can be analyzed by the following schema:

For all p, if p represents q, then p represents q simply in virtue of C

—where 'p', once again, ranges over the content of either mental states or sentences and 'q' ranges over states of affairs, facts, or the like.[20] In the present case, an accounting for analysis is a statement of illuminating necessary and sufficient conditions for the presence of the representation relation. Assuming that 'p' stands for the content of an atomic claim, 'C' might be something such as *p's being causally related to q in a certain way, p's bearing a certain kind of teleo-functional relation to q,* or *p's being about q*—where 'aboutness' is a *sui generis*, irreducible, non-causal relation. Once more, the fundamental idea here is that, if an entity is robustly representational, it is so in virtue of its bearing any of these (or similar) relations to that which it represents. At any rate, we can then say that something is a *non-robust representation relation* if and only if it is a representation relation, but not a robust one.

With this terminology in place, we can now state the 'minimal core' of deflationary views of representation thus:

The Minimal Core Regarding Representation: (i) Representation terms are not robust representation predicates, and (ii) there are representation relations, but they are non-robust.

There are plenty of details to fill in and qualifications to add regarding the minimal core regarding representation. I limit myself to the following two observations.

First, I shall assume that representation terms are what I called earlier 'quasi-predicates'. That is to say, I assume that while representation terms do not function to designate a substantial relation (or relations), they at least

---

[20] I've stated the schema for an accounting for analysis in such a way that it is the content of our mental states or sentences (as opposed to concepts or terms) that is representative. This is an oversimplification. A more adequate formulation of the schema would allow for the fact that entities other than the content of mental states and sentences can be representative (e.g. concepts and terms).

play many of the types of logical and grammatical roles played by standard predicates.

Second, at this point in the discussion, I assume that expressivists are committed to there being a representation relation. My reason for assuming this, once again, is that expressivists such as Blackburn seem to believe that the conditions for there being properties and relations are met easily; where we have terms that behave like predicates, we simply ascend from these predicates to corresponding properties and relations.[21]

In summary: The third component of the deflationary package tells us that epistemic thought and discourse are representational. This, however, should be understood to mean that epistemic thought and discourse are representational only in the foregoing deflationary sense.

The fourth component: facts

Thus far I've presented three components of the deflationary package—claims that concern the nature of epistemic discourse, truth, and representation. I've claimed that expressivists are committed to there being epistemic propositions, epistemic truths, and genuine representation relations of a certain kind. I want now to put the last component of minimalist expressivism into place by exploring what is meant when it is claimed that epistemic facts exist in some deflationary sense.

Definitive of expressivism of all varieties, I've maintained, is the denial that there are epistemic facts strictly so-called. Yet I've also stressed that nontraditional expressivism is more latitudinarian than its traditionalist cousins, as it countenances the existence of what I have called 'quasi-facts'. Although expressivists have little to say about the nature of these entities, I submit that we can better understand what they are if we bring to mind the account of epistemic facts assumed by the epistemic realist.

Recall that, according to the realist, epistemic facts have at least these two characteristics: In a broad range of cases, they are what make the content of epistemic claims true and are what are represented by such

---

[21] Horwich writes regarding reference: 'This is certainly not to deny that there really is such a relation as reference. For one might well employ a liberal notion of property (and of relation) according to which every logically normal predicate expresses a property (or relation). However, the question of whether or not this relation of reference is constituted by some underlying causal relation—or by some other non-semantic relation—is an entirely separate issue. And part of the deflationary position, as I see it, is that the reference relation is very unlikely to have any such underlying nature' ([1998a], 123).

claims. Epistemic quasi-facts, according to expressivists, are also facts of a certain kind; however, they are neither truth-makers nor what is represented by epistemic claims. That epistemic quasi-facts are not truth-makers is implied by what minimalist expressivists say about epistemic discourse and truth; for according to expressivists, there is nothing that accounts for the fact that a quasi-proposition is true. That epistemic quasi-facts are not represented by epistemic claims is also implied by what minimalist expressivists say about epistemic discourse; for according to what minimalists say, epistemic claims are not in the business of representing epistemic states of affairs. (Recall that representation in this case is understood to be robust.) However, if quasi-facts are neither truth-makers nor what is represented by epistemic claims, we're left with the question of why expressivists would bother claiming that quasi-facts exist. After all, if quasi-facts play neither of these explanatory roles, then why would expressivists include them in their ontological inventory?

I think the short answer to this question is that minimalist expressivists hold that, once we admit that epistemic claims are true, then epistemic 'facts' come 'for free'.[22] Now it certainly does seem right to say that if the content of epistemic claims is true, then there are epistemic facts. For consider the following version of the T-schema:

The proposition that p is true if and only if p.

It is plausible to believe that the occurrence of the schematic-letter 'p' on the right-hand side of this schema is necessarily (logically) equivalent to 'it is a fact that p'. For example, suppose that we substitute for this occurrence of 'p' the noun-phrase 'that lemons are sour'. It is very plausible to believe that this occurrence of the phrase 'that lemons are sour' is necessarily (logically) equivalent to 'it is a fact that lemons are sour'.[23]   So, suppose that there are epistemic truths as The Expressivist's Modified Alethic Thesis tells us. It follows that there are epistemic facts of some kind.

Epistemic realists hold that this implication gives us good reason to believe that, if there are epistemic truths, then there are robust epistemic facts. Expressivists deny this, holding that this is an inflationary reading of the T-schema. I am now going to suggest that minimalist expressivists are

---

[22] The phrase comes from Blackburn (1998), 80.   [23] See Alston (2002), 24.

best understood to avoid this inflationary reading by accepting a radically deflationary account of epistemic facts according to which epistemic quasi-facts are 'virtual facts' or what Bertrand Russell called 'logical fictions'.[24] If this view is correct, epistemic facts are such that we can afford them a nominal form of existence inasmuch as we ostensibly speak and predicate things of them. But any complete, correct, and perspicuous account of reality would not contain a term that designates or applies to them. I present two arguments for this account of the character of quasi-facts.

The first argument is one from elimination. Fundamental to expressivism, we might say, is a double rejection: On the one hand, expressivists stand in the lineage of Moore insofar as they reject the thesis that epistemic facts are natural facts—where such facts are understood to be (roughly) those entities that pull their weight in the natural sciences.[25] On the other, expressivists stand against Moore insofar as they reject the claim that epistemic facts are non-natural facts—where these are understood to be those facts that are not natural. Moreover, it is very plausible to assume that, were there moral facts, they would supervene on descriptive features. And, by extension, it is very plausible to assume that, were there epistemic facts, then they too would supervene on descriptive facts. If the argument of Chapter 3 is correct, however, expressivists are committed to the claim that the supervenience of epistemic facts on non-epistemic ones is as deeply problematic as the supervenience of moral facts on non-moral ones; to paraphrase Blackburn on the matter, supervenience is not part of the solution of placing epistemic facts in a natural world, but part of the *problem*.[26] Assuming, however, that the natural/non-natural distinction is

---

[24] See Russell (1956). In what follows in the paragraph, I draw upon Van Cleve (1999), Ch. 1, van Inwagen (1990), Sect. 11, and Cortens (1999), Ch. 2.

[25] For more on the natural/non-natural distinction, see Copp (2003), Shafer-Landau (2003), 58–65, Timmons (1999), 46–9, and Hampton (1998), Ch. 3. When speaking of David Lewis's favored version of ethical naturalism, Blackburn writes: 'projectivism shares the metaphysics of Lewis's dispositional theory. But it objects to his relocation of ethical content (the substitution of a naturalistic predicate). The reason is that we must be able to combine a naturalistic metaphysics with a place for an activity—moralizing—that does not confine itself to delineating natural features' ([1993a], 23). See, also, Blackburn (1993), 180–1. Gibbard (2003) is difficult to assess on this issue. In some places, Gibbard identifies normative with natural facts (pp. x, 100). In other places, he appears to deny the identification (p. 182). At the end of Chapter 7, I voice my reservations about identifying normative with merely descriptive natural facts.

[26] Blackburn (1993), 145. Blackburn (1993), Ch. 7 offers a quasi-realist account of the supervenience of moral concepts on natural ones. But I take this issue to be orthogonal to the one we're now considering.

exhaustive and that epistemic facts would have to be supervenient were they to exist, this leaves no place for epistemic facts in the expressivist's ontology. For, if such facts were to exist, then they would have to be either natural or non-natural ones that supervene on non-epistemic features.

So, we need a way to understand the expressivists' claim that there are epistemic facts that is consistent with their polemic against realism. I suggest that the best way to do so is to interpret the expressivist's talk of epistemic 'facts' as adverting to what I've called 'virtual facts'. If this suggestion is on the mark, then minimalist expressivism does not inherit the problems intrinsic to realism. For epistemic quasi-facts are like smiles, moving shadows, or fake passports, which is to say, not genuine objects at all.[27]

The second argument I offer is textual in nature. Among nontraditional expressivists, one frequently finds it said that there is an 'internal' and 'external' perspective on what we are doing when we engage in normative thought and discourse.[28] When applied to the epistemic realm, the distinction runs as follows: The internal epistemic perspective is one of an engaged participant in ordinary epistemic discourse and practice. From the internal perspective, we say that we respond to epistemic facts, claim that epistemic judgments are true in virtue of representing these facts, and so forth. The 'external' perspective, by contrast, is that of the observer not engaged in 'epistemicizing'—in Blackburn's case, the perspective of the philosopher committed to a robust version of naturalism who is diagnosing what agents do when they engage in epistemic thought and discourse. From the external perspective, the philosopher denies that there are epistemic facts and interprets what happens from the internal perspective as simply the 'adjusting,

---

[27] It is helpful to note a difference between those views according to which smiles, moving shadows, and fake passports are virtual objects and those views according to which epistemic quasi-facts are virtual objects. Distinctive of the view that, say, smiles are virtual objects is the thesis that we can paraphrase all talk of smiles in terms of *smilings*; any apparent reference to smiles can be understood (when reference is pulled off) as making reference to smilings. But, if what I've called the expressivists' 'double rejection' accurately characterizes their view, we cannot offer similar paraphrases of discourse that invokes epistemic quasi-facts: any such paraphrase that is faithful to what Timmons calls 'the thesis of semantic unity' could offer only a paraphrase of quasi-fact discourse in terms of naturalist or non-naturalist predicates, which is precisely what the double-rejection precludes.

[28] See especially Blackburn (1993), Ch. 9, Ch. 8, 157, (1984), 247, and (1998), 50. See, also Timmons (1999) and Korsgaard (1996), 124–5. For a reading of Korsgaard according to which her view is broadly expressivist, see Gibbard (1999).

improving, weighing, and rejecting [of] different sentiments or attitudes'.[29] From the external perspective, there are no epistemic 'properties ... made for or by sensibilities', and the 'only things in this world are the attitudes of people'.[30] Expressivism of this variety 'deserves to be called anti-realist' because it avoids the view that when we engage in epistemic thought and discourse 'we respond to, and describe, an independent aspect of reality'.[31]

The natural question to raise about this way of thinking about the epistemic domain is: How should we understand claims to the effect that epistemic facts exist when such claims are made from the internal perspective? The correct interpretation doesn't appear to be that epistemic facts exist relative to the internal perspective. Blackburn, for example, shows no sympathy for the idea, made popular by Hilary Putnam, that existence is a dyadic, scheme-relative property.[32] That is to say, Blackburn shows no sympathy for the idea that epistemic facts exist relative to the internal perspective, but fail to exist relative to the external perspective. Rather, the best interpretation of what Blackburn says seems to be that, according to expressivists, epistemic facts do not exist at all—although we speak of them as existing from the internal perspective. Here is Blackburn once again. Quasi-realism regarding the moral domain is aptly named

because it starts from an emotivist ... account of the fundamental elements of what we are doing when we moralize. ... But we talk as if there were a truth in that talk, that's why the *quasi*. We talk as if there were a reality, a normative reality, the kind that Plato believed in.[33]

And again:

the quasi-realist has no problem with talking of moral facts, and even of our own sensitivity to them. We can even say, if we want, that moral facts leap to the eye. But all the quasi-realist sees in such talk is another expression of attitude, an

---

[29] Blackburn (1993), 173–4. Here and in what follows I transpose what Blackburn says about the moral realm into what a quasi-realist would say about the epistemic realm.

[30] Blackburn (1993), 174. I assume Blackburn is here engaging in hyperbole!

[31] Blackburn (1993), 157. Blackburn goes on to suggest that a realist view of moral obligation is 'unintelligible or marks a mistake about explanation' (ibid., n. 9).

[32] See Blackburn (1989). Nor, might I add, does Timmons express sympathy with this view.

[33] This quotation comes from a 2002 interview with Blackburn. Text available online at http://www.cfh.ufsc.br/ethic@/ETICA1~1.PRN.pdf). Blackburn (2005) offers a rather different account of his view.

exercise of the conative disposition that, according to him, constitutes our moral commitments.[34]

Of course talk of moral and epistemic facts has its place from the internal perspective. But it should be understood loosely, as affording epistemic facts a nominal sort of existence in the way we afford existence to smiles and fake passports.[35]

We now have the final component of the deflationary package in place. This fourth component tells us that there are epistemic quasi-facts, where quasi-facts are understood to be virtual objects. Having now explored these four components of the deflationary package, we should have a better idea of the extent to which minimalist views can appropriate what epistemic realists say about the epistemic domain. Realists claim that epistemic discourse is assertoric, that some such discourse is true and representative, and that there are epistemic facts. With all this, minimalists agree—so long as we understand these notions in the requisite deflationary sense.

III. Against minimalism: two objections

As philosophical folklore would have it, there was once a day in which it was quite clear what separated moral realists from their expressivist rivals. A theme one hears increasingly voiced in contemporary metaethics is that those days are gone: Given the ways in which expressivism can capture the realist-looking features of ordinary moral thought and discourse, some philosophers have suggested that the distinction between these two views threatens to collapse.[36] Or, more modestly, given the ways in which expressivism is able to mimic the realist-looking features of ordinary moral thought and discourse, some philosophers have claimed that we do not have any grounds to believe that realism better explains the presence of these features than does expressivism.

In this chapter thus far, my attention has been focused on the sort of mimicry in which minimalist epistemic expressivists engage and, in

---

[34] Blackburn (unpublished), 8. For examples of other passages along these lines, see Blackburn (1984), Ch. 6, (1993), 57, 111, 156–7, 175, 177, and especially Chs. 6 and 7.

[35] For a similar view about quasi-propositions, see Horgan (2002), 229–30 and (1989), 135.

[36] See, for example, Blackburn (1993), 4 and Ch. 1, Dreier (2002), (2004), and Gibbard (2003), Ch. 9.

particular, what minimalists mean when they claim that there is a sense in which there are epistemic assertions, that the content of these assertions is true, that they represent epistemic reality, and that there are epistemic facts. The question I now want to pursue is whether this mimicry is so thorough as to capture everything we could plausibly mean when we engage in ordinary epistemic thought and discourse without implying that such discourse and thought are systematically in error. I will contend that the answer is 'no'. My argument rests on two objections that I raise against minimalism—what I call the 'modal' and the 'perspective' objections respectively.

The modal objection

If minimalists are to be believed, expressivists can help themselves to all the realist-seeming appearances of moral thought and practice without any substantial ontological investment. The modal objection rests on the suspicion that this is too good to be true. In philosophy, one often gets what one pays for, and I now wish to urge that the present case is one in which the theoretical dividends do not exceed the investment.

To set the stage for this objection, let me return to last chapter's discussion. In that discussion, I presented two platitudes regarding the epistemic domain that any adequate position should honor. The platitude most relevant for present purposes is:

The Prime Epistemic Platitude: Epistemic merit concepts properly apply to a mental state non-derivatively only if it expresses representational content.

I noted that for this platitude to be genuinely platitudinous, it needs to be understood in such a way that it is neutral between different views regarding the nature of representation, including so-called robust and deflationary views about representation. My argument last chapter was that traditional expressivist views fall afoul of this platitude, even when they are broadly understood. Now it might be thought that nontraditional expressivism is not vulnerable to this concern, as it allows that epistemic claims can be representative in a deflationary sense. I contend, however, that in this case the appearances mislead. Minimalist expressivism also fails to satisfy The Prime Epistemic Platitude.

The argument for this claim has two parts. First, consider any epistemic claim that p that purports to 'represent' a correlative fact *that p*. (Unless the context indicates otherwise, I shall put terms in quotation marks when they stand for deflationary notions.) We want to know: With respect to what type of fact is this claim 'representational'? Presumably, the answer is that epistemic claims are 'representational' with respect to what I've called epistemic 'quasi-facts'. For if The Expressivist's Modified Ontic Thesis were true, epistemic facts in any other sense do not exist.

Suppose, then, epistemic claims are 'representational' with respect to epistemic quasi-facts. Let's now take a case in which all goes well and the epistemic claim in question succeeds in 'representing' the epistemic quasi-fact *that p*. If 'representation' is a genuine relation—albeit not a substantial one—it follows that this epistemic quasi-fact has the property of *being 'represented' by the claim that p*. Fundamental to my argument in the last section, however, is the thesis that minimalist expressivism is not ontologically serious about the existence of epistemic quasi-facts: Since epistemic quasi-facts are virtual objects, a complete, correct, and perspicuous account of reality would not contain a term that designates or applies to an epistemic quasi-fact. And if I understand minimalist expressivists correctly, this is not because they are ontologically unserious about *everything*; expressivists don't purport to be global antirealists.[37] Nor is it because expressivists deny that there are more or less perspicuous ways of talking about reality—ways of talking about reality that, while correct, may more or less appear to imply falsehoods. (Think, for example, of the ways in which we talk about smiles or pains.) To the contrary, if I understand the view correctly, minimalist expressivism is committed to the thesis that there are perspicuous representations of reality, viz., those from what they call the 'external' perspective of naturalism.

The ingredients of a problem are now before us. For a very plausible claim about what sorts of things can have properties is:

Nothing can have a property unless it possibly exists.

This claim is very weak: So-called possibilists (such as David Lewis) who believe that there are possibilities that do not exist, actualists (such as Kit Fine) who believe that there neither is nor could be things that do not exist, and serious actualists (such as Alvin Plantinga) who believe that there

---

[37] See Blackburn (1993), 166. As Timmons says in one place, such a view would be 'crazy' ([1999], 154).

is no case in which an object exemplifies a property in a world in which it does not exist—all of these philosophers would accept it.[38] However, if the claim stated above is true, it follows that since the quasi-fact *that p* bears the property of *being 'represented' by the claim that p*, it possibly exists. Fundamental to minimalist expressivism, though, is the conviction that, strictly speaking, epistemic quasi-facts do not exist in the actual world or, for that matter, in any other; they are virtual entities. It follows from this that minimalism is committed to two incompatible claims: on the one hand, that possibly epistemic quasi-facts exist and, on the other, that necessarily such facts do not exist. These claims imply by *reductio*, however, that it is false that epistemic claims 'represent' epistemic quasi-facts.

Now for the argument's second part. Consider the following plausible claim: Epistemic merit concepts such as *being a case of knowledge* properly apply non-derivatively to only those (predicative) claims that represent or 'represent' some correlative fact. The plausibility of this claim is underscored by connections we assume to hold between knowledge and representation. Assume that there is no other sense of the term 'represent' than that captured by substantive or deflationary accounts of representation terms. It would be paradoxical to say that I know some state of affairs *that p*, but there is *no* sense in which my judgment that p is about this state of affairs.[39] If this is right, two options present themselves.

In the first place, one might accept the plausible assumption that we regularly apply epistemic merit concepts such as *being a case of knowledge* to epistemic claims. However, if the foregoing is correct, then the conditions for the proper application of these concepts are not satisfied, for there is no sense in which epistemic claims either represent or 'represent' correlative states of affairs. And, accordingly, it follows that ordinary epistemic discourse is systematically in error; it is discourse wherein we systematically misapply epistemic concepts of certain kinds. The second option is simply to deny that we apply epistemic merit concepts such as *being a case of knowledge*

---

[38] See Lewis (1986), Fine (1985), and Plantinga (1979) and (1985). Van Inwagen (forthcoming) maintains that Lewis is not a possibilist. If van Inwagen is right, then what I say should be modified so that it says that possibilism is a view commonly attributed to Lewis.

[39] In my judgment, it is also plausible to assume that alethic concepts such as *being true* properly apply non-derivatively to only those (predicative) claims that represent or 'represent' some correlative fact. If the foregoing is correct, it follows that (given a few additional assumptions) The Expressivist's Modified Alethic Thesis is false, as there would be no epistemic claims that could properly admit of alethic concepts.

to epistemic claims in a non-derivative way. While there appears to be conceptual space for this position, it doesn't particularly recommend itself, for it is difficult to see how such a position could capture everything we could plausibly be doing when we engage in ordinary epistemic thought and discourse. Neither option recommends itself.

The upshot of this argument is that minimalist expressivism no better satisfies The Expressivist's Challenge than does traditional expressivism: Given a plausible claim about the application conditions of epistemic concepts, minimalism implies that either ordinary epistemic discourse is systematically mistaken or that expressivism fails to capture adequately what we are doing when we engage in ordinary epistemic discourse. Admittedly, the argument does not imply that, according to minimalism, epistemic discourse is systematically false. But, as I suggested in the last chapter, there are many ways in which a domain of discourse can be mistaken, and we shouldn't assume that being systematically false is the only type of mistake that we should be concerned to protect against.

While I find the modal objection cogent, it is not unassailable. It does, after all, rest on several assumptions that not all philosophers would accept. Still, I do not think there is any premise of the argument that minimalist expressivists should be comfortable rejecting. Consider, for example, the following three responses to the argument.

First, one might reject the claim that nothing can have a property unless it possibly exists. Philosophers who reject this claim endorse a form of Meinongianism according to which there are things that have 'being', but do not possibly exist. Apparently, on this view, it is possible for things that have mere 'being' to display properties. I have little to say about Meinongianism except that I share the puzzlement expressed by many philosophers regarding what Meinongian 'being' could amount to.[40] Between being and existence I can see no difference. In any event, I trust that accepting Meinongianism will not seem at all attractive to expressivists wary of baroque and 'queer' ontologies.

---

[40] See, for example, van Inwagen (2005). On a related note, suppose we return to the discussion in Chapter 2 and distinguish epistemic *states of affairs* from epistemic *facts*—the latter being moral states of affairs that obtain. A minimalist could say that virtual states of affairs exist. According to such an ontology, virtual states of affairs would be *impossible* states of affairs—states of affairs such that it is not possible for them to obtain. Still, even if minimalists were to say this, they could not claim that virtual *facts* exist. For then they would be committed to the claim that there are impossible states of affairs that obtain.

Second, one might reject the assumptions, built into The Minimal Core Regarding Representation, that 'representation' is a property or relation of some sort and that representation terms function predicatively. (I assume these two assumptions come in a package: To adopt the latter but not the former, would imply that representation discourse is systematically mistaken. To adopt the former but not the latter, would undermine the motivation for believing that representation terms function impredicatively.) To adopt a position such as this is presumably to embrace a view with regard to representation terms that is an analogue to the redundancy theory of the truth term. According to such a view, representation terms are not used to describe anything, but are simply devices for commendation or executing grammatical maneuvers such as anaphoric reference.[41] Without going into detail regarding the positions that advocate such a view regarding representation terms, it is difficult to see how such a view could be made to work. The problems in this case are parallel to those that afflict redundancy theories of the truth term, of which I shall mention only one.

It is frequently pointed out that, if redundancy theories of truth were correct, then claims such as 'the proposition that Sam is irrational is true' and 'that Sam is irrational' would have the same propositional content or be 'cognitively equivalent'.[42] (If they didn't, simply furnishing the latter sentence would not establish that we can say everything said by the first without recourse to the truth predicate.) But these claims do not have the same propositional content; the first, for instance, contains the concept of a proposition, while the second doesn't. As we might put it, the first sentence is about a proposition, while the second is about Sam.[43]

A similar problem afflicts redundancy-style accounts of representation terms. Suppose we were to hold that the following schema governs our use of the truth term:

(T) It is true that p if and only if p.

---

[41] Brandom (1984) and Field (2001), Ch. 4, advocate this view. Blackburn (1998), 79, also expresses sympathy with this position. But see Blackburn (1996), 86, 92, for what appears to be a different view.

[42] This phrase is Field's; see Field (2001), Ch. 4.

[43] Here I follow Alston (1996), 46–7. The point is made by Künne (2002), 181–2, Soames (1997), 12, McGinn (2000), Ch. 5, and Wiggins (2002), 323, among others. I take this objection to be germane with respect to not only so-called classic deflationary views, but also with respect to more sophisticated prosentential views.

Suppose, also, we were to believe that a substitution instance of (T) such as:

It is true that Sam is irrational if and only if Sam is irrational

is identical in sense with:

Sam is irrational if and only if Sam is irrational

since the sentential operator 'it is true that' can be eliminated from the first sentence without loss of meaning. As best I can tell, however, there is no analogue to schema (T) with respect to representation terms. That is, to my knowledge, there is no schema in which representation terms such as 'represents the facts' or 'refers to' function as sentential operators such that they are eliminable from sentences in which they embed without loss of meaning. Admittedly, as Horwich points out, we can formulate equivalence schemas regarding representation terms of certain kinds. For example, there is the following schema regarding reference:

(y)(The singular concept N refers to y if and only if y = n).[44]

But no one, I would think, holds that a substitution instance of this biconditional is such that the propositional content expressed by its right-hand side is identical with the propositional content expressed by its left-hand side.[45] Suppose, for example, 'N' is the singular concept *being the mayor of New York City*. It is not very tempting to believe that the claim that Michael Bloomberg (in the year 2006) is identical with the mayor of New York City is identical in sense with the claim that the singular concept

---

[44] See Horwich (1998a), 30. Horwich does not say how we should understand the relation between the schematic letters 'N' and 'n'. Presumably, however, the schema presupposes that for every referring singular concept N there is some thing n to which it applies—call it an 'n-correlate'. So, for example, if the singular concept 'being the current mayor of New York' refers, there is some n-correlate to which it refers, in this case, Michael Bloomberg (in the year 2006).

[45] This point is important for assessing quietism about the normative. While philosophers use the term 'quietism' in different ways, in one of its central uses it denotes a position about the normative according to which we can say everything that normative realists do, but deny that these sayings have any theoretical or metaphysical import (or that it makes sense to offer second-order theories about their content). As Blackburn (2005a) puts it, according to quietists, philosophical worries about whether ethical commitments are really true are not worries about whether they correspond to some order of Platonic 'Forms and Norms'. Rather, they are simply expressions of an ethical sensibility, a first-order ethical concern about the status of one's ethical commitments. The route to this position, in Blackburn's case, runs through what he calls 'Ramsey's Ladder': It is because locutions such as 'p', 'it is true that p', 'it is a fact that p', and ' "p" accurately represents the facts' all mean the same thing, that quietists can deny that saying 'it is a fact that p' carries with it any more ontological commitment than saying 'p'. The simple reply to this rationale for accepting quietism, however, is to point out that the supposed meaning-equivalences fail to hold. For more on this matter, see Cuneo (forthcoming).

being the mayor of New York City refers to Michael Bloomberg. The first claim includes the concepts of a singular concept and reference, while the second does not. Accordingly, a person could coherently accept the first claim while rejecting the letter claim if, for example, she were ignorant of the sense of the concept *being the mayor of New York City* or how singular concepts work. If this is right, one might be able to construct a broadly deflationary account of representation terms on the basis of schemata such as the one stated above (as Horwich attempts to do). But it is another matter altogether to construct a *redundancy* theory of representation terms that captures what we mean when we use these terms.[46] And since embracing a redundancy view regarding representation terms is required if we reject a central premise of the modal argument, I submit that expressivists ought not to reject this premise.

Third, and finally, one might reject the assumption that minimalism is committed to the claim that quasi-facts are virtual facts. For example, one might claim that the real lesson to be learned from the present objection is not that minimalism fails to meet The Expressivist's Challenge, but that minimalists are committed to the genuine existence of epistemic facts. Were minimalists to say this, then the force of the foregoing objection would be averted completely.

I have already indicated why I think that minimalists are best interpreted to claim that epistemic quasi-facts are mere virtual entities. That said, I

---

[46] In the context of defending a broadly redundancy theory of representation terms, Robert Brandom writes that 'philosophers have misconstrued the plain man's use of "refers" and hypostasized a relation of reference as the semantic interpretant of the apparently relational expressions, and have then asked for a theory of it. Such a mistake is of a piece with the search for objects corresponding to each expression that syntactically plays the role of a term—e.g. "someone" and "everyone". ... Reference is a philosopher's reification and a fiction, generated by a grammatical misunderstanding' ([1984], 488).

Brandom's suggestion seems to be that the redundancy account of representation terms is supposed to capture ordinary use of such terms. And yet it is difficult to see how this could be so. For one thing, despite what the passage just quoted seems to say, Brandom himself appears not to deny that there is a genuine reference relation ('Expressions do refer to nonlinguistic items [it is true that the one referred to by <Leibniz> is not a word and was a person]' p. 491). But if there were such a relation, the rationale for claiming that representation terms never function so as to pick it out is perplexing. Moreover—and here I paraphrase Alston—it is crucial to Brandom's own 'prosentential' account of reference terms that expressions such as 'is about', 'refers to', 'mentioned by', and the like are such that their constituents have no specifiable meanings, but function as semantically unanalyzable anaphoric expressions. But it is hard to imagine that ordinary speakers would deny that 'is about' and 'refers to' are such that they have specifiable meanings that they carry around from one context to another. Accordingly, it is difficult to see that redundancy theories really do offer a plausible account of what the plain person means when he uses representation terms. See Alston (1996), 47, for an analogous claim regarding truth.

do not deny that expressivists might say that epistemic quasi-facts exist in a perfectly ordinary sense of this term. But this is a position different from minimalism. Indeed, it is what I referred to earlier as 'maximalist' expressivism. And while I will address this view shortly, I want first to turn to the second objection to minimalism.

The perspective objection

When I introduced minimalist expressivism earlier, I said that minimalists typically employ a distinction between an internal and an external perspective with respect to epistemic thought and discourse. The second objection to minimalism I wish to develop concerns this distinction. For reasons that will be apparent in a moment, I believe that minimalists are correct to emphasize that something like perspectivalism of this sort is necessary to state their position. I suggest, however, that the distinction between these different perspectives is unsustainable.

A theme that has repeatedly surfaced in our discussion is that there are two competing theoretical desiderata that minimalists wish to satisfy: On the one hand, minimalists aspire to capture and vindicate the realist-seeming appearances of ordinary epistemic thought and discourse. On the other hand, they want to remain distinctively antirealist by not committing themselves to an ontology of epistemic facts with all its attendant problems. The minimalist solution is to appeal to perspectives with regard to the epistemic domain. The internal perspective, recall, is supposed to be the perspective that captures what it is like to be an agent engaged in ordinary epistemic thought and discourse; it is the arena in which it appears to an agent that she is giving and assembling epistemic reasons, epistemically evaluating beliefs, uttering epistemic truths, representing epistemic reality, and so forth. The external perspective, by contrast, is supposed to be the perspective of the naturalist philosopher who in Terry Horgan and Mark Timmons's words is engaged in 'metaphysical speculation' or 'theoretical inquiry', but believes that there are no epistemic reasons or facts.[47] Transposing what Blackburn says just a bit, from the external perspective, what transpires in the internal

---

[47] The quotations are from Timmons (1999), 152 and Horgan (2001), 90, respectively. The most extensive discussion of the external perspective with respect to morality is found in Timmons' discussion of assertoric nondescriptivism in Timmons (1999), 150–2. Here I transpose what an assertoric nondescriptivist about morality says about the moral realm into what an assertoric nondescriptivist about epistemology would say about the epistemic realm.

perspective is simply the 'adjusting, improving, weighing, and rejecting [of] different sentiments or attitudes'.[48]

Given the competing theoretical desiderata that minimalists wish to satisfy, the need for both perspectives should be apparent. To capture the appearances, expressivists need to appeal to something akin to the internal perspective. But to remain distinctively antirealist and to tell an explanatory 'story' about how normative 'thought functions', expressivists need to appeal to the external perspective.[49] Presumably, there must be a stance from which we can explain what it is to be a *quasi*-realist!

That there is an internal epistemic perspective few would doubt. But it is very hard to see how there could be anything like an external epistemic perspective that one could intelligibly occupy. That is to say, it is very difficult to see how there could be a perspective in which a person at once engages in theoretical inquiry and does not believe (or take it for granted) that there are epistemic reasons. After all, anything we could recognizably call 'theoretical inquiry' or 'inquiry from a naturalist perspective' involves viewing ourselves as assembling reasons, epistemically evaluating claims, offering arguments, and so forth. In short, anything we could recognizably call theoretical inquiry requires taking not the external, but the *internal* perspective. To which I add, even if it were the case that the external perspective could be coherently occupied, it is hard to see what point there might be in doing so, for it is not a perspective in which there could be—or in which we could take ourselves to offer, accept, or reject—reasons for any claim.

It is helpful to see that the problem I am identifying is one that affects any sort of perspectivalist account of the epistemic realm. Consider, for example, so-called fictionalist accounts of epistemic discourse that have some affinities with perspectival expressivism.[50] According to a fictionalist view with respect to entities of some kind K, a complete, correct, and perspicuous account of reality would not make reference to Ks. Still, the fictionalist urges, there are two types of stance one can take up with respect to Ks. One can adopt the fictive stance with respect to Ks in which one talks and acts as if there were Ks while taking it for granted that there are

---

[48] Blackburn (1993), 173–4.   [49] Blackburn (1998), 49.

[50] Some, such as Lewis (2005), interpret quasi-realism itself as a species of fictionalism. Blackburn (2005), however, maintains that the positions are distinct. Joyce (2001) and Kalderon (2005) develop fictionalist accounts of morality.

no Ks. Or one can adopt the non-fictive stance according to which one forthrightly denies that there are Ks. A distinguishing feature of fictionalism with respect to Ks is that, in the typical case, if we take up the fictive stance with respect to Ks and are pressed on the issue of whether there really are Ks, we are prone to shed the fictive stance. If, for example, you have taken up the fictive stance with respect to cartoon characters and I ask whether you really believe whether, say, Spiderman has climbed the Empire State Building, you are (all else being equal) disposed to say 'No'.[51]

Could such an account be made to work in the epistemic domain? I doubt it. The problem is not simply that we are not disposed to shed 'reason-talk' when pressed. It is rather that there is a significant sense in which we cannot do this. For if what I have argued is correct, and if there were a non-fictive stance with respect to epistemic reasons, it could not be one that an agent could occupy and coherently engage in anything resembling what we call theorizing or inquiry. Indeed, if one adopts the plausible assumption that thinking in a recognizably (mature) human fashion implies that we take ourselves to recognize considerations that favor some of the opinions we hold, the non-fictive stance is not one that we could occupy and remain engaged in a recognizably human way of life. We can put the point like this: Presumably, to 'author' or 'project' a fictional world with respect to entities of some kind, one must do so from a non-fictive stance with respect to entities of that kind.[52] However, anything resembling what we call authoring or projecting a fictional world involves viewing ourselves as offering and assessing reasons, assuming that certain propositions are evidence in favor of other propositions, and so forth. Since, by hypothesis, occupying a non-fictive stance with respect to epistemic reasons would preclude viewing ourselves as engaging in these activities, it is impossible to engage in anything resembling what we call 'authoring' or 'projecting' a fictional world with respect to epistemic reasons. And since it is plausible to believe that there can be a fictionalist view with respect to entities of some kind only if one can engage in something like what we call authoring or projecting a fictive world with respect to entities of that kind, it is plausible to believe there could not be a fictionalist view with

---

[51] See Joyce (2001), 14, see also 185.

[52] Could one non-intentionally project a fictional world? Not if an agent's projecting such a world is an illocutionary act of a certain kind and that agent occupies anything like ordinary optimal conditions. See Wolterstorff (1980) for a defense of the view that fictional projection is an illocutionary act.

respect to epistemic reasons.[53] And, accordingly, it is difficult to see how appealing to an external perspective can be of any help in meeting The Expressivist's Challenge.

Let me close this section by calling attention to why these points about the external perspective highlight a puzzling feature of what Blackburn terms the 'quasi-realist' project. Quasi-realism is, in Blackburn's own words,

> the enterprise of explaining why our discourse has the shape it does, in particular by way of treating evaluative predicates like others. ... It thus seeks to explain, and *justify*, the realistic-seeming nature of our talk of evaluations. ... Technically, in the philosophy of language, it tries mainly to justify what I call the 'propositional surface' of ethics, or the fact that we voice our reactions in very much the way in which we describe facts.[54]

The puzzling feature of this description of quasi-realism is this: Suppose we understand expressivism to offer an account not only of the character of epistemic discourse, but also of the character of the mental states expressed by that discourse. Thus understood, expressivism suggests that the mental state expressed by the phrase 'to explain and justify' should be understood in a broadly expressivist manner: In the ordinary case, were I to say 'I have explained and justified X', I would not thereby have expressed the proposition that I have provided sufficient reasons in favor of X. Rather, I would have done something else such as commend X, accept certain norms that instruct us to embrace X, or the like. Still, the mental state expressed by this sentence has what Blackburn calls 'realist-seeming' characteristics or a 'propositional surface'. If so, then the quasi-realist's project is to explain and justify this mental state's 'realist-seeming' characteristics. But, if what I have argued is correct, anything recognizable as a putative explanation and *justification* of the realistic-seeming characteristics of this mental state will presumably involve thinking that there are considerations that favor accepting that this mental state has these realistic-seeming characteristics. Any such mental state, however, essentially involves the very realistic-seeming characteristics we are trying to explain. And, thus, of any such mental state we need to ask what explains and justifies *its* realistic-seeming characteristics. And so on. The quasi-realist position

---

[53] Have we here identified an interesting disanalogy between the moral and epistemic domains? I address the issue in the last chapter.

[54] Blackburn (1984), 180 and (1996), 83–4. Italics mine.

does not look like it can gain enough theoretical traction to get off the ground.[55]

I said earlier that the aim of The Expressivist's Challenge is to offer an expressivist account of epistemic discourse that at once captures what we ordinarily mean when we engage in such discourse without implying that such discourse is in systematic error. The upshot of the 'perspectival' objection is that this is something minimalist expressivists cannot do. For to meet the challenge requires positing two perspectives: one that captures what we are doing when we engage in epistemic discourse, and another that offers an expressivist explanation of this discourse from the 'disengaged' or 'theoretical' perspective. But there is, I have urged, no such external perspective from which to offer such an explanation. Any such explanation would have to proceed from the internal perspective. This, however, leaves minimalists without the type of explanatory story they themselves believe must be furnished.

Summary

The discussion to this point has been complex, so let me summarize its main features. I began by identifying two types of nontraditional expressivist position—minimalist and maximalist expressivism, respectively. To better understand minimalist expressivism, I explored the four components of what I labeled the 'deflationary package', offering an account of the types of deflationary views to which minimalists appear committed. According to the interpretation I offered, minimalists maintain that there is a sense in which epistemic quasi-propositions, quasi-truths, and representation relations exist. But, I suggested, there is considerable evidence for maintaining that, according to minimalists, epistemic facts are mere virtual entities, enjoying at best an ersatz mode of existence. The combination of these views, I argued, presents problems for minimalism. According to the first objection I raised—what I called the 'modal objection'—minimalism fails to honor certain platitudes about the connections between representation

---

[55] In his response to Dreier (2002a), Blackburn seems to recognize an analogous problem that a different sort of objection to his view raises. If I understand his response, Blackburn seems to think that the regress is unproblematic because his project is not one of offering an 'old-fashioned' analysis of normative concepts ([2002], 166). I do not see why this response helps. Even if quasi-realism does not engage in analysis of this sort, it purports to explain and justify certain phenomena. And, if what I have argued is correct, a vicious regress of the sort identified would undermine the explanatory and justificatory task.

and knowledge. According to the second objection—what I called the 'perspective objection'—minimalists are committed to there being both an internal and external perspective with respect to epistemic thought and discourse. I claimed that there could be no such external perspective, at least none that we could coherently occupy.

Where does this leave minimalism? A central claim of the argument thus far is that, for all its sophistication, minimalist expressivists embrace an ontology nearly identical with that of epistemic nihilism. I argued in the last chapter that, inasmuch as expressivists adopt the epistemic nihilist's ontology (or something close thereto), their view is vulnerable to the charge that it implies a type of radical skepticism no better than that enshrined in what I called in Chapter 4 'the three undesirable results'. The expressivist response to this charge, recall, was to issue The Expressivist's Challenge. If the argument of the last chapter is correct, traditional expressivism fails to meet this challenge, for either it does not capture the character of such discourse or implies that such thought and discourse are in massive error. And if the argument of this chapter is correct, minimalist expressivism also fails to meet this challenge, for its construal of ordinary epistemic thought and discourse either does not capture the character of such discourse or implies that such thought and discourse are in systematic error. This result, I suggest, is a powerful reason to reject each of these views.

IV. Maximalist expressivism

The debate between realists and expressivists proceeds in epicycles. Realists charge expressivists with violating platitudes of various kinds such as The Prime Epistemic Platitude; expressivists respond by offering a deflationary account of some concept that figures centrally in these platitudes, thereby attempting to establish that their view can satisfy the relevant platitudes. A lesson that has emerged from our discussion thus far is that it is generally unhelpful for expressivists simply to embrace a deflationary conception of one or another kind of entity when responding to concerns regarding their view. It matters what *type* of deflationary view is embraced. My contention in the last section was that minimalist expressivists are best interpreted as adopting a version of the deflationary package that fails to meet The Expressivist's Challenge. But it is natural to ask whether there are other versions of the deflationary package to which expressivists can appeal. I believe there are. Maximalist expressivism develops a position that accepts a fairly robust version of the deflationary package.

In the last section, I furnished textual evidence for attributing to expressivists the position that epistemic facts are mere virtual objects. But there are also passages in which quasi-realists such as Blackburn appear to say something quite different, thereby inching closer to a realist understanding of epistemic facts. Consider the following passages for instance.

Even if we sorted truth into TRUTH and truth ... and decided that there was no moral TRUTH, this would only mean that you don't walk into rights and duties, or that they can't be cubic or solid or seen under a microscope.

Yes, I am an anti-realist; no, this does not mean that there are no facts of an ethical or normative kind ...

Quasi-realism ... refuses to give ethical facts a typical explanatory role. This is already heralded when we turn our backs on ethical representation. A representation of something as F is typically explained by the fact that it is F. A representation *answers to* what is represented. I hold that ethical facts do not play this explanatory role.[56]

There is no harm in saying ethical predicates refer to properties, when such properties are merely the semantic shadows of the fact that they function as predicates. A quasi-realist protection of ethical truth protects ethical predicates, and if our overall semantic picture is that predicates refer to properties, so be it. But ethical predication remains an entirely different activity from naturalistic predication. ...[57]

The thought expressed in this last passage seems to be that, since there are moral predicates, there are moral properties. The latter are not to be confused with the sorts of properties that exist in what Blackburn calls the 'real world' of cubic and solid things. But nonetheless these properties and facts exist, if only as the semantic 'shadows' of moral predicates.[58]

---

[56] Blackburn (1998), 319 and (1999), 216.
[57] Blackburn (1993), 181 (*see also* 177, 206). In *Ruling Passions*, Blackburn writes something similar:

If we were discontented with minimalism about representation and truth, we might wonder how the story would go with a thick theory of representation in hand. Would that deliver a contrast between 'representing the ethical facts' and 'representing natural facts'? It is hard to say. Obviously there will be some differences between 'ethical facts' and the others. The fact that there is a cannonball on the cushion explains why it is sagging in the middle. The fact that kindness is good explains no such thing. ([1998], 80.)

[58] Blackburn (1993), 177.

Unfortunately, Blackburn never says what a 'semantic shadow' of a predicate is. As a consequence, it is difficult to see what exactly distinguishes Blackburn's conception of moral facts from a realist's; after all, realists also wish to say that we don't walk into rights and duties, or see them under a microscope. In *Truth and Objectivity*, however, Crispin Wright also employs the metaphor of a shadow and specifies more exactly what he means when he says that moral states of affairs are 'shadows' of moral sentences. To my knowledge, Wright's discussion is the only extensive treatment of such issues. Accordingly, I propose to close our discussion of expressivism in this chapter by exploring Wright's view, thereby bringing maximalist expressivism into sharper focus. I am going to suggest that, while interestingly different from its minimalist cousin, maximalist expressivism does not protect ordinary epistemic thought and discourse from the charge that they are systematically in error. This is because maximalist expressivism is not a coherent view. Were we to use epistemic concepts in the way that maximalist expressivists suggest, epistemic thought and discourse would be systematically mistaken.

In what remains, I'll begin by distinguishing two ways in which Wright understands the representation relation. Having done this, I then identify how maximalist expressivists think of epistemic quasi-propositions and quasi-facts. I'll then contend that the resulting position should be rejected.

Shadows, minimal truth, and cognitive command

Our first task is to understand what Wright has in mind when he employs the metaphor of a shadow that is cast by the assertoric form of discourse. Transposing a passage from Michael Dummett, Wright says:

The states of affairs which (merely) minimally true sentences represent are no more than reflections on those sentences, sentences which behave, by simple formal criteria, in a manner analogous to sentences which are apt to depict real states of affairs, but whose senses cannot be represented as consisting in our capacity to identify states of affairs necessary and sufficient for their truth.

Wright continues by pointing out that:

the concluding part of… [this] thought might naturally be taken as an expression of (or kind of) *irrealism*. … But, again, that is not the only possible meaning. The thought can be that understanding such a sentence should not be seen as consisting in a capacity appropriately to *respond to* the relevant type of truth-conferring states of affairs. For, in parallel to the situation with abstract objects, there seems to be no question of such a state of affairs ... directly influencing the thought of someone who lacks the conceptual wherewithal to characterise it, or directly producing any other kind of effect on our consciousness, or on our bodies or non-human objects of any kind. ... Like pure abstract objects, the states of affairs purportedly depicted by merely minimally true sentences do not seem to do anything except answer to the demands of our minimally true thoughts. The irresistible metaphor is that ... the states of affairs to which ... merely minimally true sentences correspond, are no more than *shadows* cast by the syntax of our discourse. And the aptness of the metaphor is merely enhanced by the reflection that shadows are, after their own fashion, real.[59]

Coming to light in this passage are several of Wright's assumptions about what a realist treatment of entities of a kind K would have to consist in, the most important of which is that it must be such that, if Ks are represented in the content of our attitudes, then this representation consists in our *responding* to them. So, the suggestion seems to be that we can distinguish between two modes of representation: 'serious' representation, which obtains only when a claim represents a state of affairs in virtue of its being a 'response' to that state of affairs; and, what I'll call 'weak representation', which obtains when and only when a claim 'depicts' a state of affairs, but not in virtue of its being a response to it.[60] That states of affairs of a certain kind are mere shadows of true claims, then, is the thesis that these states of affairs can only be weakly represented by these true claims.

Several conditions, in Wright's view, must be met if an attitude seriously represents a state of affairs, among which is that it exerts what Wright calls 'cognitive command'. Roughly, the idea here is that if a statement seriously represents a fact, then any dispute about the truth of that statement must involve a cognitive shortcoming on the part of at least one of the participants in that dispute.[61] Wright emphasizes that this idea tries to capture two intuitions.

The first is that there is a link between realist truth, or genuine facts, and objectivity. If we are really dealing with an objective matter of fact, says Wright, then,

---

[59] Wright (1992), 181–2.   [60] 'Serious representation' is Wright's term. See ibid., 200.
[61] See ibid., 92–3, 144. Wright offers a refurbished version of cognitive command in Wright (2001). For my purposes, the differences are not relevant. For more on this matter, see Cuneo (2003).

the opinions which we form are in no sense optional or variable as a function of permissible idiosyncrasy, but are *commanded* of us—that there will be a robust sense in which a particular point of view *ought* to be held, and a failure to hold which can be understood only as a rational/cognitive failure.[62]

So, to use Wright's example, statements about what is funny do not intuitively exert cognitive command. If two persons were to sit down to watch Abbott and Costello, and if one person were to claim that their dialogue is highly amusing, while the other were to assert that it is tiresome and juvenile, neither would (all else being equal) suffer from a cognitive shortcoming. Either claim would be rationally acceptable.

The second intuition that cognitive command tries to capture is one concerning the nature of representation. Wright puts it thus:

For to think of oneself as functioning in purely cognitive mode, as it were, is, when the products of that function are to be beliefs, to think of oneself as functioning in representational mode; and that idea is then subject to a truism connecting representation and convergence—that representationally functioning systems, targeted on the same subject matter, can produce divergent output only if working on divergent input or if they function less than perfectly. The nerve of the Cognitive Command constraint is a specialization of that idea to the case where the representational system is a thinking subject engaged in the formation of belief.[63]

Think here of photography as an instructive analogy: If we take photographs with two cameras of one and the same scene in equally good conditions, and these photographs somehow represent this scene in incompatible ways, then there has to be some kind of malfunction in at least one of the cameras.[64] Similarly with cognitive systems aimed at representing the world.

Wright's contention is that a position that admits that moral statements do not exert cognitive command is consistent with 'robust kinds of reference to moral qualities'. But it

will not be possible to regard the disciplined formation of a moral view as a seriously representational mode of function, or as a mode of activity in which we respond to states of affairs which, precisely because they are at the service of explanation of other things, can be put to serious work in explaining the course assumed by those responses.

---

[62] Wright (1992), 146.   [63] Ibid.   [64] Cf. Wright (2001), 55.

And while a moral view of this sort needn't lapse into 'amoral tolerance', differences in moral opinion 'need involve nothing worth regarding as cognitive shortcoming'.[65]

The incoherence of maximalist expressivism

The ingredients for a maximalist version of epistemic expressivism are now at hand. Suppose we assume that what Wright calls 'minimalism' about truth is a close relative to what I've called 'deflationism' about truth.[66] We can then say that, according to maximalist expressivism, epistemic discourse functions to express epistemic quasi-propositions, where these are simply the content of epistemic claims that purport to weakly represent epistemic quasi-facts. Suppose, also, that if the maximalist view were right, some such content is true in a deflationary sense. Finally, and most importantly, suppose the view implies that there are epistemic quasi-facts—where these are not virtual objects, but simply those facts weakly represented by epistemic claims. Grant these assumptions and we have a maximalist understanding of the expressivist's modified speech act, alethic, and ontic theses.

I wish now to suggest that this position is not coherent.

Let's begin by focusing on the doctrine of cognitive command. This doctrine, it will be noticed, is a normative thesis: It tells us that, necessarily, if a statement seriously represents a fact, then any 'brute dispute' (this is Wright's phrase) about the truth of that statement involves a cognitive shortcoming, a rational failure, or lack of proper function on the part of at least one of the participants; at least one of the participants, as Wright says, ought to view the matter differently. Let's now distinguish between what we can call a 'robust epistemic norm' and a 'weak epistemic norm'. A *robust epistemic norm* is such that, necessarily, if one fails to conform to it (and the norm is not overridden by some other), then one thereby suffers from a rational failure. A *weak epistemic norm*, by contrast, is such that it is

---

[65] Wright (1992), 200.

[66] Let me enter three caveats, however: first, Wright himself never calls the moral analogue to the epistemic view I am describing 'expressivist'. Second, as I indicated in the Introduction, there are passages indicating that Wright himself would resist extending what I am calling an expressivist view to the epistemic realm (see Wright [1992], 201). Third, Wright is no friend of deflationary views of some kinds; see Wright (1992), Ch. 1. Still, what he calls 'minimalism' corresponds rather closely to what I have been calling 'deflationism'. For an attempt to establish that deflationary views of truth can address Wright's worries about the view, see Horwich (1998), Ch. 3.

not the case that, necessarily, if one fails to conform to it (and the norm is not overridden by some other), then one thereby suffers from a rational failure. Now, if maximalist expressivism is true, epistemic norms are weak in character; they are not such that they can be seriously represented and, thus, statements that express them fail to exert cognitive command. As I've already indicated, however, cognitive command is a normative thesis; it tells us that in cases of brute disputes, then at least one party ought to view the matter differently. If maximalist expressivism is true, then this 'ought' is weak in character, for it is an epistemic norm.

On the assumption that the foregoing is correct, the problems for maximalist expressivism are at least twofold. First, it is a very plausible claim that we can respond to states of affairs of various kinds in the world and, thus, seriously represent them. By all indications, expressivists believe this (think of what Blackburn says about the real world of cubic and solid things).[67] However, if cognitive command implies that, in cases of disputes of certain kinds, at least one party weakly but not strongly ought to view the matter differently, then there cannot be serious representation. For serious representation requires that there be strong epistemic norms—norms such that, if one fails to conform to them, one thereby suffers a rational failure. So, on the assumptions that there is serious representation and that the doctrine of cognitive command (at least in part) captures this notion, it follows that maximalist expressivism cannot be true. For if there were serious representation, it would follow that there are strong epistemic norms. Maximalist expressivism, however, denies that there are such norms.

Second, while maximalist expressivism is committed to the existence of weak epistemic norms, it is hard to see how one can make any sense of this idea. After all, it is plausible to believe that, if there are epistemic norms, then there are at least two species thereof. These are what I called in Chapter 2 'propriety' and 'responsibility' norms, respectively: norms that, on the one hand, pertain to the proper function of our cognitive faculties and those, on the other, that pertain to the formation and maintenance of our intentions to engage in action plans of certain kinds. But it appears to be a conceptual truth that some norms of these types are such that, necessarily, if one fails to conform to them (and the norm is not overridden

---

[67] See also Blackburn (unpublished) especially and Timmons (1999), 154.

by some other), then one thereby suffers from a rational failure of *some* sort. If a person firmly believes a proposition simply because of some sloppy guesswork, then it appears to be a conceptual truth that that person has violated a norm of rationality and thereby suffers a cognitive defect. However, as formulated, maximalist expressivism is not consistent with this conceptual truth. For, if maximalist expressivism were true, all epistemic norms are weak in character, and their violation does not imply that anyone suffers from a cognitive or rational defect.

Summary

Maximalist expressivism attempts to occupy a narrow band of conceptual territory. On the one hand, it denies that there are epistemic facts strictly so-called and that epistemic claims are robustly representational. On the other, it claims that there are epistemic facts more robust in character than mere virtual facts and that epistemic claims are representational in a non-robust sense. I have argued that, if we model this view on what, to my knowledge, is its only moral analogue, it is not defensible—in part because it cannot account for there being genuine or 'serious' representation. If this is right, maximalist expressivism thus understood cannot—any more than its minimalist counterpart—offer us a plausible response to The Expressivist's Challenge; it also does not yield an expressivist account of epistemic thought and discourse that both captures everything we could plausibly mean when we engage in such thought and discourse and also protects it from systematic error. Of course the fact that both minimalist and maximalist expressivism fail The Expressivist's Challenge doesn't imply that there could not be an epistemic antirealist view that satisfies this challenge. But it seems to me that the prospects for there being such an expressivist position are dim. Deflate epistemic facts and we are back to minimalist expressivism again. Inflate such facts and we are flirting either with realism or some form of reductionism. In short, there appears to be no conceptual room for a recognizably *expressivist* position that avoids both these shoals.[68]

---

[68] In a reductive spirit, Blackburn briefly develops a position (in Blackburn [1998], 56) that might appear to be a recognizably expressivist view that avoids both minimalism and realism. According to this view, judging that a cognitive system ought to function in a certain way simply consists in 'expecting' it to act in a certain way. This proposal seems to me unpersuasive, however. For, presumably, a person's 'expecting' that a cognitive system will work a certain way means that she thinks that the odds are that the system will work in a particular way. It is, however, perfectly possible—and indeed actual—that

V. Conclusion

In this chapter and the last, we have been exploring the clash between two convictions central to the expressivist project. On the one hand, there is the conviction that expressivism is not a species of error theory, but an alternative to it. Expressivism offers us an account of ordinary epistemic thought and discourse that purports to protect such thought and discourse from the charge that it is systematically in error. On the other hand, there is the conviction that expressivism does not offer us a revisionary account of epistemic discourse (or, if it is revisionary, it is only minimally so). Understood aright, expressivism is supposed to capture everything we could plausibly mean when we engage in ordinary epistemic thought and discourse—where this is taken to mean that it at least captures what I've called the 'content platitudes' with respect to epistemic facts. A reoccurring theme of our discussion is that, given the resources with which expressivists allow themselves to work, honoring both these convictions proves to be very difficult: As I've put it, protecting ordinary epistemic thought and discourse from error yields the result (given other commitments of expressivists) that expressivism fails to capture what we actually do when engaging in such thought and discourse. But capturing crucial features of what we actually do when engaging in ordinary epistemic thought and discourse implies (given other commitments of theirs) that such thought and discourse is systematically in error. Still, might there be a way to navigate between these two tendencies? Suppose, for instance, we were simply to surrender the two convictions that drive it. Might not this be less damaging than we think? Rather than view the speech act thesis and its variations as descriptive claims about the character of ordinary epistemic discourse, might we not instead construe them as *proposals* for how we ought to reform epistemic discourse?

Yes, we could. But one wonders what the nature of the recommendation could be. It doesn't seem very plausible to say that we ought to reform epistemic discourse in the manner suggested for either prudential, aesthetic, or moral reasons, as it isn't at all clear that reforming it in this way would

---

we expect a cognitive system not to work in a certain way and still judge that it ought to. I do not see, then, how we could plausibly construe judgments about what ought to be the case simply in terms of our expectations.

be advantageous along any of these normative dimensions. And if it is supposed to be epistemic considerations that motivate the reform, then there is a puzzle to face.

Consider the sentence 'There is excellent epistemic reason to reform epistemic discourse in such a way that it is expressivist in character.' When understood in an expressivist fashion, this sentence is presumably a case of the very sort of discourse that is being recommended. As such, the sentence expresses not an epistemic proposition, but a pro-attitude toward reform or a quasi-proposition. (I assume that the latter sort of entity should be understood in a minimalist fashion; a maximalist understanding, if I am right, is not coherent.) According to expressivism, however, the content of this sentence thus used does not give anyone a reason to reform epistemic discourse—there being, strictly speaking, no epistemic reasons that could favor the reform. And if we are clear about what we are actually doing when we use this sentence in this way, then it would not even be the case that its content is *represented* to us as counting in favor of reform. Rather, we would find ourselves in a situation analogous to when we are confronted with an optical illusion: The oar in the water appears to us bent; but because we are aware of the nature of the illusion, we do not represent it as such. Likewise, the attitude or quasi-proposition expressed may appear to us a consideration that favors reform; but because we are clear about the nature of the mimicry, neither is represented to us as favoring reform (there being, strictly speaking, no favoring relations of this sort). And so we have our puzzle: If, strictly speaking, there are neither considerations that actually favor reform nor (when we are clear about what we are saying) considerations that are represented to us as favoring reform, what could recommend revising epistemic discourse in the way expressivists propose?

7

Epistemic Reductionism

In the last three chapters, I have been concerned primarily with views that flatly deny that there are epistemic facts ('maximalist' expressivism being the exception). There are, however, ways of developing epistemic antirealism that shy away from such a strong claim, preferring instead to admit the existence of epistemic facts of a kind less robust than realists favor. Positions of this sort I shall call 'reductionist' versions of epistemic antirealism. What qualifies them for this title? Recall that in Chapter 2 I said that epistemic facts irreducibly exist only if two conditions are met: First, they must satisfy certain content platitudes—platitudes to the effect that an attitude can display an epistemic merit or demerit non-derivatively only insofar as it is representational. Second, they must satisfy authority platitudes—platitudes that tell us that epistemic facts are, imply, or indicate reasons for us to behave in certain ways and that some of these reasons govern us independently of any particular desires, concerns, or projects we may have. To use the terminology employed earlier, epistemic realists are committed to there being categorical epistemic reasons.[1]

Epistemic reductionism, then, is the view that epistemic facts exist, but fail to satisfy our commonsensical conception of epistemic facts—the latter being comprised of both the content and authority platitudes with respect to epistemic facts. If this is right, there are in principle two main ways to be an epistemic reductionist. The first is to claim that there are epistemic facts, but to deny the content platitudes; the second is to claim there are epistemic facts, but to deny the authority platitudes. I am not aware of any position that takes the first route. To be sure, there are positions according

---

[1] As I use the locution, 'categorical' reasons are identical with what are often called 'external' normative reasons. Likewise, as I use the locution, 'hypothetical' reasons are identical with what are often called 'internal' normative reasons. I have chosen to use the terms 'categorical' and 'hypothetical' so as not to multiply externalisms and internalisms beyond necessity.

to which 'evaluating systems of cognitive processes' is done simply in terms of broadly pragmatic considerations.[2] As I indicated in Chapter 2, however, I believe that such positions are better characterized as versions of epistemic nihilism. It is, after all, a plausible claim that the representation platitudes are constitutive of our epistemic notions; to deny that notions such as justification or knowledge should be understood in terms of these platitudes, accordingly, is simply to deny that they are epistemic notions.[3] (I am aware that there are broadly pragmatist positions according to which the goal of our believings is not to represent reality aright, but to be able to offer reasons for what we believe.[4] While I find such views unconvincing, they are not in conflict with the authority platitudes. One can affirm that our central epistemic concepts must be understood in terms of the notion of representation, but deny that representing reality aright is the (or even a) goal of belief.)

Consequently, I propose that we understand epistemic reductionism to be a position that at once admits the existence of epistemic facts that satisfy the content platitudes, but denies that their character is captured by the authority platitudes. For present purposes, we can think of epistemic reductionism as being committed to three central claims. On the one hand, epistemic reductionism mirrors epistemic realism insofar as it adopts:

The Epistemic Realist's Speech Act Thesis: Some epistemic discourse is assertoric;

and:

The Epistemic Realist's Alethic Thesis: The contents of some predicative epistemic claims are true and, if the contents of such claims are true, then they are true in the realist sense.

On the other hand, the view breaks with realism insofar as it embraces:

The Epistemic Reductionist's Ontic Thesis: Epistemic facts exist, but fail to satisfy the authority platitudes with respect to epistemic facts. That is,

---

[2] Stich (1990), 131.   [3] But see the discussion of 'radical' reductionism at the end of this chapter.

[4] See Rosenberg (2002), Ch. 6. Rosenberg argues that not truth, but justification, or the ability to give reasons for one's beliefs, is the goal of belief. The problem with claiming that truth is the goal of belief, according to Rosenberg, is that we could never ascertain whether we reliably achieve it (p. 218). For reasons that should become clear shortly, I think this view will not appeal to adherents of the reductionist views I consider in this chapter.

either such facts are not prescriptive or all epistemic reasons are hypothetical in character.[5]

I will unpack the reductionist's ontic thesis in a moment. However, before I do so, let me highlight a defining characteristic of epistemic reductionism thus understood.

Epistemic reductionism is a theoretically conservative enterprise. Its aim is not so much to overturn our theoretically entrenched or ordinary understanding of epistemic notions, but to preserve them as best possible. In this sense, it shares a great deal in common with epistemic realism. Indeed, witness just how much from realism reductionism takes on board! Unlike realism, however, reductionism is driven by the conviction that an epistemic antirealist view can deliver everything we could sensibly want of a theoretical account of the epistemic realm. This is not to suggest that reductionists would deny that repudiating the authority platitudes comes at a theoretical price. I suspect that many sympathetic with reductionism would not deny this. But the reductionist reply is that their view preserves enough of our theoretically entrenched or commonsensical conception of epistemic facts, and jettisons enough of the unattractive features of realism, to be a powerful rival to realism. To paraphrase David Lewis in another context, reductionists propose that we accept imperfect, but good-enough deservers of the name 'epistemic fact'.[6] My contention in this chapter is that we should resist such a proposal. Reductionism, I will argue, preserves rather less and gives up rather more of a plausible understanding of the epistemic realm than it should.

My argument for this claim proceeds by dividing reductionist views into two kinds—what I call 'moderate' and 'radical' reductionist views, respectively. The difference between these positions is that they reject different components of the authority platitudes: The moderate view claims that there are epistemic reasons but denies that any are categorical, while the radical view denies that epistemic facts are prescriptive in any sense. For reasons I will highlight later, I am going to engage extensively with only moderate reductionism on this occasion. Against this position, I am going

---

[5] In presenting the second disjunct of this thesis as a general claim about epistemic reasons, I follow Laudan (1990a) when he says that 'good reasons are instrumental reasons; there is no other sort' (p. 318). See also Kornblith (1993) and Railton (1992), 49.

[6] Lewis (1995), 469. The context is a discussion of qualia.

to argue, first, that it fails to preserve some theoretically entrenched and plausible ways of understanding the nature of epistemic merits, such as those adopted by both externalists and internalists with regard to justification. Second, I will argue that the motivations offered for embracing this position are unpersuasive. In closing, I turn my attention to radical reductionist views, suggesting that we do well to resist a position that wishes to do away altogether with the normative dimensions of epistemic facts.

I. Moderate reductionism

The driving idea behind moderate reductionism is the claim that epistemic reasons are so-called hypothetical imperatives. As such, moderate reductionism is rooted in a conviction that has exercised considerable influence in western philosophy, i.e. that normativity is a function of what we desire. It is not surprising, then, that in contrast to epistemic nihilism and expressivism, moderate reductionism—or at least something approximating it—is a position with which numerous philosophers have expressed sympathy.[7] Toward the end of this chapter, I'll be discussing more specifically why philosophers have been attracted to the view. At this stage of the discussion, let me introduce two items of terminology that will help us to formulate the position better.

The first piece of terminology is that of a 'cognitive goal'. An agent S has a *cognitive goal* at some time, I'll stipulate, just in case S is, at that time, dispositionally or occurrently motivated to implement a doxastic policy (a strategy for forming and governing belief) whose end is that some range of her beliefs display one or another property (the instantiation of which) S finds desirable. Thus understood, there are a huge variety of cognitive goals. And I will assume that an agent can have many of them at a given time. For example, an agent may have the cognitive goals of forming justified beliefs, to avoid forming beliefs that threaten her political convictions, to achieve understanding, to believe only what is scientifically respectable, and so forth.

---

[7] Field (2001), Ch. 13, Giere (1989), Kornblith (1993), Lammantra (1988), Laudan (1987), (1990), (1990a), and (1996), Maffie (1990) and (1990a), Quine (1986), Railton (1992), Rosenberg (1999), and Wrenn (2004) all express sympathy with the view or something close thereto. Field, I think misleadingly, calls his position a version of 'expressivism'.

The second piece of terminology I wish to introduce is that of an 'epistemically basic cognitive goal'. An agent S has an *epistemically basic cognitive goal* at some time, I will assume, just in case S is, at that time, dispositionally or occurrently motivated to implement a doxastic policy whose end concerns the aim of believing what is true. The basic idea here is that a doxastic policy of this sort explicitly specifies how an agent will orient herself with respect to the end of forming and maintaining true beliefs.[8] And the assumption is that goals of this sort are epistemically basic inasmuch as they make reference to alethic properties, which provide a non-epistemic anchor by which we can elucidate epistemic properties such as *being a case of knowledge*.[9] At any rate, as I will indicate shortly, I assume that agents can have numerous epistemically basic cognitive goals of this sort at any given time. For example, at some time, an agent may have the goals to form only well-confirmed true beliefs, to avoid holding obviously false beliefs, to hold only those true beliefs that are practically important, and so forth. Unless the context indicates otherwise, I will assume that occurrences of the phrase 'cognitive goal' refer to cognitive goals of this sort.

With the concept of a cognitive goal in hand, I suggest that we think of moderate reductionism as a two-tiered position. The first and more fundamental tier contains the following claim concerning the nature of epistemic reasons:

The Application Thesis: S has an epistemic reason to Φ at t only if and because S has cognitive goal(s) Ψ at t.

The second tier of the view builds upon the first inasmuch as it contains a thesis regarding the presence of epistemic merits. This thesis, first introduced in Chapter 2 and amenable to epistemic realists and reductionists alike, is:

The Generation Thesis: S's attitude p has epistemic merit X at t if and only if and because p is an appropriate response to epistemic reasons at t.[10]

---

[8] To be more exact, epistemically basic cognitive goals should probably be formulated in terms of the aim of forming and maintaining true beliefs *and* not false ones, or representing reality aright *and* not failing to represent it aright. In what follows, I shall speak simply of forming and maintaining true beliefs for simplicity's sake.

[9] For more on this, see David (2001).

[10] Recall that the notion of a reason in play is capacious; it encompasses both veridical and nonveridical reasons. For more, see the discussion in Chapter 2.

Taken together, these claims imply:

The Conditional Claim: S's attitude p has epistemic merit X at t only if and because S has cognitive goal(s) Ψ at t.

It should be acknowledged that The Conditional Claim is a thesis that is not ordinarily explicitly formulated by philosophers sympathetic with moderate reductionism. As I read these philosophers, this is mostly because their attention typically is fixed on the nature of epistemic norms or reasons and the epistemic merit of 'rationality', rather than on epistemic merits as such. Still, The Conditional Claim is implied by a pair of claims to which, I take it, moderate reductionists would not object. In any case, let me now add several refinements to this formulation of moderate reductionism that concern the concept of a cognitive goal.

First, as I have already indicated, I will not assume that if an agent has an epistemically basic cognitive goal she thereby endeavors to believe only those propositions that are true. Rather, I will assume that truth-relevant cognitive goals can be and often are more nuanced (and idiosyncratic!) than this. For example, it wouldn't be unusual if an agent deeply concerned with her own moral character and who aims at forming true beliefs generally were not to desire to know anything about the specific contents of the Marquis de Sade's lurid *The 120 Days of Sodom and Other Writings*. Moreover, there are agents who are particularly anxious not to be 'taken in' and, thus, are more deeply concerned about not believing false propositions than believing only true ones. Furthermore, and somewhat differently, there are (presumably) agents who aim at forming true beliefs generally, who nonetheless refuse so much as to entertain evidence against their conviction that the pronouncements of a particular religious authority are true or that a spouse is faithful. Finally, some agents appear to believe propositions of certain kinds precisely because the evidence for them is not strong. Kierkegaard, for example, seems to have advocated such an approach with respect to religious belief. If this is right, epistemically basic cognitive goals can be quite varied, hedged, and qualified in all sorts of different ways.

Second—and this ties in with the last point—I will assume that an agent's cognitive goals can be more or less admirable from an epistemic point of view. That is, I'll assume that an agent's cognitive goals can be more or less concerned with forming true beliefs or representing reality aright. Without trying to specify exactly what renders a cognitive goal admirable, I'll simply assume that occurrences of the term 'cognitive goal' in the schemata stated stand for only admirable cognitive goals. Furthermore, I'll stipulate that two cognitive goals are incompatible just in case if one such goal is admirable, then the other is not.

Third, I am going to assume that any plausible account of the nature of cognitive goals will imply that they are often not objects of awareness or consciousness. This implies that cognitive goals are very different from, say, fund-raising goals inasmuch as the former are often such that we neither consciously and intentionally formulate them nor are consciously aware of having them. To return to a case just mentioned, an agent might be strongly motivated not even to consider evidence that his spouse is unfaithful, even though he is not conscious of having this goal. Indeed, even if made aware of this goal, he may not repudiate it given its putative importance to his psychological well-being.

Fourth, I assume that a plausible account of cognitive goals will imply that, during our ordinary activity of forming and maintaining beliefs, such goals often remain merely dispositional. So, while the acceptance of a proposition may sometimes be an act motivated by an occurrent desire to believe the truth, often the formation and maintenance of our beliefs are not. To the contrary, I assume that given certain kinds of experiential inputs, many beliefs are formed in us, as it were, automatically; they do not form by virtue of our having any occurrent (or non-occurrent) desire to believe what is true.

In summary, I shall assume that for agents such as us, cognitive goals are often comprised of non-conscious, non-occurrent motivational states regarding the forming and maintaining of true beliefs with respect only to certain domains of propositions. In the next section, I am going to develop an argument against the position that such goals are determinative of the presence of epistemic reasons and merits. The argument comes in three parts. In the first part, I contend that moderate reductionism is incompatible with an externalist view of justification. In the second part, I maintain that moderate reductionism is also incompatible with an internalist view regarding justification. Finally, in the third part, I argue that moderate reductionism yields an unattractive form of epistemic relativism. The combined thrust of these arguments is that The Conditional Claim and, thus, The Application Thesis are false.

II. Against moderate reductionism

Central to the debate among contemporary epistemologists is the question of whether we ought to understand the concept of epistemic justification as standing for an 'internal' or an 'external' epistemic merit. As I use these terms, the difference between them is this: According to an internalist account of justification, the only sort of thing that can justify a (human) person's belief is mental states that have their source in sense experience, introspection, memory, broadly logical intuition, and the like.[11] As such, internalists understand states of only these types to be evidential and, thus, what justify our propositional attitudes. So, for example, if internalism were true, a person's belief *that it is presently snowing* is justified if and only if and because it is based on adequate evidence of this sort.[12]

According to an externalist account of justification, by contrast, entities other than mental states can justify an agent's attitude. For example, according to certain types of externalist accounts of justification, a person's belief *that it is presently snowing* is justified if and only if and because it is produced by a reliable belief-forming mechanism in an appropriate environment, where justification in this case supervenes on the causal origin and the manner in which a belief is produced rather than simply the mental states that occasion it. Externalists, then, work with a wider notion of evidence than do internalists in at least this sense: Whether a mental state of a certain kind or a state of affairs of a certain type counts as evidence for a person to believe a proposition is a function of whether

---

[11] See Steup (2001). I use the term 'states' broadly also to cover mental events and conditions.

[12] Two points: First, let me remark on my use of terminology. Unless the context indicates otherwise, I will use the terms 'evidence' and '(epistemic) reason' more or less interchangeably. This use is, in part, based on what I take to be the linguistic data. It would be odd to say, for example, that S has evidence to believe p, but no reason to believe p. Likewise, it would be odd to say that S knows or is justified in believing p, but has no reason to believe p.

  Second, what I am calling 'internalism' is what Conee and Feldman (2004), Ch. 3, call 'mentalist' internalism and Steup (2001) calls 'evidentialist' internalism (which, incidentally, the authors defend as the most defensible form of internalism). This view is to be distinguished from 'access' internalism or the position that an agent's belief is justified only if he has epistemic access to the reasons that justify his belief (see BonJour [2003], Part I, for an explication of this view). I have chosen to focus on a mentalist version of internalism in part because it corresponds more closely to what goes by 'internalism' in the debate concerning practical reasons. I should note, though, that what I say about the incompatibility of mentalist internalism and moderate reductionism should apply equally to the combination of access internalism and moderate reductionism.

mental states and states of affairs of these kinds reliably produce true beliefs in an environment such as ours.[13]

It is not my purpose here to weigh in on whether internalists or externalists offer a more nearly adequate account of epistemic justification. I introduce the dispute between these two views to highlight three assumptions I will make in the subsequent discussion.

I will assume, in the first place, that beliefs and other propositional attitudes can be both internally and externally justified.

Second, I will assume that in addition to justification there are other epistemic merits, many of which can be understood in either an internalist or externalist fashion. I assume, then, that internalism and externalism are not simply positions with regard to justification, but general views that specify the type of evidence that confers a given epistemic merit on one or another propositional attitude. Somewhat more exactly, when understood in its broadest sense, internalism tells us that, for some range of epistemic merits E, what confers E on a person's attitude are only mental states of that person that have their source in sense experience, introspection, memory, broadly logical intuition, and the like. Externalism denies this, claiming that sources other than mental states of these types can confer an epistemic merit E on a mental state.

Finally, I will assume that the epistemic merit of *being a case of knowledge* in particular is (at least in part) an external merit.[14] This assumption is grounded in the following oft-recognized point: Suppose knowledge consists in true belief in addition to some other feature—call it 'warrant', following Alvin Plantinga's terminology.[15] It is possible for a person's true belief to be justified in an internal sense—that is adequately grounded in her mental states—and for it not to count as knowledge; the belief may, after all, be the product of massive deception or a cognitive malfunction of which she could not be aware. If this is right, justification understood in

[13] I don't deny that there is another sense in which the notion of evidence with which externalists work is narrower than that employed by internalists. According to externalists, a feature counts as evidence for a proposition in the sense of justifying that proposition only if it reliably indicates that that proposition is true. Internalists deny this, opting for a more liberal account of justification-conferring evidence.

[14] Here I assume that there is one concept of knowledge that epistemologists are analyzing. This is a somewhat controversial assumption. For those skeptical of this assumption, what follows can be viewed as an exercise regarding one particular conception of knowledge with which many epistemologists work.

[15] See Plantinga (1993) and (1993a).

the internalist sense is not identical with warrant; it is not that feature that single-handedly converts true belief into knowledge. This is not to claim, let me note, that warrant should be understood to be simply an external epistemic merit. It may be, as numerous philosophers have insisted, that it should be thought of as having both external and internal ingredients.[16]

At any rate, return now to what I've called 'The Generation Thesis' or the claim that:

S's attitude p has epistemic merit X at t if and only if and because p is an appropriate response to epistemic reasons at t.

If we focus on the occurrence of the term 'appropriate' in this schema, we can see that it will have different senses depending on whether the merit in question, X, is internal or external. In the case of internal merits, the appropriateness of the response will supervene simply on the mental states of the agent in question (the mental states of an agent being necessary and sufficient for the presence of whatever internal epistemic merits that agent's attitude may display). To use the conceptuality of Chapter 2, the appropriateness may reside in the awareness of having satisfied a responsibility norm she countenances—a norm to the effect that an agent ought, in forming or maintaining a given belief, to intend to implement one or another action plan with respect to the forming or maintaining of that belief. In the case of external merits, however, the appropriateness of the response will not simply supervene on the mental states of the agent in question. To use the terminology introduced at the end of the second chapter again, the appropriateness may reside in the satisfaction of a propriety norm—a norm to the effect that an agent with properly functioning cognitive faculties would respond in such-and-such manner to features of certain kinds in her environment.

The first two arguments I want to develop trade on this ambiguity of what an 'appropriate response' to reasons consists in. In the first argument, I will argue for a pair of conclusions: First, if we understand the occurrence of 'appropriate' in The Generation Thesis as referring to the presence of a paradigmatic external epistemic merit, moderate reductionism is incompatible with externalism with respect to such an epistemic merit; and, second, this conclusion is strong incentive to reject moderate reductionism.

---

[16] See Alston (1988), Part III on what he calls 'justification' and Steup (2001) among others.

In the second argument, I will argue for a pair of parallel conclusions: First, if we understand the occurrence of 'appropriate' as referring to the presence of a paradigmatic internal epistemic merit, then moderate reductionism is incompatible with internalism with respect to such an epistemic merit; and, second, that this does not bode well for moderate reductionism. I begin with the argument from the nature of external epistemic merits and then turn to the argument from internal merits.

The argument from external merits

As I formulated it earlier, externalism with respect to epistemic merits is the view that considerations other than an agent's mental states can confer epistemic merits of certain kinds on her attitudes. In its classic formulation, externalism is more or less synonymous with reliabilism or the view that what confers justification on a belief is that belief's having been (non-accidentally) produced by a reliable belief-forming faculty (i.e. a faculty that produces a preponderance of true beliefs) in an appropriate environment.[17] Suppose we call beliefs thus produced 'E-justified' (for 'externalist-justified'). And suppose also we assume that when we speak of a belief's being 'produced' we mean 'produced by a cognitive faculty aimed at forming true beliefs' (as opposed to forming beliefs with other sorts of virtues such as pragmatic ones). Definitive of any account of E-justification is what I will call:

The Epistemic Externalist's Supervenience Thesis: The E-justificatory status of a person's belief strongly supervenes on how it was produced in an appropriate environment: Necessarily, if the beliefs of any two possible individuals in such an environment are produced in the same way (and if they have no undefeated defeaters for their beliefs)[18] at t, then these beliefs are E-justificatorily alike at t, i.e. E-justified to the same extent.

Let's call any position that adopts this thesis an instance of 'paradigmatic' externalism. Some philosophers sympathetic with moderate reductionism

---

[17] See, for example, Goldman (1979) and (1986) and Sosa (1991) and (2003). For reliabilism with a twist, see Greco (2000) and, somewhat differently, Plantinga's proper function theory in Plantinga (1993), (1993a), and (2000). I use the locution 'appropriate environment' in a deliberately vague way. Reliabilists of different stripes will understand the appropriateness in question differently.

[18] As they are typically understood, defeaters are (roughly) considerations that either count against the truth of a belief or the reasons one has for holding a belief (or appear to do so). Plantinga (2000), Part IV.II.1 offers an extended treatment of defeaters. The supervenience thesis and its parallel regarding internalism find their inspiration in Conee and Feldman (2004), 56.

appear to believe that their position is compatible with externalism.[19] I want now to contend that this is not so. To make my case, I appeal to a pair of cases inspired by Linda Zagzebski's book *Virtues of the Mind*.[20]

Suppose that in world W, Ella is a nosy neighbor who keeps a close eye on her immediate neighbors to the east, a group of rowdy college students of whom she is suspicious. Accordingly, Ella regularly sits by the easternmost window of her apartment carefully observing the behavior of the students. While nosy and suspicious, Ella's cognitive goal with regard to those propositions regarding the activity of her neighbors is nonetheless admirable, for she aims to form only true and not false beliefs about their activities. As it happens, one evening she sees her neighbors engaging in all manner of illegal activity, which includes defacing her car with a can of spray paint. Upon so witnessing these events, she forms a cluster of beliefs, including the belief *that the neighbors are defacing my car with a can of spray paint*. Ella immediately lets her other neighbors know about the activities of the disreputable students.

Suppose that in world W*, Ella also lives in the apartment immediately adjacent to rowdy college students and from her easternmost window keeps a keen eye on their activity. Ella in W*, we can suppose, is identical with Ella in W in all relevant respects with this exception: In W*, Ella regularly sits by the easternmost window of her apartment observing the behavior of the students not because she is interested in forming only true beliefs about their activity, but because she wishes to glean whatever appears to be information that will help her to make these students seem highly disreputable to her other neighbors. Gleaning apparent information of this sort and forming beliefs on the basis of this apparent information is Ella's cognitive goal with respect to propositions that concern the activity of these neighbors. As it happens, one evening she sees her neighbors engaging in all manner of illegal activity, which includes defacing her car with a can of

---

[19] Maffie, for example, claims both that 'epistemic…facts become reason-giving…only when relevant to our ends' ([1990], 286) and that standard reliabilism is true ([1990a], 336–7). Likewise, Wrenn (2004) writes that it is possible that S knows p, but it is false that S ought to believe p. On the assumption that there is a conceptual connection between epistemic oughts and reasons such that if S epistemically ought to believe p, then there is some ground that epistemically favors his believing p, Wrenn's claim is that it is possible that S knows p, but it is false that there is any ground that epistemically favors S's believing p. If what I argue is correct, neither of these positions is coherent.

[20] See Zagzebski (1996), 314 ff. In employing these cases, I don't wish to imply that Zagzebski would approve of the moral I draw from them; she may not (cf. p. 281). In what follows, I'm indebted to Baehr (2002).

spray paint. Upon so witnessing these events, she forms a cluster of beliefs, including the belief *that the neighbors are defacing my car with a can of spray paint*. Ella immediately lets her other neighbors know about the activities of the disreputable students.

Let's now stipulate that in each world Ella's cognitive goals are compatible, her cognitive faculties are working well, her environment is epistemically hospitable, there are no available defeaters for her beliefs, and what she sees happening is as vividly presented as one might hope. It follows from The Externalist's Supervenience Thesis that in both worlds Ella's beliefs concerning her neighbors are E-justified. This implication is (in part) a function of The Epistemic Externalist's Supervenience Thesis, which tells us that since Ella's beliefs in both worlds are produced in the same way (and she has no undefeated defeaters for her beliefs), then these beliefs are E-justificatorily alike. Indeed, given the stipulations just mentioned, it is plausible to assume that in both worlds she not only has E-justified beliefs concerning her neighbor's activities, but *knows* what her neighbors have been up to.

But now let's suppose The Conditional Claim is true and that, for any epistemic merit, an agent's cognitive goals are determinative of whether her beliefs exhibit that merit. If The Conditional Claim is true, however, then the following must also hold: If two otherwise identical epistemic agents in identical conditions have incompatible cognitive goals with respect to some proposition at some time, then their beliefs regarding that proposition cannot exhibit the same E-justificatory status at that time.[21] This additional claim is (in part) the conceptual fallout of the thesis that an agent's cognitive goals are determinative of the epistemic status of her beliefs. At any rate, in the cases I have described, Ella in W and W* has incompatible cognitive goals with respect to propositions concerning the activities of her rowdy neighbors and believes the same propositions regarding her neighbors on the same grounds; in W, Ella's cognitive goals with respect to her neighbor's activities are admirable, while in W*

---

[21] More pedantically put: If worlds W and W* are identical with the exception that S has cognitive goal G at t with respect to a range of propositions p in W and goal G' at t with respect to p in W*, where G and G' are incompatible, and in both worlds S believes p at t only on account of being aware of some ground g, then S's beliefs regarding p in W and W* at t cannot display the same E-justificatory status.

I want to note that this principle is one that pertains only to what I called earlier 'paradigmatic' versions of externalism. I don't wish to deny that Ella's belief in W may be epistemically non-virtuous, where such an epistemic demerit is not a paradigmatically external, but nonetheless an external demerit.

they are not. It follows that, if moderate reductionism is true, then Ella's beliefs concerning her neighbors do not display the same E-justificatory status. However, if externalism is true, then Ella's beliefs do display the same E-justificatory status, for they are both E-justified. It follows that, if moderate reductionism is true, a paradigmatic form of externalism is false.

It strikes me as a bizarre result of moderate reductionism that Ella's beliefs concerning her neighbors fail to exhibit the same E-justificatory status. After all, in both worlds, Ella occupies qualitatively identical environments, her faculties are working equally well, she engages in the same cognitive activity, she has the same vivid visual experiences of her neighbors, she forms the same beliefs on account of these activities and experiences, and so forth. Moreover, as I indicated earlier, I don't think an adequate reply to this concern would be simply to deny that beliefs can be E-justified. Any position that seeks to accommodate a theoretically viable account of knowledge, for example, cannot turn its back on external merits of this kind, for the presence of such merits is (if the standard analysis of knowledge is correct) indispensable for having knowledge. If this is right, and The Conditional Claim is true, a moderate reductionist should furnish a reductionist account of a merit such as E-justification. Given The Conditional Claim, the view would presumably look something like this:

S's belief p is E-justified if and only if and because (i) p is (non-accidentally) produced by a reliable belief-forming faculty of S's in an appropriate environment (and S has no undefeated defeaters for p); and (ii) S has cognitive goal(s) Ψ.

While I do not wish to deny that the cognitive goals a person harbors may in some cases abet or impede the reliability of her cognitive faculties, I doubt that they always do. And, accordingly, it seems to me that moderate reductionism could offer us only a highly strained account of E-justification: If we are thinking of reliability in anything like its ordinary sense, in many cases, the cognitive goals we possess have no bearing upon whether a belief is E-justified. Indeed, one moral to draw from the case of Ella is that one can have epistemically *disreputable* goals and still form E-justified beliefs or acquire knowledge. However, if this is right, then clause (ii) in the foregoing reductionist analysis is, in a wide range of cases, explanatorily misplaced; some beliefs are E-justified but not because of what we are motivated to do or what goals we possess. It follows from this that The

Conditional Claim is false: It is not the case that a person's attitude has an external epistemic merit such as being E-justified only if and because she has one or another truth-relevant cognitive goal. The having of such a goal, in a wide variety of cases at least, goes no distance toward explaining the presence of external epistemic merits.[22]

The argument from internal merits

A reaction one might have to the foregoing line of argument is to claim that while moderate reductionism is not well-placed to offer us a plausible analysis of external epistemic merits, it can nonetheless offer us a promising account of internal epistemic merits. The second stage of the argument I am pressing aims to show that this is not the case.

According to the characterization I offered earlier, internalism is the view that, with respect to a certain range of epistemic merits E, what confers E on a person's attitude are only mental states of that person that have their source in sense experience, introspection, memory, broadly logical intuition, and the like. Thus understood, internalism is typically taken to advance a view regarding the nature of justification, fundamental to which is the claim that justification is simply the property of being supported by adequate evidence or reasons understood in the internalist manner. Suppose we say that when a belief is thus supported by reasons it is 'I-justified' (for 'internalist-justified'). And suppose, furthermore, we restrict our attention to I-justification as it concerns our occurrent beliefs. Constitutive of any such view of justification is what I will call:

---

[22] Two concerns: First, might it be that the reason the moderate reductionist holds that Ella's beliefs have different E-justificatory status is that disreputable cognitive goals function as a defeater for a belief's being E-justified? I don't think so. Such goals would not be considerations to think that Ella's beliefs concerning her neighbors are false. Nor would they function so as to undercut the grounds Ella has for believing what she does about her neighbors—especially if Ella were unaware of them. For more wrinkles regarding this issue, see the discussion of strongly non-conscious cognitive goals in the next section.

Second, might the objection under consideration be avoided were we to allow that cognitive goals can also be non-actual in character—goals that agents would have under certain conditions? Perhaps. But new problems would surface. In the first place, this suggestion does not fit well with some of the main motivations offered in favor of moderate reductionism, since these motivations appear to require that our cognitive goals be ones that we actually have (see Sect. IV of this chapter). Moreover, the non-actual goals in question would presumably be ones that agents have under idealized conditions. (That an agent simply happens to have cognitive goals of a certain kind in a different possible world is, presumably, not relevant to determining the E-justificatory status of that agent's beliefs in this world.) I argue toward the end of this section—when I consider the second way to avoid the so-called relativist result—that such a view is not promising.

The Epistemic Internalist's Supervenience Thesis: The I-justificatory status of a person's belief strongly supervenes on that person's mental states: Necessarily, if any two possible individuals are mentally alike in the relevant respects at t, then they are I-justificatorily alike at t, i.e. the same beliefs are justified for them to the same extent.

This statement of the supervenience thesis includes a clause about individuals being mentally alike 'in the relevant respects'. How should we think of this proviso?

For our purposes, we needn't fix upon a precise account of what the relevant respects are, but can simply identify those mental states that are clearly not relevant for an occurrent belief's being I-justified. My suggestion is that among those mental states not relevant for an occurrent belief's being I-justified are those that are strongly non-conscious and dispositional for an agent.

By way of clarification, suppose we say that a mental state M is strongly non-conscious for an agent S at some time t if (at that time) S is in M, S is not conscious of M, and M is not easily brought to S's consciousness.[23] Likewise, let's say that a mental state M is weakly non-conscious for S at t if (at that time) S is in M, S is not conscious of M, but M is fairly easily brought to S's consciousness. The intuitive idea behind the 'in all relevant respects' clause, then, is that a person's occurrent beliefs cannot at some time be evidentially supported or undercut by mental states whose content she has virtually forgotten, lies buried deep in the recesses of her mind, or is otherwise not easily accessible at that time.[24] For example, suppose it seems to me that Ella's testimony regarding her neighbors is accurate and nothing in my experience suggests otherwise. Suppose, also, that I had been told quite some time ago that Ella tends toward exaggeration. Suppose, finally, that I have no occurrent recollection of this latter bit of testimony, although with help I could probably remember it. According to the present understanding of 'relevant respects', the prima facie evidence I have (at some time) for believing Ella's testimony cannot be defeated (at that time) by what someone had told me some time ago and what I (at that time) don't easily

---

[23] I am using the preposition 'in' here in a loose sense to capture the idea, which is common enough, that agents can have doxastic attitudes such as beliefs, some of which are non-conscious. See Pollock and Cruz (1999), 45, on the distinction between (stored) beliefs and 'thoughts'.

[24] I assume, then, there is at least this much connection between mentalist and access internalism: Mentalist views will ordinarily incorporate some sort of accessibility condition.

recollect.[25] To which it is worth adding that this claim is compatible with the thesis, defended by some internalists, that non-conscious, dispositional beliefs can themselves be justified—'dispositionally justified'—and that the evidence for these beliefs can consist in non-conscious, dispositional mental items.[26]

Let me now try to bring out why internalism of the sort under consideration is incompatible with moderate reductionism. Once again, I proceed by adducing a pair of cases.

Consider a world W in which Ella, who in addition to being a nosy neighbor, is also a nepotistic sister and has the highest opinion of the moral character of her twin sister Elma. Ella's nepotism runs sufficiently deep that she tends to avoid entertaining the thought that Elma is not a morally upstanding person. Still, Ella's cognitive goal with regard to propositions that concern her sister is admirable, as she desires to believe only true and not false propositions regarding Elma's moral character. As it happens, the morning after the incident with her rowdy neighbors, Ella opens the local newspaper wherein she sees a photo of Elma defacing a public monument with a can of spray paint. The brief article accompanying the photo, which she reads, records details of the case and the efforts of the police department to crack down on this sort of behavior. Upon reading the article and viewing the photo, Ella finds herself (perhaps contrary to what we may have expected, given her nepotism) believing that her sister is not of upstanding moral character.

Now consider a different world W* in which Ella's mental states are identical with those had in W, with this exception: Ella's nepotism runs so deep that she has the cognitive goal not so much as to entertain the thought that Elma is of disreputable character. And while this cognitive goal forms part of a coherent set of such goals and helps to explain Ella's behavior at times, it (like some of her other cognitive goals) often remains dispositional and is strongly non-conscious; protective mechanisms prevent her from seeing it clearly, though we can assume she wouldn't disavow it were she to be made aware of it. As things go, the morning after the incident with her rowdy neighbors, Ella opens the local newspaper

---

[25] Although we can say that mental states that are not easily-accessible function as *potential* defeaters. See Plantinga (2000), 361.

[26] Conee and Feldman (2004), Ch. 3, for example, claim to be open to the proposal that beliefs can be dispositionally justified.

wherein she sees a photo of Elma defacing a public monument with a can of spray paint. The brief article accompanying the photo, which she reads, rehearses details of the case and the efforts of the police department to crack down on this sort of behavior. Upon reading the article and viewing the photo, Ella finds herself (perhaps contrary to what we may have expected, given her nepotism) believing that her sister is not of upstanding moral character.

Internalism implies that in worlds W and W* Ella has identical prima facie evidence that Elma is not of upstanding moral character. And, thus, the view implies that, since in both worlds Ella's beliefs regarding her sister's character are based on this evidence, they are I-justified to the same extent. This implication is a function of The Epistemic Internalist's Supervenience Thesis, which tells us that since Ella's mental states are, in W, in all relevant respects identical with her mental states in W*, her beliefs concerning her sister enjoy the same I-justificatory status. True, Ella's mental states in W* are in one obvious respect different from her mental states in W; Ella in W* has the cognitive goal not to entertain thoughts that her sister Elma is not of upstanding character. But the supervenience thesis tells us that this is a difference that makes no I-justificatory difference, for the difference in question concerns a strongly non-conscious dispositional state, which as such can have no bearing on the evidence that Ella has for believing that Elma is not morally reputable. However, if The Conditional Claim is true, Ella's cognitive goals are determinative of any epistemic merit her beliefs may enjoy. Moreover, if this claim is true, then the following must also hold: If two otherwise identical epistemic agents have incompatible cognitive goals with respect to some proposition at some time, then their beliefs regarding that proposition cannot exhibit the same I-justificatory status at that time. In the cases I have described, however, Ella in W and W* has incompatible cognitive goals with respect to propositions concerning her sister's character and believes what she does about her sister's less-than-upstanding character on the same grounds. It follows that, if moderate reductionism is true, then Ella's beliefs concerning the moral character of her sister do not display the same I-justificatory status. However, if internalism is true, then Ella's beliefs do display the same I-justificatory status, as they are both I-justified. It follows that, if moderate reductionism is true, a paradigmatic form of internalism is false.

This result, I believe, speaks strongly against the plausibility of moderate reductionism. So long as we are thinking of justificatory evidence in the internalist fashion, it is a highly counter-intuitive result of moderate reductionism that Ella in W should have evidence different from what she has in W* and that her beliefs concerning her sister should enjoy a different I-justificatory status. After all, in both worlds, Ella's cognitive goals are coherent, she has the same vivid visual experience of reading the newspaper article and of viewing the photo of her sister, forms the same beliefs on the basis of this experience, and so forth.

Now a dismissive reply to the foregoing cases might insist that the incompatibility between moderate reductionism and internalism is innocuous since internalism with regard to justification is false. But I think any reasonably ecumenical approach to the character of epistemic merits should recognize that beliefs can be epistemically meritorious in numerous ways. And one such way that a belief can be meritorious is its being based on evidence—evidence of the sort internalists countenance as evidence. Granted, a belief's being meritorious in this fashion may not be a necessary component of knowledge, but that in itself does not give us any reason to believe there is no such merit as being I-justified. In any event, if this is right, and The Conditional Claim is true, then moderate reductionism should provide a reductionist account of I-justification. Presumably, any such account would look something like this:

S's belief p is I-justified at t only if and because (i) p is based on evidential mental states of S at t that indicate that p is true; and (ii) S has cognitive goal(s) Ψ at t.

My complaint regarding this schema echoes what I said earlier about the moderate reductionist's attempt to amend reliabilism: It may be true that in some cases an agent has a reason to believe a proposition or pursue a line of inquiry because of the cognitive goals he has. Indeed, some philosophers have developed theories of rationality that tell us exactly this.[27] But if we are thinking of evidential relations in anything like the ordinary sense, then, in many cases, the cognitive goals we harbor—especially ones that are strongly non-conscious and dispositional—have no bearing upon whether a belief is I-justified. And if this is true, we have another reason for believing The Conditional Claim is false: It is not the case that for an internal merit such

[27] See Foley (1987), Ch. 1, for example.

as being I-justified a person's attitude has that merit only if and because she has one or another truth-relevant cognitive goal.

The relativity argument

Take two prominent ways in which epistemologists think of the nature of epistemic merits of certain kinds, I have argued, and it becomes evident that they are incompatible with The Conditional Claim or the thesis that epistemic merits are a function of the cognitive goals we possess. The incompatibility, I've also suggested, is not benign. So long as we hold that moderate reductionism aspires to capture the main lines of our theoretically entrenched ways of thinking about the nature of epistemic merits, we have good reason to believe that the view fails to supply (to echo Lewis) good enough candidates for whatever answers to our conceptions of the epistemic merits. I want now to extend this line of criticism by turning to a third argument, which has been lurking just below the surface of the discussion thus far.

Moderate reductionism, I have been suggesting, is committed to at least these two theses: first, The Application Thesis or the claim that epistemic reasons are a function of our cognitive goals; and, second, for any cognitive goal G, it is possible that an agent S has G and another agent S* lacks G. The combination of these claims yields a very strong version of epistemic relativism.

The form of relativism is not simply the view that different persons placed in different circumstances may have different epistemic reasons—although, of course, it is compatible with this. Nor is it the view according to which it is possible that there be cases in which, for some proposition p, believing p displays an epistemic merit at some time while believing p lacks that merit at some other time—although it is compatible with this too. Rather, the type of relativism at issue is one according to which it is possible that an agent's simply having or failing to have a cognitive goal of some kind is determinative of whether she has an epistemic reason to believe a proposition or not. Somewhat more exactly, the view implies that it is possible that the following claims are all true at some time t:

Some ground g in circumstance C implies or indicates that some proposition p is true.

Agents S and S* occupy C and are aware that g implies or indicates that p is true.

S and S* are exactly mentally alike apart from the fact that S desires to believe p if supported by the evidence, but S* does not.

S has an epistemic reason to believe p, while S* does not.

Suppose we assume for argument's sake that desiring to form only true (and not false) beliefs regarding some range R of propositions is a necessary condition of having reasons to believe any member of that range of propositions (and, thus, of her beliefs exhibiting one or another epistemic merit). Now return to the case of Ella and her twin sister (and assume the propositions they believe fall within R). Given the aforementioned assumption, moderate reductionism implies that, although Ella in W and in W* is aware of the very same grounds in her environment, Ella in W* fails to have prima facie reason to believe Elma is not morally upstanding, while Ella in W does. Of course one can rightly point out that if moderate reductionism were true, Ella's goals in W would be (all else being equal) more likely to help her achieve a preponderance of true beliefs regarding her sister. And because of this one would like to say that Ella's goals in W are epistemically *better* than those she has in W*. But this is not the sort of thing that moderate reductionism allows us to say—at least if we take 'better' to mean something like 'more admirable from an epistemic point of view'. For there is no sense in which Ella would be epistemically irrational or make any sort of epistemic mistake in failing to believe p. (By hypothesis, she has no reason to believe p.) Likewise, there is no sense in which Ella would be epistemically irrational or make any sort of epistemic mistake in rejecting the goals she has in W in favor of those she has in W*. If moderate reductionism is true, at most what can be said is that, relative to the goal of believing what is true with respect to some range of propositions, Ella's beliefs in W* are irrational and her goals in W are epistemically better than those she has in W*.[28]

If there is an implication of moderate reductionism that fits especially poorly with our ordinary ways of thinking about and conducting ourselves in the epistemic realm, this is probably it. As I indicated back in Chapter 2, in a large range of cases, we do not behave as if an agent's failing to desire to believe the truth about some issue implies that she fails to

---

[28] Might one respond that Ella in W is epistemically superior to Ella in W* for this reason: Constitutive of being an epistemic agent is having the goal of believing what is true with regard to any proposition whatsoever? I'll address this position in a moment.

have an epistemic reason to consider that issue carefully. Indeed, epistemic relativism of the kind under consideration is arguably in conflict with a fairly plain necessary truth, viz., that if an agent S is aware that some set of considerations implies that a proposition is true or likely to be true, and there are no considerations that suggest otherwise, then S has an epistemic reason to believe p. (Of course the reason needn't be overriding.)

The foregoing is a simple but, I think, damaging line of argument against any reductionist view that wishes to preserve something close to our ordinary ways of thinking about epistemic concepts. The problem the argument highlights, to paraphrase William Frankena in a slightly different context, is that moderate reductionism looks to trim epistemic reasons to the size of what cognitive goals we happen to have.[29] That said, the line of argument just developed is not wholly uncontroversial, as some philosophers deny that grounding epistemic norms in motivational states has any objectionably relativistic implications. There are three such denials of which I am aware. Let me close this section by considering them.

Three denials

In his article 'Epistemic Normativity', Hilary Kornblith endeavors to marry the broadly reductionist claim that epistemic reasons are hypothetical in character with the non-relativist position that they are universal in scope.[30] His argument runs thus: Suppose we accept the plausible claim that every agent has intrinsic desires—desires to bring about or maintain certain states of affairs, but not simply because doing so would satisfy some further desire. And suppose we agree that there are epistemic norms of various kinds—norms that enjoin us to form, maintain, or jettison beliefs of certain types in certain circumstances, pursue certain lines of inquiry in various types of conditions, and so forth. We can ask: When are these norms binding on us? The answer Kornblith proffers is that epistemic norms are binding on us only when conforming to them offers us our best chance at satisfying our intrinsic desires over the long run. This claim, in turn, is grounded in the general principle that, if a person intrinsically desires to Φ, and Ψ ing is, over the long run, the most likely way to satisfy her intrinsic desire to Φ (and she is capable of desiring to Ψ), then she should desire to Ψ. Forming true beliefs, however, is our best bet at satisfying our intrinsic

---

[29] Frankena (1976), 73.   [30] Kornblith (1993).

desires over the long run. It follows from this that we should desire to conform to epistemic norms, for doing so is our best bet to satisfy our intrinsic desires. As Kornblith puts it, such norms are thereby 'universal in their applicability'.[31]

About this argument, let me make two comments. First, the position for which Kornblith argues is not, strictly speaking, a variant of moderate reductionism. The reason for this is that Kornblith's view attempts to ground epistemic reasons not in the possession of cognitive goals, but in the possession of intrinsic desires—where these two things are not identical. That said, Kornblith's view and moderate reductionism are quite similar, since both positions reject the existence of categorical epistemic reasons and attempt to ground epistemic reasons in the conative states of agents.[32] Given this similarity, I take it to be worth considering Kornblith's position as a view very much in the spirit of moderate reductionism.

While Kornblith's position is a view in the spirit of moderate reduction-ism—and this is the second point I wish to make—I do not think it is an improvement over moderate reductionism, as I fail to see that it avoids the force of the argument from relativism.

Let me argue the point by working with the following case: Suppose in world W* Ella intrinsically desires only psychological contentment. Suppose also in W* she is extraordinarily psychologically fragile; for her to be psychologically content implies that she must isolate herself from most others and engage in very simple tasks. Most importantly, she must 'wall-off' from consideration a huge number of propositions about her own psychological state, the general state of the world, the status of her family and friends, and so on, as she finds considering any of these subject matters profoundly disturbing. Imagine, finally, she is very effective at doing this over the long run. Granting the above and the soundness of Kornblith's argument, it follows that epistemic norms that enjoin us to consider carefully the available evidence are not binding on Ella, for she has reason *not* to desire to form true beliefs about a large number of propositions. So, the general principle to which Kornblith's argument

---

[31] Kornblith (1993), 372, see also 359.

[32] As Hampton (1998) and others have pointed out, it is not as if a position such as this rejects categorical reasons altogether. Presumably, the general principle on which Kornblith's argument rests—i.e. if a person intrinsically desires to Φ, and Ψing is, over the long run, the most likely way to satisfy her intrinsic desire to Φ (and she is capable of desiring to Ψ), then she should desire to Ψ—specifies not a hypothetical, but a categorical reason.

appeals—if an agent intrinsically desires to Φ, and Ψ ing is, over the long run, the most likely way to satisfy her intrinsic desire to Φ (and she is capable of desiring to Ψ), then she should desire to Ψ—can be used equally well to show that, for a large domain of propositions, some agents have reasons *not* to care about believing them to be true—even if the likelihood of their being true is very high (and this likelihood is fairly easily seen). If this is right, the line of argument we just considered does not imply that there are epistemic norms that are universally binding. For it does not rule out cases in which (i) two agents are exactly mentally alike apart from the fact that S lacks certain intrinsic desires (ii) both are aware that a proposition p is decisively supported by the evidence, but (iii) only one agent has an epistemic reason to believe p. At most, Kornblith's argument implies that, since every agent has intrinsic desires, every agent has reason to conform to epistemic norms of some sort or other, however idiosyncratic they may be.

A second strategy used to avoid the relativistic result is to defend a view that is the epistemic analogue to what Bernard Williams has called 'internalism' about normative practical reasons.[33] The basic idea behind Williams's view in the practical realm is that we can reject the authority platitudes regarding moral (and other practical) reasons, but not thereby be forced to embrace any objectionable form of relativism. More exactly, Williams's proposal in the practical realm is that an agent has a reason to act only if and because he is motivated to so act or would be so motivated to act were he to deliberate soundly from his existing motivational states. Suppose we call the epistemic counterpart to this view 'sophisticated' moderate reductionism. And suppose we let the symbol Ψ stand for the fundamental cognitive goal of believing only what is true (and not believing what is false). When formulated, the view says this:

S has an epistemic reason to Φ at t only if and because (i) S has cognitive goal(s) Ψ at t, or (ii) S would have Ψ were he to deliberate rationally from his existing cognitive goals.

[33] Williams's view should not be confused with what I've been calling internalism about epistemic merits. His position is developed in Williams (1981), Ch. 8 and (1995), Ch. 3. Williams, himself, I should note, develops several different positions about reasons that he calls 'internalism'. The view I formulate here is modeled on a robust form of internalism, according to which reasons existentially depend on our goals. For a discussion of these matters, see Dancy (2000), 17–20 and FitzPatrick (2004). For an example of an attempt to be a sophisticated moderate reductionist with respect to epistemic merits, see Lammantra (1988).

I think we ought not to be attracted to this view: As discussions of its practical analogue make evident, it is presumably the case that if S deliberates rationally, then the beliefs with which he deliberates must have epistemic merits such as being justified.[34] But if these beliefs are justified, then they are based on reasons—indeed, epistemic reasons. However, the schema stated above purports to offer an explanatorily informative account of the nature of epistemic reasons, and this cannot be done if what is doing the explaining invokes the very concept needing to be explained, viz., that of an epistemic reason.

A third strategy for avoiding the relativistic result is what we might call 'the-constitutive-aim-of-belief' approach.[35] According to this view, constitutive of being an epistemic agent with respect to a proposition is having the aim of believing that proposition with the aim of thereby accepting a truth. (According to those who appear sympathetic with this view, such as David Velleman, these aims can be had by agents themselves or their belief-generating systems.[36]) To fail to have this aim with respect to a range of propositions is not to be irrational with regard to those propositions. Rather, it is to fail to be an epistemic agent altogether with respect to those propositions.[37] So, the contention goes, it is true that Ella in W has epistemic reasons to believe the propositions constitutive of R, while Ella in W* does not. But this does not imply an objectionable form of epistemic relativism according to which we are constrained to assess epistemic agents only relative to their contingent cognitive goals.

[34] See Joyce (2001), 100. Joyce is drawing upon Michael Smith's development of Williams's position in Smith (1994), Chs. 5 and 6. Incidentally, I assume that considerations such as these give us excellent reason to believe that we cannot create plausible epistemic analogues to so-called Kantian versions of internalism with respect to practical reasons. For more on Kantian views, see Shafer-Landau (2003), Ch. 7.

[35] Something like this position is defended in Velleman (2000), Chs. 8 and 11 and Korsgaard (unpublished). But see n. 37.

[36] See Velleman (2000), 183–8. Velleman's view, then, allows for cases in which a *person* lacks the desire to believe a proposition p inasmuch as it is true, but a cognitive system of hers is inclined to produce the belief that p inasmuch as it is true. While I think this view generates puzzling cases, they won't affect the substance of what I claim.

[37] 'So when we say that indicators of truth are reasons for belief, we aren't making a normative judgment about whether to be inclined toward truth; we're saying that they're reasons for someone only if he is inclined toward the truth, since we're identifying them as reasons of a kind whose universe of application is the set of potential believers, who are constitutively truth inclined' (Velleman [2000], 186). This statement of the-constitutive-aim-of-belief position appears to allow that so long as an agent is a *potential* believer with respect to a proposition, she is an epistemic agent with respect to it. This gives me some reason to doubt that the view I am describing is Velleman's and, thus, that Velleman's position is not in any interesting sense 'internalist' about reasons.

Relativism is implied only if Ella in W* is an epistemic agent relative to those propositions that constitute R. But since Ella in W* is not such an agent, it would make no more sense epistemically to assess Ella's conduct in W vis-à-vis her conduct in W* than it would to assess Ella's conduct in W vis-à-vis, say, a thermometer.[38]

If this is true, the-constitutive-aim-of-belief approach yields an interesting result: One can be a moderate reductionist about epistemic reasons and also capture everything epistemic realists have wanted to say about the authority of epistemic reasons. For, according to the constitutive aim approach, hypothetical epistemic reasons behave, for all intents and purposes, exactly like categorical ones. For epistemic agents, epistemic reasons (of a fairly large range, at least) simply cannot 'evaporate' if one lacks the appropriate cognitive goals, since one cannot both be an epistemic agent and lack the appropriate cognitive goals.

Let me offer a two-part response to this position.

The constitutive-aim-of-belief approach tells us that constitutive of believing a proposition is accepting it with the aim of thereby accepting a truth. I myself am dubious of this claim.[39] But suppose the claim were true. If it were true, however, this claim would be consistent with there being a range of attitudes—call them 'acceptings'—that behave a lot like beliefs, but are not produced by cognitive faculties aimed at truth.[40] To illustrate, consider the following two cases.[41]

Sam has assumed for many years that he will live a long life. Today he gets the bad news that he is very sick, the statistics indicating he has only a couple of months to live. Rather than believe it is likely that he will die soon, what we might call 'the optimistic overrider' cognitive system kicks in, and he finds himself compelled to accept the proposition that he will live much longer than a couple of months.

Encountering a barrage of skeptical arguments, Margaret becomes convinced that there are no other minds. For some time, she is able to stand by the courage of her convictions. But, in an unguarded moment, when Sam asks her for medical

---

[38] I assume that, in the case of Ella in W*, her beliefs are not produced by some cognitive sub-faculty of hers that is aimed at yielding true beliefs.

[39] I am dubious about this claim because it seems to me that what I call in the next paragraph 'acceptances' have a legitimate claim to be called beliefs. I should note that Velleman himself expresses doubts regarding this claim about the connection between truth and belief (see Velleman [2000], 247, n. 5). Velleman claims that this admission does not affect the overall thrust of his view, however.

[40] Here I use the term 'acceptance' in a sense different from that of Chapter 2.

[41] Here I draw inspiration from Plantinga (2002), Sect. A.

advice, 'the Humean overrider' cognitive system kicks in, and Margaret finds that she can't help but accept that Sam also has a mind.

As I understand these scenarios, Sam and Margaret accept propositions without believing them with the aim of thereby believing a truth. These belief-like states are generated by non-alethic cognitive mechanisms—in this case, the optimistic and the Humean overrider systems. Can we assess the belief-like states produced by these systems by employing epistemic criteria, ascertaining whether they are warranted, justified, rational, or the like?

Well, suppose an agent were of the sort who can form true beliefs, govern to some extent the formation and maintenance of a large range of her beliefs, and so forth. Call an agent of this sort a 'creedal agent'. To deny that a creedal agent's acceptances are open to epistemic assessment, one would have to accept the following assumption:

The Alethic Assumption: If a cognitive state of a creedal agent is not produced by a cognitive mechanism aimed at yielding true beliefs, then it is not amenable to epistemic assessment.

But this is a very implausible assumption. If it were true, we could not epistemically assess the attitudes produced by the optimistic and Humean overrider systems, let alone those mental states produced by unreliable cognitive mechanisms such as wish-fulfillment or guess work.[42] However, we *do* epistemically assess cognitive states that are the product of such mechanisms; indeed, by most philosophers' lights, mental states of the latter sort are paradigmatic cases of irrational attitudes. If this is right, we have strong reason to believe it is false that accepting a proposition with the aim of thereby accepting a truth is constitutive of being an epistemic agent with respect to that proposition.

This is an important result for our purposes. Recall that the advocate of the constitutive-aim-of-belief approach claimed that the argument from relativity goes through only if we assume that an agent such as Ella is an epistemic agent. Only if Ella has this status, it was pointed out, could the argument from relativity establish that Ella in W and in W* is subject to epistemic appraisal, but only relative to her contingent cognitive goals in each world. We have seen, however, that the costitutive-aim-of-belief

---

[42] At least this is true if we assume that creedal agents such as Sam and Margaret do not harbor the general cognitive goal of accepting all and only those propositions that are true and, thus, can be assessed in terms of this general goal. I will assume that Sam and Margaret do not harbor such a goal.

approach gives us insufficient reason to believe that Ella in W* fails to be a cognitive agent. If so, then the argument from relativity stands: In both W and W*, Ella is a cognitive agent. By hypothesis, Ella in W has the appropriate cognitive goals with respect to those propositions that belong to range R, while Ella in W* does not. On the assumption that moderate reductionism is true, Ella in W has epistemic reasons to believe these propositions, while Ella in W* does not. Ella, moreover, is subject to epistemic assessment in both worlds—although only relative to her own contingent cognitive goals in those worlds.

This is the first part of my response. Here is the second: Suppose we grant that because Ella in W* lacks the relevant cognitive goals, she thereby fails to be an epistemic agent with respect to the propositions that constitute R. Now, it seems to me, there is still an interesting question to be addressed, and that is whether Ella has reason to believe that she *ought* to be an epistemic agent with respect to the propositions constitutive of R. (For my purposes, it doesn't matter whether the 'ought' in question is the all things considered ought, the epistemic ought, the prudential ought, the moral ought, or the like.) Suppose, for argument's sake, that she lacks the cognitive goal to believe this proposition. If the-constitutive-aim-of-belief approach is true, then Ella in W* has no epistemic reason to believe that she ought to be such an agent, for she is not even an epistemic agent with respect to this proposition. But then it cannot be said that the-constitutive-aim-of-belief approach captures everything worth capturing in the realist's view. For, according to the realist, if Ella is not an epistemic agent, then it is true both that Ella ought to be such an agent with respect to the propositions that constitute R and that she can become aware of this. (I suppose any number of reasons could be offered for the former claim, among which is that her beliefs are more likely to represent reality better.) It follows (all else being equal), according to the realist view, that Ella has an epistemic reason to believe that she ought to be an epistemic agent. Nothing comparable can be said according to the-constitutive-aim-of-belief approach, however. According to this view, it may be true both that Ella ought to be an epistemic agent and that she can become aware of this. But there is, nonetheless, no epistemic *reason* for Ella to believe that she ought to be such an agent.

In sum: If the foregoing is right, the-constitutive-aim-of-belief approach neither answers the argument from relativity nor captures everything we should say about the character of epistemic reasons.

III. Engaging the motivations

I began this chapter by claiming that reductionism is a theoretically conservative position. Its goal is to offer an account of epistemic concepts that
is at once theoretically adequate and goes a considerable distance toward
preserving our commonsensical conception of the epistemic realm. I have
argued that it is unsatisfactory on both counts. As far as providing a theoretically adequate account of central epistemic notions such as knowledge,
justification, and warrant, the view does not rate well; moderate reductionism is incompatible with both paradigmatic externalist and internalist
understandings of these concepts. And as far as capturing the idea that some
epistemic reasons govern us regardless of the character of our motivational
states, moderate reductionism fares no better. Rather, the view implies
an unlovely form of epistemic relativism, which some of those attracted
to the reductionist picture themselves have not been enthusiastic about
endorsing.

So far forth, this is to launch a more or less frontal assault on the idea
that epistemic reasons as such are a function of our cognitive goals. But to
this point, I have offered no specific indication about why someone would
be attracted to moderate reductionism in the first place. I wish to close
our discussion of moderate reductionism by identifying two important
arguments offered for this view and why I find them problematic. The
first argument is modeled on a popular argument employed to establish a
broadly reductionist view regarding practical reasons. The second is not so
modeled, but offered directly in favor of epistemic reductionism.

The first argument

In the context of arguing for what he calls 'internalism' about reasons,
Bernard Williams appeals to the idea that categorical reasons are objectionable because they could not explain behavior done for reasons. The
argument, which I shall label 'The Explanation Argument', hinges on the
so-called Explanatory Constraint:[43]

Necessarily, if x is a normative reason for an agent S to Φ, and S acts for that
reason, then x can figure in a correct explanation of why S Φs.

---

[43] The label comes from Dancy (2000), 101. Dancy's statement of the principle differs slightly from
what appears above. My statement of the principle follows Joyce (2001), Ch. 5, more closely.

However, the argument continues, if reasons are categorical and apply to us independently of motivational states, then they cannot figure in a correct explanation of why agents act at all. This is because a reason can figure in a correct explanation of action only if it can motivate an agent. And a reason can motivate an agent only if it is (or is constituted by) a conative state such as a desire. But, as the realist styles them, categorical reasons are not conative states, but facts—indeed, facts that often don't have motivational states as their constituents. As such, they fall afoul of The Explanatory Constraint. It follows that reasons for action are not categorical.

To investigate this argument properly, I first need to address an interpretational issue. While Williams's argument makes liberal use of the modal term 'can', the manner in which it is used is unclear. The term, after all, cannot plausibly be used in the argument to denote metaphysical or even nomic possibility. How would one go about establishing that there are no possible worlds, even nomically possible worlds, in which categorical reasons are explanatory of action? Without exploring all the interpretational options available regarding Williams's argument, I propose to follow Russ Shafer-Landau and assume the locution embedded in The Explanatory Constraint

A normative reason X can figure in a correct explanation of an action

means something like:

An agent is or would be motivated by X were her cognitive faculties functioning well or were she to deliberate soundly from her existing motivations.[44]

Understood thus, several problems with the argument emerge. I limit myself to identifying two.

First, Williams's argument concerns reasons for action; by this he is commonly interpreted to be speaking of reasons for intentional action. Suppose we assume likewise. If we do so, there is a fairly obvious problem with the argument, as the formation and maintenance of beliefs of many sorts (and other types of propositional attitudes) are not naturally viewed as intentional actions—actions we undertake in any sense. Ella, let's suppose, looks up from reading her paper and upon having a visual experience of a certain kind forms the belief *that the shirt her neighbor is wearing is red.* In such a

---

[44] See Shafer-Landau (2003), 172. Shafer-Landau's formulation differs slightly from mine.

case, her forming this belief amounts to no more than a belief's forming concerning the color of her neighbor's shirt. And, as such, to explain why she forms this belief, one would no more attribute to her any sort of motivational state than one would attribute to her a motivational state to explain why she winces when she stubs her toe. Were she to lack, for instance, the desire to form true beliefs about instances of the colors, it wouldn't be as if she would have thereby failed (or even tended to fail) to form the type of belief in question. This much I take to be uncontroversial.[45] But, if this is true, the argument we're now considering offers us no rationale for believing that epistemic reasons to believe propositions are grounded in our cognitive goals, for in a wide variety of cases, when our cognitive faculties are working well, our cognitive goals do not explain why we form, surrender, or maintain the beliefs we do.

Let me pursue this matter a bit further. I emphasized in Chapter 2 that epistemic reasons are not simply theoretical reasons or reasons to believe propositions; they can often be practical in nature, favoring the pursuit of certain lines of inquiry, the assembling or weighing of evidence, and so forth. Consequently, even if what I have said about the irrelevance of cognitive goals to the formation of beliefs of various kinds is correct, something more needs to be said in response to the argument we're considering, for Williams's argument may very well establish that at least practical epistemic reasons are hypothetical in nature.

But—and this is the second point I wish to make—the argument does not establish that practical reasons of any sort are a function of our motivational states, as Williams's argument depends on a contentious understanding of one of its key premises. We can bring this understanding to light as follows: Suppose we grant the broadly (albeit controversial) Humean picture of motivation that Williams assumes in his argument, according to which motivational reasons (i.e. considerations that incline us to act) are belief/desire amalgams. And suppose we understand facts to be states of affairs in an agent's environment that are not themselves belief/desire pairs. The Action Explanation Argument rests on an inference from:

Facts or an agent's grasping thereof do not explain why an agent acts

---

[45] For a more detailed argument on the issue, see Audi (2001) and Alston (1988), Ch. 5. To forestall misunderstanding, let me note that I do not deny that, in some instances, the formation, maintenance, or repudiation of a belief can be under an agent's direct voluntary control.

to:

So, facts or an agent's grasping thereof are not normative reasons.

But, on the assumption that The Explanatory Constraint is true, this inference has plausibility only if we read the premise stated above as saying that:

Facts or an agent's grasping thereof *alone* do not explain why an agent acts.

Now, in fact, error theorists with respect to morality such as Richard Joyce interpret the premise stated above in this fashion.[46] But thus understood this premise expresses a terribly controversial and, I believe, implausible claim. Why think that, if some consideration genuinely counts in favor of responding to it in a certain way, it alone must explain why an agent responds to it in that way? We don't, to fix upon a parallel case, think that something is a cause only if it alone can causally explain some event. We're happy to acknowledge the explanatory power of partial causes and almost always cite only them in causal explanations. It is hard to see why we should treat normative reasons any differently. Accordingly, if we take the parallel with causation seriously, there is no apparent reason why the categoricity of categorical normative reasons bars them from explaining actions done for reasons, at least partially. Indeed, in something of an ironic reversal of Williams's argument, some philosophers have gone so far as to claim that desires never (or almost never) explain actions done for reasons. Their claim is that normative reasons are states of affairs and they alone explain why we act for reasons.[47]

The second argument

Judging from what those sympathetic with moderate reductionism say, the second argument I am going to consider is the deepest reason why philosophers find themselves attracted to the view. It is also the most elusive argument marshaled in favor of moderate reductionism to assess. The core idea of the argument, first expressed in Chapter 3, is that there is something metaphysically odd about there being categorical reasons that govern our behavior. When one surveys the cold, hard world of facts, it is difficult to see what sort of things such reasons could be. But

---

[46] See Joyce (2001), 110.   [47] See Dancy (2000), Chs. 5–8.

there is nothing metaphysically odd about hypothetical imperatives or 'the engineer's ought', as Quine puts it.[48] After all, desires are familiar elements of our psychology, and there is no mystery in the idea that they supply reasons for us to act. On the assumption that we should want to remove the mystery from epistemic norms as much as possible, we have powerful reasons to believe that epistemic norms are not categorical, but hypothetical reasons.[49]

As far as I can see, the charge that categorical, but not hypothetical, reasons are objectionably mysterious expresses at least one of three claims.

First, the claim may be that categorical, but not hypothetical reasons are mysterious because the former, but not the latter, are vulnerable to the types of argument offered against epistemic realism in Chapter 3. If this is the claim, though, then it is not well-directed. In Chapter 3, we saw that putative epistemic facts are supposed to be objectionably mysterious for at least the following two main reasons: We have no explanatorily informative account of either the supervenience of epistemic features on merely descriptive ones or the way in which we grasp epistemic features. Merely grounding epistemic reasons in motivational states does not speak to these concerns, however. Simply claiming that epistemic reasons are hypothetical, for example, does not demystify the supervenience relation that holds between normative and mere descriptive features or explain how we grasp hypothetical oughts.[50] This is not to say, let it be added, that there are not plausible replies to these arguments of which moderate reductionists might avail themselves. It is to say, however, that these replies cannot simply appeal to the fact that desires underlie reasons. Indeed, I suspect that when replying to such arguments reductionists and realists alike will have to lock arms against more radical antirealist views.

The second thing that could be meant by saying that categorical, but not hypothetical epistemic reasons are objectionably mysterious is that

[48] Quine (1986), 358.

[49] For expressions of these claims, see Kornblith (1993) and Maffie (1990a).

[50] At least this is true if the supervenience of the normative on the merely descriptive is not a species of identity. For arguments that it cannot be, see Dancy (2004a), Majors (2005), Oddie (2005), Ch. 5, Shafer-Landau (2003), Ch. 4, and the discussion of radical reductionism in the next section. Might it be said that hypothetical reasons better explain the intimate connection between normative judgments and motivation, since the truth-makers for these judgments are states of affairs comprised of an agent's desires? Well, it is worth noting that we are often motivated by false normative judgments. In these cases, it can't be that hypothetical reasons better explain the intimate connection between normative judgment and morality, since these judgments have no truth-makers. So, insofar as we want a general explanation of this phenomenon, the appeal to hypothetical reasons appears unhelpful.

the former, but not the latter, fail to fit into a broadly naturalistic world view. While some philosophers sympathetic with moderate reductionism seem to make this claim, it seems to me puzzling nonetheless. After all, moderate reductionism doesn't deny that there are bona fide epistemic reasons—considerations that genuinely favor responses of certain kinds on our part. It simply claims that epistemic reasons are a function of our motivational states. But, if I understand aright the types of things that naturalists say, it is precisely because reasons are *normative* that they are objectionable. For example, when discussing the concept of rationality in *Wise Choices, Apt Feelings*, Gibbard claims that there is a sense in which 'a person is rational only if he tends to be guided by reasoning that is good. This sense is normative, and so ... not straightforwardly naturalistic'.[51] If Gibbard is expressing a paradigmatically naturalist view, then, as far as naturalism is concerned, it shouldn't much matter whether reasons themselves are categorical or hypothetical; reasons of both sorts equally fit or fail to fit into the world naturalistically described.[52] If, however, Gibbard is expressing a non-paradigmatic, highly restrictive version of naturalism, it is unclear why categorical, but not hypothetical reasons are suspect. For example, it would be strange to say that hypothetical, but not categorical reasons pull their explanatory weight in the sciences. It is just not apparent what it could be about the categoricity of categorical reasons that renders them, but not hypothetical reasons, explanatorily impotent in scientific explanation in particular.

The third thing that could be meant by claiming that categorical, but not hypothetical reasons are mysterious is that there *is* something uniquely objectionable about the categoricity of categorical reasons. This is the line of thought one encounters in Richard Joyce's *The Myth of Morality*, for example.[53] Joyce does not claim that categorical reasons are mysterious in some brute, ineffable sense. Rather, his claim is that categorical reasons are objectionably mysterious because they cannot explain why particular agents have reasons for acting or how such reasons could explain action. Now I suppose, if correct, this might support the claim that categorical reasons are naturalistically unacceptable because they fail to pull their explanatory weight in the sciences. (Of course, if the considerations to which Joyce

[51] Gibbard (1990), 49.   [52] This argument is developed at greater length by Hampton (1998).
[53] Joyce (2001).

appeals are correct, categorical reasons would fail to pull their weight in any type of bona fide reason explanation.) But I doubt the type of consideration to which Joyce appeals is correct. It is, after all, nothing other than the Williams–style argument we just considered. And if what I have said earlier in this section is true, this sort of consideration does not provide us with much incentive to adopt moderate reductionism.

IV. From moderate to radical reductionism

As far as I can tell, then, there is no sense of the descriptive phrase 'objectionably mysterious' such that categorical, but not hypothetical epistemic reasons can be plausibly said to satisfy it. I do not deny that there are referential uses of the term 'epistemic reason' such that those entities that satisfy the term are non-mysterious. For instance, there are what we might call 'radical' reductionist views, sometimes attributed to Hume, Quine, and others, that seek to reduce reasons to mere descriptive, non-normative, causal (or at least nomic) features.[54] As its name suggests, this type of view is radical not simply because it repudiates the claim that there are categorical epistemic reasons, but because it denies that epistemic facts are in *any* sense normative, according to a common understanding of this concept. (Of this understanding, I'll have something to say in a moment.) It should be emphasized that radical reductionism thus understood does not imply that we ordinarily think of reasons as non-normative features; in fact, some philosophers appear sympathetic to the thesis that, while reasons themselves are mere descriptive features, *concepts* of these reasons are not simply descriptive.[55] In any event, if we

---

[54] See Kim (1993), Ch. 12, on Quine, and Hampton (1998), Ch. 3, and Korsgaard (1997) on Hume. See, also, Jackson (1998) for a position that would endeavor to identify putatively normative considerations with merely descriptive ones. While so-called Cornell Realists, such as David Brink and Nicholas Sturgeon, claim that normative facts are natural, I do not interpret them as maintaining that they are merely descriptive.

[55] See, for example, Gibbard (2003), Ch. 2. Gibbard focuses his attention on the concept of *being the thing to do*, which, he says, is a 'plan-laden' concept that expresses a decision (p. 8). About this concept, he says, first, that it pertains not to normative properties, but merely descriptive ones, and, second, that it functions much like non-naturalists believe the concept *being good* functions. While I find it puzzling how a decision could designate properties of any sort, my main concern about this proposal is that I do not see how a plan-laden concept could function in the way that many ordinary normative concepts do. Suppose, for example, an agent were to think that an object deserves to be appreciated. To think

understand radical reductionism to offer a merely descriptivist account of epistemic facts, but a normative account of epistemic concepts, there is a sense in which the view is both more and less revisionary in character than moderate reductionism. It is more revisionary because it denies that epistemic facts are normative. But it is arguably less revisionary because it does not imply that epistemic 'reasons' are all hypothetical (although it is compatible with this) or that we ordinarily think of such 'reasons' as being either hypothetical or non-normative in character. Since this type of position appears to have some currency among philosophers, let me complete our discussion of reductionism by indicating why I take it to be unattractive.

What I have to say about radical reductionism is brief (no doubt overly so!) and rests on the following five assumptions.

First, I assume that substance monism is false; the world is not simply one substance, thought under different descriptions, but composed of entities of different kinds bearing different properties. Accordingly, discourse that makes apparent reference to properties is not simply a matter of an agent's thinking about this substance, under different descriptions.

Second, I assume that it is impossible for something to be both a normative and a merely descriptive, non-normative property—at least if we use the term 'normative' in anything like a standard way. (Incidentally, I don't wish to claim that it is impossible for something to be both a normative and a natural property; this is mostly because I am unsure what the category of the 'natural' amounts to.) So, for instance, suppose it is true—as I think it is—that fundamental to the normative domain are reasons—where such entities are ones that favor or justify responses of various kinds on our part. The claim expressed by this second assumption implies that the property of *being such as to favor such-and-such response* cannot be identical with a merely descriptive feature such as the property of *being the cause of such-and-such response, being such as to imply such-and-such response, being likely to produce something desired,* or the like. For, according to anything like our ordinary understanding of favoring, something can cause someone to do something but not favor his doing it (and vice versa); imply that he does it but not favor it (and vice versa); be such as to

---

this is not, as best I can tell, to express an action plan or decision-like state; rather, it is to think that that object *favors* a response of a certain kind on her part (which might, depending on the case, be an action plan).

be likely to produce something desired but not favor it (and vice versa), and so on.[56]

Third, I assume that our epistemic concepts are normative in this sense: Ordinary agents who are competent with epistemic concepts typically (if only implicitly) assume that epistemic reasons are those things that count in favor of, justify, permit, or obligate us to respond to the world in certain ways and that epistemic merits are those qualities that are appropriate responses to reasons thus understood.

Fourth, I assume that a broadly Fregean view of concepts is correct; predicative concepts are ways of thinking of properties or features of the world.[57] Accordingly, a property *falls under* a predicative concept just in case it corresponds to that concept or way of thinking of that property.

Fifth, I assume that the sincere and competent utterance of an epistemic sentence such as 'John's belief is irrational' involves intending to ascribe a genuine property of some kind to John's belief by way of the attributive use of some predicative concept. So, consider an agent S who is competent with epistemic concepts. Given the above, we can say that S's sincerely uttering an epistemic sentence of the form 'x is F' involves thinking there

---

[56] This, at any rate, is the grain of truth I find in Moore's open question argument. Schroeder (2005), interestingly enough, believes that reasons are excellent candidates for reduction. His argument has two stages. First, suppose we assume (with many realists) that reasons are the most basic normative entity. Second, suppose we do not have a very stable grip on the concept of a reason since, 'around the edges, our intuitive judgments about when there is or is not a reason for someone to do something are bound to be systematically misleading' (p. 15). Schroeder suggests that, if we can reduce all other normative features to reasons, and our grip on the notion of a reason is not stable, it looks as if reasons are excellent candidates for reduction.

I find myself not persuaded. In the first place, while I believe reasons are paradigmatic normative entities, I do not believe that they are the most basic normative entity (see Ch. 2, Part II). Second, I fail to see why the fact that 'around the edges' our judgments about the nature of reasons are unstable or indeterminate (I think 'misleading' is not the appropriate term here) is evidence that reasons are good candidates for reduction. After all, it is difficult to find any philosophically interesting concept that fails to share this feature. For example, in the essay I quote from, Schroeder contends that identifying (the Christian) God with the strong nuclear force isn't at all plausible, given our understanding of (the Christian) God. But surely, around the edges, our understanding of God is also unstable. We ask: Does God's everlastingness consist in an atemporal or a never-ending mode of existence? Can God forfeit his power or is it essential to him? And so forth. But it does not follow from this that our intuitions about the nature of God are systematically unstable, indeterminate, or misleading. If this is right, our unsteady or indeterminate intuitions about the more controversial or obscure features of a concept shouldn't significantly count toward our believing that the putative feature it stands for is amenable to reduction.

[57] If one is not comfortable with the Fregean view, substitute whichever view about concepts that captures the phenomenon of our being able to think of the same thing under different descriptions.

is some property F exemplified by an object x that falls under f and, thus, whose character is at least consistent with that way of thinking of F that the concept f expresses.

We are by now familiar with cases in which different concepts pick out the same property. We are also familiar with cases in which the properties that fall under concepts have natures rather different from what those who wield those concepts could imagine. The gap between concept and property that radical reductionism countenances, however, is different from these. We can see this as follows: Assume for a moment that epistemic facts are as the radical reductionist says, i.e. mere descriptive facts. If the aforementioned assumptions are true, the consequence is that radical reductionism implies that there are epistemic 'facts', but all our predicative epistemic claims (about objects that exist at least) are false. For take any predicative epistemic claim whose predicative component f purports to pick out some epistemic property F of x. If radical reductionism is true, then F is a mere descriptive property. But if F is a mere descriptive property, then it fails to fall under the predicative concept f, since *ex hypothesi, f* expresses a way of thinking about F according to which F is not merely descriptive.[58] So, on the broadly Fregean assumptions that propositions are the content of our thoughts and composed of concepts, it follows that it is not the case that there is an x such that x is F. And, according to a realist conception of truth, this implies that (Strawsonian scruples about reference failure aside) any such predicative claim is false. On the further assumption that a broadly realist conception of truth is correct, it follows that radical reductionism implies what I called in Chapter 4 'The Epistemic Nihilist's Alethic Thesis' or the claim that, if the content of a predicative epistemic claim is true, then it is true in the realist sense, and no such content is true.

Radical reductionism, then, is a form of epistemic nihilism (or at least occupies the conceptual shadowlands that stretch between outright epistemic nihilism and reductionism). As such, I don't have much else to say about it beyond what was said in Chapter 4 about nihilism itself. If

---

[58] Might the reductionist claim that F is normative, albeit in a revisionist sense of this term? She might. (Perhaps, for example, she holds that x is normative for an agent just in case it produces what that agent desires.) But this sense of 'normative', I am assuming, fails to correspond to anything like the ordinary sense according to which normative considerations favor or justify responses of certain kinds. And if it is the ordinary sense of 'normative' that informs our normative concepts, then it will still be the case that our normative concepts fail to apply to normative features.

one is a cognitivist and embraces a broadly Fregean way of thinking of concepts, there are two ways to avoid such a view: The first is to reject the claim that epistemic facts are merely descriptive in character, which is the way of both the realist and the moderate reductionist. The second is to propose that we revise our epistemic concepts in such a way that epistemic 'facts' fall under them. Of this last option, I can say only that I can imagine such a revision, but not what would favor accepting it.

objectionable features and other properties such as *being indispensable for theorizing*. (A parallel: It may be that, were sets and universals to exist, they would both have numerous theoretically objectionable features that would create a presumption against allowing them into our ontology. But it may be that only sets have the property of *being indispensable for theorizing*. And, thus, we may have reason to believe that of these two sorts of entity, only sets exist.) If this is right, the assumption that we should adopt is not the unqualified claim: If moral facts do not exist, then there is nothing that has the objectionable features. Rather, it is the more moderate: All other things being equal, if moral facts do not exist, then there is nothing that has the objectionable features. If we grant that epistemic facts are indispensable for theorizing, though, then all things are not equal. And, so, if this strategy were correct, the argument for the parity premise is wide of the mark.

There are, then, two conclusions we might draw from the claim that epistemic facts exist: One according to which moral facts exist and another according to which the argument for the parity premise does not go through. You have given us no reason to prefer the first conclusion to the second. Indeed, for all you've said, taking the second route is just as reasonable as taking the first. If so, for all you've said, the argument you have offered for the parity premise fails.

I believe this objection is unsuccessful. To develop my response, let me first sharpen the objection somewhat, and then state why I am not persuaded by it.

Consider a type of property that we can call an 'elimination stopper'. For our purposes, let's say that an elimination stopper is a feature of a type such that, necessarily, were an entity to possess it, we would have excellent reason to believe that that entity exists—even if it were to display one or another objectionable feature. Call any feature of this type 'F'. Now return to the assumption, fundamental to the argument I offered for the parity premise, viz., that if moral facts do not exist, then nothing has the objectionable features. With the concept of an elimination stopper in hand, we can more exactly state the way in which we ought to qualify this assumption. Rather than say that, if moral facts do not exist, then nothing displays the objectionable features, we say instead that:

If moral facts do not exist, then nothing displays the objectionable features, unless it possesses F.

In principle, there is any number of properties that might function as elimination stoppers. The one with which the present objection is particularly concerned, though, is this:

Being necessary for engaging in anything we would ordinarily recognize as theorizing.

Theorizing—that is, accepting, evaluating, and formulating theories (however inchoate in character) of various kinds—is arguably an unavoidable practice for ordinary human agents; it is difficult to imagine a recognizably human way of life in which we do not engage in it. If this is right, it follows that epistemic facts are indispensable in at least this sense: They are such that participation in certain practices that are themselves practically unavoidable commits us to their existence.[1]

Suppose, then, we qualify the general premise we are considering along the lines I have suggested. The pertinent question to raise is: On the assumption that epistemic facts exist, which of the two conclusions identified in the objection ought we to embrace? Should we conclude that moral facts exist or should we qualify (in the manner just indicated) the claim that nothing has the objectionable features?

My reply is: It doesn't much matter. Either conclusion is one that moral realists can endorse. Embracing the first conclusion leaves the argument for the parity premise that I offered intact. Embracing the second conclusion requires us to abandon that argument in its present form, but gives us sufficient reason to believe that moral facts exist. Let me explain.

Consider what we can call 'ordinary sub-optimal epistemic conditions'. Ordinary sub-optimal conditions are those in which there are truths and epistemic reasons to believe those truths, but the apprehension of those truths and reasons can be and often is rather difficult. For example, in such conditions there are true propositions that we do not yet grasp whose discovery requires us to assemble and assess evidence with great care. Moreover, in such conditions, there are true propositions that we do grasp, but the evidence for which remains obscure and whose discovery requires us to exercise considerable diligence and attentiveness. Ordinary sub-optimal conditions are the conditions that ordinary human beings occupy in a world such as ours. And, as such, they are the conditions in which we theorize.

A pervasive theme in western philosophy, explicitly articulated by philosophers such as John Locke among others, is that in conditions such

---

[1] For a developed argument along these lines with regard to normative facts in general, see Enoch (2003). I develop a similar line of argument in Cuneo (unpublished a).

as these there are 'rules for the conduct of the understanding' to which we should conform.[2] These norms are broadly practical in nature. They concern how we should guide and govern our believings, acceptings, and withholdings of assent to propositions, how we should conduct inquiry, assemble and appraise evidence, and so forth. Conforming to norms such as these, thought Locke, is the best strategy we have by which to arrive at a more nearly accurate representation of reality when theorizing. If we were to state norms such as these, we might compile a list with members such as the following. For any proposition p that is of sufficient theoretical or practical importance for an agent S when theorizing:

If S believes p merely on the basis of wishful thinking, then (all other things being equal) S ought not to persist in believing p.

If S's evidence for p is ambiguous, then (all else being equal) S ought carefully to assemble and consider the evidence in favor of and against p.

If S has excellent evidence for p, then (all else being equal) S ought not willfully to ignore that evidence.

If S believes p, but becomes aware of excellent evidence in favor of not-p, then (all else being equal) S should not simply discount this evidence because it conflicts with his present beliefs.

There are live questions regarding how best to interpret these conditionals, as it is unclear whether, for each of these conditionals, there are actually multiple 'oughts' in play. But we needn't venture any specific claims on this score to see that at least this much is the case: Were an agent to fail to conform to these norms, then (all else being equal) she would exhibit defects such as being intellectually negligent, careless, dishonest, or lacking appropriate objectivity or fairmindedness. However, as I stressed in Chapter 2, according to a fairly intuitive conception of the moral realm, defects such as these are moral in character—failures such as negligence, carelessness, dishonesty, undue partiality, close-mindedness, and lack of courage leave an agent open to appropriate correction, reproach, admonishment, blame, or the like. Norms such as those stated above, then, are what we might call 'bridge conditionals' that link ordinary epistemic reasons with appropriate ways of governing our mental conduct. They are

---

[2] Locke's view is presented in Bk IV of *An Essay Concerning Human Understanding.*

an example of what I have called the entanglement between the moral and epistemic domains.

Suppose, then, that there are ordinary epistemic facts, ones that favor accepting or believing propositions. The claim I have made is that, in ordinary sub-optimal epistemic conditions, indispensable for anything that we would ordinarily recognize as theorizing is the conformance to norms of the sort articulated. It follows from this that not only do norms of this kind exist, but also that moral facts of a certain range exist. And, so, we can affirm that, if epistemic facts exist, then so also do moral facts, for an agent's failure to conform to these norms implies that she suffers from one or another moral demerit or dis-excellence. But—and this is the important thing to see for our present purposes—this implies (by contraposition) that the parity premise is true: If moral facts do not exist, then epistemic facts do not exist.

Admittedly, moral realists believe that, in addition to there being moral facts of the kind that I've just mentioned, there is also a whole range of other prosaic moral facts, ones that concern the benevolent or compassionate treatment of others, for example. And, it might be noted, if the argument from the bridge conditionals to the existence of moral facts is sound, it does not imply the existence of moral facts of these other kinds. These facts do not, it seems, figure in our theorizing.

It is true that the aforementioned argument doesn't straightforwardly imply the existence of these more prosaic moral facts. And, strictly speaking, that is compatible with the core argument. But it is difficult to see what principled reason there could be at this point for not admitting such facts into our ontology. For, if what I have argued is correct, not only have we admitted that there are entities other than moral facts that possess the objectionable features, but we have also admitted that there are moral facts of a certain range that display these features. Presumably, then, the philosophical advantage of not admitting what I've called the more 'prosaic' moral facts into our ontology is not a matter of admitting fewer types of a given entity into our ontology. Once again, we have at this point already admitted the existence of moral facts that display the objectionable features. Might there not, however, be other theoretical advantages to not allowing these facts into our ontology? For instance, might the advantage of not admitting these facts into our ontology be that we don't allow scores of *tokens* of facts of this type into our ontology—perhaps an indefinite or infinite amount of them?

I doubt it. In the first place, if there were an indefinite or infinite number of moral facts already, adding more tokens of the type hardly seems a consideration sufficient to tip the scales in favor of the position favored by the proponent of the objection we're considering. Second, recall that the objection we're considering concedes that the arguments for the thesis that epistemic facts exist go through. But if these arguments are sound, they have at least the following implication for the moral realm: If moral nihilism or expressivism were true, then we could not know putative moral truths such as *that one ought not to kill innocents for the mere fun of it*. For, according to these views, there are no facts of this sort to know. (Nor, in the case of expressivism, are there acceptable paraphrases of the sentence 'one ought not to kill innocents for the mere fun of it'.) However, the proponent of the objection we are considering has accepted the claim that epistemic facts exist on the basis of the arguments offered in Chapters 4 through 7. Presumably, then, she is not dismissive of the claim that an adequate theory regarding the epistemic realm ought to capture the commonsensical appearances, for those arguments are predicated on this assumption. But, if our objector takes the commonsensical appearances of our normative thought and practices at all seriously, it is difficult to see why she should admit that we can know:

(a) If S has excellent evidence for p, then (all else being equal) S ought not willfully to ignore that evidence,

but not:

(b) One ought not to kill innocents for the mere fun of it.

Likewise, if moral reductionist views are correct, it is not apparent why such a theorist should read a conditional such as (a) to make essential reference to categorical reasons, while a conditional such as (b) to make essential reference to mere hypothetical ones. Now, admittedly, trade-offs between honoring different theoretical virtues such as theoretical parsimony and what David Lewis calls saving our 'less-than-Moorean commonsensical opinions' are not always easy to adjudicate.[3] But at least this much seems plausible: If we are to choose between complicating our ontology to a certain extent by allowing more tokens of a type of entity that we have

---

[3] The phrase is from Lewis (1983), 353.

already admitted into our ontology or ensuring that certain claims that
seem obviously true do not come out false (or lacking a truth value), then
we ought to complicate our ontology by allowing more tokens of that type
of entity.

Let me add to this a final point: I can imagine our imagined objector
formulating the revised assumption:

If moral facts do not exist, then nothing displays the objectionable features, unless
it possesses F

in such a way that it implies that there is one and only one value for F, i.e.:

being necessary for engaging in anything we would ordinarily recognize as
theorizing.

Were we to read the aforementioned principle in this fashion, then arguably
there would be conceptual space for a position according to which there
are epistemic facts, but no prosaic moral facts such as *that one ought not to
kill innocents for the mere fun of it*—facts such as this not being necessary for
engaging in what we would ordinarily recognize as theorizing.

In reply, I say the price for carving out the conceptual space for this
view is too high.

In the first place, there are very few entities that haven't been at some
point the object of a philosopher's animus; moral facts are hardly unique in
being singled out as being objectionable. And, second, rather few entities
are such that we have good reason to believe that their existence is necessary
for engaging in anything we would ordinarily recognize as theorizing.

Take, for example, a case in which a philosopher adopts the presently
orthodox position that, if there are ordinary inanimate and animate objects
such as chairs and persons, then they are material, and that any such entity
is composed of simple material items (that is, physical entities that have no
proper parts). Suppose, moreover, that philosopher were to hold that to
believe in the existence of such composite objects (and their non-simple
parts) is highly problematic simply because we have no plausible account
of what it would be for them to be composed of simples. Now consider
that philosopher as he sits in his office chair. Common sense seems to tell
us that there is exactly one person sitting in his office chair. But given
some plausible assumptions regarding material composition, there is equally
good reason for believing that there are multiple persons sitting in this

chair—there being no reason to think that the simples that occupy the region of space directly adjacent to his chair compose just one person.[4] On account of this problem—the 'composition problem' as we may call it—imagine that it is proposed that we eliminate all putative composite material objects from our ontological scheme, inanimate and animate alike. And to the incredulity that might be provoked by the suggestion that one proposes to eliminate *oneself*, a putatively material object, from existence, imagine the following familiar-looking thesis is provided:

Eliminate all composite material objects only unless some such putative object is such that we could not engage in anything we would ordinarily recognize as theorizing were it not to exist.

It is, however, plausible to believe that the only composite animate material object that is strictly necessary for an agent to engage in anything resembling ordinary theorizing is herself—and perhaps those with whom she theorizes. Accordingly, the resulting position is a fairly radical form of nihilism with respect to the material world. It tells us that there are no composite material objects save for oneself and perhaps those with whom one theorizes. (Of course we can grant that the existence of other composite material objects is necessary for engaging in anything resembling ordinary theorizing about ordinary objects. But this is a different matter.)

It seems to me that a position such as this is unacceptable, one to be avoided at nearly all costs.[5] And, accordingly, I assume that a type of principle that would recommend the elimination of a putatively objectionable entity only unless its existence were necessary for theorizing is likewise unacceptable. (The assumption *if moral facts do not exist, then nothing has the objectionable features, unless it has F*, under the present interpretation, I assume, is merely one case of this type of principle.) Indeed, I would suggest that accepting a principle of this type would be considerably out of step with how we actually theorize. After all, a principle of this type is not itself built into our ordinary conception of theorizing. Nor is it one to which we conform when engaging in ordinary scientific or philosophical

---

[4] For a crisp statement of the problem, see Hudson (2001), Ch. 1.

[5] Whether the view is incoherent is a more complicated matter. For a discussion, see Dorr and Rosen (2002), Sect. 6. An alternative conclusion to draw from the composition problem is that persons are physical simples. To my knowledge, Roderick Chisholm and E. J. Lowe are the only contemporary philosophers to have countenanced this position. See Chisholm (1978) and Lowe (2001).

theorizing. Nor, as far as I can tell, is its employment likely to allow us to honor theoretical virtues such as saving the appearances, theoretical conservativeness, theoretical fecundity, explanatory power, or the like. In fact, aside from something like a fascination with the theoretical virtue of simplicity, it is difficult to see what principled rationale there could be for accepting the idea that a putative entity's being necessary for theorizing is the single feature that ensures that that entity should not be eliminated from one's ontological scheme.

In summary, suppose there are two conclusions that one might reasonably draw from the claim that epistemic facts exist—one according to which the argument for the parity premise remains as it is, the other according to which it does not. I've argued that the moral realist can accept either conclusion.

II. The second objection

The objection we have been considering maintains that we ought not to accept the core argument's first premise. The second objection I wish to consider is directed toward the core argument's second premise. This objection concedes that we should accept the parity premise. It also concedes that the argument developed in Chapters 4 through 7 reveals that epistemic antirealism is a deeply problematic position. However, it charges that the argument I have developed is importantly incomplete. According to this objection:

Moral and epistemic antirealism are beset by their share of theoretical liabilities. But in this respect these antirealist views are no different from their realist counterparts. After all, realist views have their own, albeit different, set of problems with which to cope. Simply pointing out that the problems that afflict epistemic antirealism are especially pressing, however, does not imply that they are worse than those that afflict epistemic realism. Comparison is called for. And nothing that you've said indicates that epistemic antirealism is in worse theoretical shape than epistemic realism. Hence, even if you have exposed deep problems with the claim that epistemic facts do not exist, it doesn't follow that we have stronger reasons than not to accept that such facts exist.

In its main lines, this objection seems to me correct: Comparison between the views we are considering is called for. And to this point in the discussion, while I have developed a case for thinking that epistemic facts exist, I have said relatively little—at least explicitly—about why we ought to favor this position over its antirealist counterparts. Let me now develop what I take to be the most expedient way of making the case that we have better reason than not to accept the core argument's second premise.

When it is said that we ought to compare epistemic realism vis-à-vis its competitors, I understand this to mean that we should assess whether epistemic realism is more epistemically probable than its competitors.[6] If the standard accounts of epistemic (conditional) probability are correct, doing so requires us to assess each position on the evidence available for it. However, if a comparison between the positions under consideration requires that we assess the evidence in favor of each, I suggest we can see how a response to the present objection should go. Let me divide this response into two stages.

The first stage

Recall, first, that the objection we are considering does not dispute the claim that the overarching argument against epistemic antirealism has been on the mark. I submit that if we grant this, it follows that, if we engage in the process of assessing whether epistemic realism is more probable on the evidence than is epistemic antirealism, then the claim that there are no (irreducible) epistemic facts is false.

Consider epistemic nihilism and expressivism as cases in point. To assess epistemic nihilism on the evidence implies—at least if we interpret the locution 'to assess on the evidence' as factive—that there are epistemic reasons with which we can assess either position. Epistemic nihilism, though, denies there are such reasons. So, to assess this view on the evidence implies that it is false. A similar conclusion holds for epistemic expressivism. To assess expressivism on the evidence implies either that there are bona fide reasons or there is a plausible expressivist paraphrase of the apparently factive locution 'to assess on the evidence' that does not imply that there are genuine epistemic reasons. If the argument in Chapters 5 and 6 is correct, however, expressivism implies both that there are no bona fide epistemic reasons and that there is no plausible expressivist construal of the locution 'to assess on the evidence'. That is, the argument

---

[6] Of course there are other ways to compare theories, say, along aesthetic lines.

implies (i) that there are no bona fide epistemic reasons, and (ii) that there is no expressivist construal of such a locution that both captures what we could mean by ordinary uses of such a locution and does not imply that the uses of such a locution are in error. It follows that, if the arguments offered in Chapters 5 and 6 are correct—as the proponent of the present objection concedes—to assess expressivism on the evidence implies that it too is false.

Admittedly, this line of argument simply sponges off of arguments offered earlier against the more radical versions of epistemic antirealism; it offers no new reasons to reject epistemic antirealism. Be that as it may, it will be noticed that epistemic reductionism is not vulnerable to the argument just offered, for reductionists admit the existence of epistemic reasons of a certain kind. But here we should note a wrinkle in how we go about assessing such a position vis-à-vis epistemic realism.

In his discussion of epistemic probability in *Warrant and Proper Function*, Alvin Plantinga points out that the concept of epistemic probability ordinarily has two sides. On the one hand, an epistemically probable proposition is typically *objectively* probable; it is evidentially supported by other propositions, but supported in a way independent of what humans think, their habits of thought, and so forth. On the other hand, an epistemically probable proposition is *belief-worthy*; it is such that it deserves to be held with one or another degree of confidence.[7]

In a wide range of cases, these two sides of epistemic probability run in tandem. For example, to claim that it is probable *that the sun will rise tomorrow* is to claim both that it is objectively likely that the sun will rise tomorrow and that this claim thereby deserves one or another degree of confidence. But as Plantinga also notes, these two sides of epistemic probability needn't run together. And the case we are considering is one such instance. For, presumably, if either epistemic realism or reductionism were true, then it is necessarily so; the objective intrinsic probability of each position is either 0 or 1, respectively. But claiming that epistemic realism is more probable than epistemic reductionism is not perforce to claim that the evidence for it is maximal or 1 on the evidence. Accordingly, it is doubtful that, when we assess the probability of a philosophical view such as epistemic realism, we

<hr/>

[7] Plantinga (1993a), Ch. 9. Here Plantinga follows Hacking (1975). Plantinga emphasizes that the objective probability in question may be of different types and that there is no one degree of confidence with which an epistemically probable proposition should be held. See p. 162.

are saying anything about the objective intrinsic probability of the position. Rather, we seem to be saying something different about epistemic realism's status—viz., that the view is the rational one to accept, given our evidence. In this case, the first, objective aspect of epistemic probability drops out, leaving only the second element.

If the foregoing is correct, the claim that epistemic realism is more epistemically probable than (moderate) epistemic reductionism is true only if accepting the former position is rational given our evidence in some unspecified sense of 'rational'. I don't propose to offer a precise account of the type of rationality in question. I assume only what appears to be relatively uncontroversial: The type of rationality in question will incorporate externalist elements. To ask whether a proposition p is supported by the evidence, we shouldn't appeal to whether an epistemically unreliable agent would accept p—no matter how it seems to him from the 'inside'—but to whether a (non-accidentally) reliable agent who is a competent judge with matters regarding p would accept p in an environment such as ours.[8]

However, a central claim of the last chapter's argument is that a reductionist account of epistemic facts is incompatible with externalism ordinarily understood, as some attitudes that display external epistemic merits are appropriate responses to epistemic reasons that are not themselves hypothetical. It follows that, if we engage in the process of assessing whether epistemic realism is more probable on the evidence than epistemic reductionism, then reductionism is false. For suppose, to simplify things, we assume that either reductionism or realism is true. To assess the claim that epistemic facts of any sort exist on the evidence implies—assuming we interpret the locution 'to assess on the evidence' as factive—that either reductionism or realism is such that, were a rational agent to consider it, she would accept it. But if the type of rationality in question incorporates externalist elements, it follows that it is possible that epistemic merits are appropriate responses to epistemic reasons that are not themselves hypothetical, which is incompatible with epistemic reductionism.

To this last argument, let me add a clarification. The argument I have just offered for believing that epistemic realism should be favored over reductionism may seem as if it unduly weights the broadly Aristotelian

---

[8] For a finer-grained analysis of the normative component of epistemic conditional probability, see Plantinga (1993a), 166–8.

theoretical virtue of saving the appearances, assuming that if a view cannot capture our ordinary account of epistemic probability, then it is unworthy of serious consideration. But the reply I have offered is not intended to be as simple as that. Rather, what I assume is this: Epistemic realism, but not reductionism, is compatible with our ordinary and theoretically entrenched account of epistemic merits and epistemic probability. Moreover, there is no sense in which epistemic reductionism displays other theoretical virtues so as to offset this manner in which epistemic realism is theoretically superior to reductionism. For example, if the argument of Chapter 7 is correct, there is no evident sense in which epistemic reductionism is less mysterious than realism. Nor is there any clear sense in which epistemic reductionism is more theoretically simple than realism, countenancing fewer types of entities or fewer tokens of those types. Perhaps it is right to say that realism is ontologically more profligate than reductionism inasmuch as it countenances both categorical and hypothetical reasons, while reductionism accepts only the latter type of reason. (I say 'perhaps' because some realists deny that there are any hypothetical reasons.[9] And, although I won't argue the point here, it seems to me that there is a sense in which reductionism is ontologically less modest than realism, as it countenances more tokens of whatever relation it is that generates hypothetical imperatives.) But even if this is true, I doubt that it tips the scales in favor of reductionism.

My main reason for saying this echoes what I claimed earlier about the nature of competing theoretical virtues. There are cases in which it is not easy to tell whether we ought to accept the more parsimonious or the more commonsensical theory. For example, an extraordinarily elegant theory that doesn't fit particularly well with Moorean common sense may deserve very serious consideration. But the case at hand is not like that. Were reductionism accepted, the gains in theoretical parsimony would be pretty modest; we would enjoy a theory that eliminates one type of reason—a type of reason, moreover, that is not in any evident sense philosophically more 'mysterious' than that which reductionists accept. However, the costs of accepting reductionism would be comparatively high: On the assumption that the argument in Chapter 7 is cogent, we would have thereby surrendered some rather deeply entrenched understandings of the

[9] See Dancy (2000), Ch. 2, for example. I am told Derek Parfit accepts this view as well.

character of epistemic merits and reasons. Given the options, it seems as if realism should win.[10]

In summary, the first stage of my response to the objection under consideration consists in pointing out that, provided the argumentation in Chapters 4 through 7 is correct, to assess whether epistemic realism is more probable on the evidence than are the various types of epistemic antirealism we considered implies that antirealist views of these types are false. This conclusion follows because these antirealist views reject the existence of (irreducible) epistemic facts; were they not to reject such facts, comparisons of the sort would not imply this result. It follows that, provided the argumentation in Chapters 4 through 7 is correct, to compare epistemic realism with its antirealist rivals implies that it is false that there are no (irreducible) epistemic facts.

The second stage

Kant is commonly credited with having vividly pointed out that there are cases in which, by our best lights, the evidence in favor of two incompatible claims is on par. The second stage of response to the objection we're considering consists in arguing that we are not in a situation analogous to a Kantian antinomy, for the reasons to believe that there are epistemic facts are better than those to believe there are not.

Toward the beginning of this chapter, I pointed out that fundamental to the argument in Chapter 3 is the following conditional claim regarding the ways in which moral and epistemic facts are alike: Were the standard objections to moral realism to establish moral facts not to exist, then (when suitably modified) these arguments would also establish epistemic facts not to exist. An equally important assumption of that chapter is that the standard objections represent all and only the relevant potential reasons for rejecting the existence of both moral and epistemic facts. However, if we grant that

---

[10] It might be worth adding that reductionists of certain kinds appear to face a certain kind of paradox. Imagine that a reductionist had the cognitive goal of accepting views that better save the appearances (all else being equal). If such a person were to accept this goal, and it is true that reductionism fails in important ways to capture the appearances with respect to the epistemic realm—say, because it cannot account for the existence of external epistemic merits—then this person's own cognitive goals would generate reasons for him to surrender the view that all his epistemic reasons are generated by his cognitive goals (all else being equal). Of course the reasons in question may not be decisive. Still, this is some indication that the resistance to realism should come earlier; the place to press will be on the objections to reductionism itself.

(i) the argumentation offered against epistemic antirealism in Chapters 4 through 7 provides us with strong reasons to believe that epistemic facts exist, and (ii) we can establish that the standard objections do not provide us with reasons of equal strength to believe that epistemic facts do not exist, then we shall have better reason than not to believe that there are facts of this kind.

There are two ways to proceed with the second stage of the argument, one more expeditious than the other. The less expeditious way of proceeding is to work carefully through the standard objections offered against epistemic realism so as to establish that these arguments are less damaging to realism than are the arguments offered in Chapters 4 through 7 damaging to epistemic antirealism. My own conviction is that this is a promising tactic to employ, for it seems to me that there are good—indeed, compelling—replies available to the standard objections to epistemic realism that exactly parallel those offered in reply to the standard objections to moral realism. For example, I see no reason to believe that epistemic facts would have to be intrinsically motivating, or that they could play no legitimate causal explanatory role, or that disagreement about epistemic matters constitutes good evidence against their existence.[11] At any rate, while I believe this to be a promising strategy to implement, it is also a cumbersome one, requiring detailed consideration of the standard objections.

The more expeditious manner of proceeding, which I shall adopt, is to concede that the standard objections to epistemic realism considered in Chapter 3 have some evidential force. But, I suggest that, even if we concede that at least a subset of these arguments creates problems for epistemic realism, then at best what these arguments establish is that the epistemic realist must countenance some metaphysical mysteries. If we grant, for example, that the standard objections are right to assume that supervenience relations are brute determination relations not amenable to explication, or that we have no informative account about how we apprehend epistemic facts of certain kinds, or that epistemic facts fail to play a wide explanatory role, then it follows that epistemic realism implies the existence of phenomena that are impenetrable—at least to agents with a cognitive

[11] A treatment of the more or less full range of the objections can be found in Shafer-Landau (2003). I try my hand at responses to the epistemological objection in Cuneo (2003a) and (forthcoming), the explanatory objection in Cuneo (2003a) and (2006a), and the motivational objection in Cuneo (1999) and (2002).

constitution in an environment such as ours. (If the argument of the last chapter is correct, epistemic reductionism is really no different from realism in this respect; it is no less mysterious in these respects than is realism.) I submit that countenancing mysteries of these types, while perhaps not very attractive in some respects, is a significantly better theoretical option than embracing wholesale epistemological skepticism. Accepting mysteries of these types is, for example, not as such irrational; indeed, arguably, were there mysteries of this sort, they would be among many other mysteries that philosophers must accept (issues regarding the nature of intentionality, qualia, free choice, numbers, and so forth, spring to mind.) Embracing radical skepticism, by contrast, is irrational, for one cannot be a minimally rational agent and accept that there is no reason to believe anything. And on the plausible assumption that, if given a choice between accepting two incompatible positions, the acceptance of only one of which is compatible with being minimally rational, then we should accept that position.

If what I have just said is true, I submit that the objection we are considering does not hit its mark. For if we grant that the main lines of argument offered against epistemic antirealism are on target, then we have strong reason to believe that the rejection of epistemic facts comes at the cost of implying a sweeping version of epistemological skepticism. And even if we suppose that the standard objections to epistemic realism have some force, at best they imply that accepting the existence of epistemic facts commits us to metaphysical mysteries of certain kinds. Since, though, accepting the latter conclusion is considerably more palatable than the first, we have better reason than not to accept the core argument's second premise, which tells us that epistemic facts exist. Moreover, if I am right to assume that reductionism is no less mysterious than realism, and that realism better captures our ordinary, theoretically entrenched conception of the epistemic realm, it also follows that (all else being equal) we should accept realism rather than reductionism.

III. The third objection

Central to my case for the claim that epistemic facts exist is the thesis that the denial of this claim comes at a prohibitively high cost. The third objection I wish to consider concedes this and, thus, disputes neither the core argument's first nor second premises. Nonetheless, the objection takes issue with the core argument's fourth premise in the following way:

Suppose that you're right to claim that moral facts exist. Even if you've established this, you haven't shown that we have better reason than not to believe that moral *realism* is true. This latter position contains claims about the nature of moral discourse and truth that are not implied by the claim that moral facts exist. Thus, at best, the conclusion of your argument should be stated more modestly as a claim about the existence of facts of this kind and not about the truth of moral realism.

This objection correctly points out that what I've called 'paradigmatic' moral realism is a view that implies not only that moral facts exist, but also that moral discourse is assertoric and that the content of some such discourse is true in the realist sense. Now, there is a sense in which anyone sympathetic with moral realism ought not to be too troubled with the present objection. The objection, after all, concedes that moral facts exist. And anyone sympathetic with realism may reasonably be content with an argument that establishes this claim, letting the chips with regard to moral discourse and truth fall where they may. Still, as I pointed out in Chapter 1, there is a sense in which assembling a case for the fourth premise of the core argument is mostly a matter of explicitly teasing out some implications from the thesis that moral facts exist.

In its main lines, the argument I offered from the existence of moral facts to the claim that some moral discourse is assertoric goes as follows. Suppose there are moral facts. If this is true, then there are good reasons to believe that a cognitivist or descriptivist account of moral discourse is correct. In the first place, such an account of moral discourse captures the way in which moral discourse appears to function and, thus, has the virtue of fitting well with the appearances. In the second place, as I pointed out in Chapter 1, rejecting such a position on the assumption that moral facts exist has consequences we should like to avoid. For one thing, if an agent were at once to adopt the view that there are moral facts and that moral discourse is not assertoric, then she would be committed to the Moorean paradoxical claim that moral facts exist, but that she doesn't believe them to exist. For another, accepting the existence of moral facts would leave one without a rationale to embrace rival versions of moral discourse; as I pointed out in Chapter 5, expressivist views are embraced nearly without exception because it is held that moral facts do not exist.

Some philosophers such as Allan Gibbard, admittedly, offer reasons to accept an expressivist position with regard to moral discourse that do not explicitly hinge on the assumption that there are no such facts. To return to a passage I quoted in Chapter 5, Gibbard writes:

What, though, of the special element that makes normative thought and language normative? There is such an element, I am claiming, and it involves a kind of endorsement—an endorsement that any descriptivistic analysis treats inadequately. The problem is not merely that every time one loophole in the analysis is closed, others remain. It is that a single loophole remains unpluggable by descriptivistic analysis.[12]

I believe that what Gibbard says here is incorrect; normativity is not a matter of endorsement, but more nearly a matter of what *merits* endorsement.[13] But, as I suggested in Chapter 1, even if what Gibbard says in this passage were true, it does not provide us with a reason to accept an expressivist account of moral discourse. At best, it provides us with a reason to hold a position with respect to moral discourse according to which such discourse functions *both* to express moral propositions and to 'endorse' states of affairs of certain kinds. To be sure, a purely expressivist account of moral discourse is more theoretically streamlined than such a hybrid position. But this needn't favor the expressivist view since the hybrid position appears to have a great deal of explanatory power: It nicely captures both the claims that moral discourse often plays an endorsing function and purports to be about moral reality.[14]

Once we agree that moral facts exist, then, the inference to the claim that some moral discourse is assertoric is fairly straightforward. The step from these two claims to the further thesis that the content of some moral claims is true in the realist sense is similarly straightforward. Recall that the reasoning I offered in Chapter 1 in favor of this inference went like this: If we grant that moral discourse is assertoric, then the content of a predicative moral claim such as that Sam's treatment of Margaret is wrong purports to represent the correlative moral fact *that Sam's treatment of Margaret is wrong*. And if we grant there are moral facts such as *that Sam's treatment of Margaret is wrong*, then everything necessary and sufficient for a moral claim's being true in the realist sense is in place, with this stipulation:

---

[12] Gibbard (1990), 33.   [13] Gibbard (2003), Ch. 1 seems to me to better capture this claim.
[14] This type of view has been developed by Copp (2001) and Hare (2001).

The propositional content of the claim that Sam's treatment of Margaret is wrong must succeed in representing the fact *that Sam's treatment of Margaret is wrong*. But it is difficult to see any reason to believe that once we've admitted that moral discourse is assertoric and that there are moral facts, such discourse systematically fails to represent these facts. Indeed, to assert that moral claims systematically fail to succeed in representing correlative moral facts, we would need to embrace the following proposition:

Moral facts exist, but we cannot represent them.

An agent's accepting this proposition, however, is no less paradoxical than her accepting the thought that moral facts exist, but that she does not believe them to exist. After all, the person who sincerely utters this claim is committed to affirming both its conjuncts. However, the claim expressed in its second conjunct ('we cannot represent moral facts') undercuts her justification or warrant for accepting the claim expressed in its first conjunct ('there are moral facts') and vice versa. And no realist, I think, would be enthusiastic about accepting a paradoxical claim of this sort. Indeed, it is difficult to see any reason why, given her other commitments, she should.

I add to this a final observation. I indicated in Chapter 5 that there are deflationists who would resist the sort of argument I just offered from the realist's ontic and speech act theses to the realist's alethic thesis. The complaint is that, while we can concede that the content of some predicative moral claims represent moral reality, we should not concede that the truth of such claims *consists* in their being about a correlative moral fact. While I myself am not persuaded by considerations such as these, I believe we can address them without taking a highly controversial stand on issues regarding the nature of truth.[15]

One way to do so is to distinguish between different conceptions of truth. Suppose we call that property of a (predicative) truth-bearer that consists in its representing reality aright 'truth in the realist sense'. And suppose we call whatever it is (if anything) that the truth property consists

---

[15] Dodd (2000), for example, claims that truth has nothing to do with mind/world relations, seeming platitudes such as 'a proposition is true just in case things are as it says they are' is a mere 'anodyne gloss' on <p> is true if and only if *p* (p. 129). I find it difficult to believe that these two claims are identical in sense, the latter being a mere 'anodyne gloss' on the former. If they are not, and it is true that it is platitudinous that a proposition is true just in case things are as it says they are, then it seems to me the deflationary theorist's insistence that truth is nothing more than a logical device fails to honor a central feature of our ordinary understanding of the concept of truth.

in according to deflationists 'truth in the deflationary sense'. The thesis that I claimed is constitutive of moral realism, recall, is:

The Moral Realist's Alethic Thesis: The contents of some predicative moral claims are true and, if the contents of such claims are true, then they are true in the realist sense.

This thesis, however, is compatible with these very same contents also being true in a deflationary sense. However, if one is uncomfortable with claiming that there are different conceptions of truth, then the basic strategy I am recommending can easily be restated. Call that property of a truth-bearer that consists in its representing a correlative fact mere 'truth'. (Recall that deflationists such as Horwich don't deny there is such a relation.) And call that property of a truth-bearer that consists in its being true in a deflationary sense genuine 'Truth'. Then the thesis I have defended is that the content of some moral claims is merely 'true'. As far as I am concerned, it doesn't matter what we call the relation of correct representation in question—we can call it mere 'truth', if we like; what matters is that there is such a relation and that the content of some moral claims bears this relation to correlative moral facts.

In any case, I submit that the third objection we've considered is also not persuasive. If we grant that moral facts exist, there is a fairly straightforward path both to the claim that some moral discourse is assertoric and to the claim that the content of some such discourse is true in the realist sense. This, I submit, entitles us to the core argument's fourth premise or the claim that if moral facts exist, then moral realism is true. But since the core argument tells us that such facts exist, it follows that we should embrace the claim that moral realism is true.

IV. The many moral realisms

The argument I have offered in favor of moral realism in this book is not discriminating in character. If sound, the argument establishes that we have good reason to believe that moral realism of a paradigmatic sort is true. However, it does not establish whether we have good reason to believe that any particular version of moral realism of this type is likely to be true. As such, the argument should be (all else being equal) equally attractive to proponents of different types of realist position, whether they be so-called non-naturalist, naturalist, constructivist, response-dependent, non-theistic, or theistic versions of moral realism. This is a result I welcome. It seems fitting that, if there are reasons to embrace one such version of moral realism over another, these arguments should be part of an interfamilial dispute, coming at a later stage. Naturally, I have leanings and convictions on these issues. But, as far as I can tell, they do not affect the substance of what I have argued for here.

Bibliography

Adams, Robert M. 1985. 'Involuntary Sins'. *Philosophical Review* 94: 3–31.

——. 1987. *The Virtue of Faith and Other Essays*. Oxford: Oxford University Press.

——. 1999. *Finite and Infinite Goods*. Oxford: Oxford University Press.

Alston, William P. 1988. *Epistemic Justification*. Ithaca, NY: Cornell University Press.

——. 1993. 'Epistemic Desiderata'. *Philosophy and Phenomenological Research* 53: 527–51.

——. 1996. *A Realist Conception of Truth*. Ithaca, NY: Cornell University Press.

——. 2000. *Illocutionary Acts and Sentence Meaning*. Ithaca, NY: Cornell University Press.

——. 2002. 'Truth: Concept and Property'. In Richard Shantz, ed., *What Is Truth?* New York: Walter de Gruyter.

Armstrong, D. M. 1997. *A World of States of Affairs*. Cambridge: Cambridge University Press.

Audi, Robert. 2001. 'Doxastic Voluntarism and the Ethics of Belief'. In Matthias Steup, ed., *Knowledge, Truth, and Duty*. Oxford: Oxford University Press.

Ayer, A. J. 1936. *Language, Truth, and Logic*. London: Gollancz.

Baehr, Jason. 2002. 'On the Epistemological Role of the Intellectual Virtues'. Ph.D. Dissertation, University of Washington.

Baker, Lynne Rudder. 1987. *Saving Belief: A Critique of Physicalism*. Princeton, NJ: Princeton University Press.

Bennett, Jonathan. 1993. 'The Necessity of Moral Judgments'. *Ethics* 103: 458–72.

Blackburn, Simon. 1981. 'Reply: Rule-Following and Moral Realism'. In Steven Holtzman and Christopher Leich, eds., *Wittgenstein: To Follow a Rule*. New York: Routledge.

——. 1984. *Spreading the Word*. Oxford: Oxford University Press.

——. 1989. 'Manifesting Realism'. In Peter French, Theodore Uehling, and Howard Wettstein, eds., *Midwest Studies in Philosophy* 15. Notre Dame, IN: University of Notre Dame Press.

——. 1993. *Essays in Quasi-Realism*. Oxford: Oxford University Press.

——. 1993a. 'The Land of Lost Content'. In R. G. Frey and Christopher Morris, eds., *Value, Welfare and Morality*. Cambridge: Cambridge University Press.

——. 1996. 'Securing the Nots'. In Walter Sinnott-Armstrong and Mark Timmons, eds., *Moral Knowledge?* Oxford: Oxford University Press.

Blackburn, Simon. 1998. *Ruling Passions*. Oxford: Oxford University Press.

———. 1999. 'Is Objective Moral Justification Possible on a Quasi-realist Foundation?' *Inquiry* 42: 213–28.

———. 2001. 'Reply by Simon Blackburn'. *Philosophical Books* 42 (symposium on Blackburn's *Ruling Passions*): 1–32.

———. 2002. 'Replies'. *Philosophy and Phenomenological Research* 65: 164–76.

———. 2002a. 'Précis of *Ruling Passions*'. *Philosophy and Phenomenological Research* 65: 124–35.

———. 2005. 'Quasi-realism, No Fictionalism'. In Mark Eli Kalderon, ed., *Fictionalism in Metaphysics*. Oxford: Oxford University Press.

———. 2005a. *Truth: A Guide*. Oxford: Oxford University Press.

———. 2006. 'Antirealist Expressivism and Quasi-Realism'. In David Copp, ed., *The Oxford Handbook of Ethical Theory*. Oxford: Oxford University Press.

———. Unpublished. 'Pragmatism, Minimalism, and the Space of Reasons'.

Boghossian, Paul. 2003. 'The Normativity of Content'. In Ernest Sosa and Enrique Villanueva, eds. *Philosophical Issues*, 12, 2003: *Philosophy of Mind*. Boston, MA: Blackwell.

BonJour, Laurence. 2003. 'A Version of Internalist Foundationalism'. In Laurence BonJour and Ernest Sosa. *Epistemic Justification: Internalism vs. Externalism, Foundations vs. Virtues*. Malden, MA: Blackwell.

Boyd, Richard. 1995. 'How to Be a Moral Realist (with Postscript: Materialism and Realism in Metaethics)'. In Paul K. Moser and J. D. Trout, eds., *Contemporary Materialism: A Reader*. New York: Routledge.

Brandom, Robert. 1984. 'Reference Explained Away'. *Journal of Philosophy* 91: 469–92.

———. 1987. 'Pragmatism, Phenomenalism, and Truth Talk'. In Peter French, Theodore Uehling, and Howard Wettstein, eds., *Midwest Studies in Philosophy* 12. Minneapolis, MN: University of Minnesota Press.

———. 1994. *Making it Explicit*. Cambridge, MA: Harvard University Press.

Brink, David. 1989. *Moral Realism and the Foundations of Ethics*. Cambridge: Cambridge University Press.

Butchvarov, Panayot. 1996. 'Moral Realism'. In Donald M. Bouchert, ed., *The Encyclopedia of Philosophy*, suppl. New York: Macmillan.

Carson, Thomas and Paul Moser. 1996. 'Relativism and Normative Nonrealism: Basing Morality on Rationality'. *Metaphilosophy* 27: 277–95.

Cartwright, Richard. 1987. 'A Neglected Theory of Truth'. In *Philosophical Essays*. Cambridge, MA: MIT Press.

Chisholm, Roderick. 1977. *Person and Object*. LaSalle, IL: Open Court Publishing.

———. 1977a. *Theory of Knowledge*, 2nd edn. Englewood Cliffs, NJ: Prentice Hall.

Chisholm, Roderick. 1978. 'Is There a Mind–Body Problem?' *Philosophical Exchange* 2: 25–34.

———. 1991. 'Firth and the Ethics of Belief'. *Philosophy and Phenomenological Research* 51: 119–28.

Churchland. Paul. 1989. *A Neurocomputational Perspective: The Nature of Mind and the Structure of Science.* Cambridge, MA: MIT Press.

Cohen, L. Jonathan. 1992. *An Essay on Acceptance and Belief.* Oxford: Clarendon Press.

Conee, Earl and Richard Feldman. 2004. *Evidentialism.* Oxford: Oxford University Press.

Copp, David. 2001. 'Realist-Expressivism: A Neglected Option for Moral Realism'. In Ellen Paul, Fred Miller, and Jeffrey Paul, eds., *Moral Knowledge.* Cambridge: Cambridge University Press.

———. 2003. 'Why Naturalism?' *Ethical Theory and Moral Practice* 6: 179–200.

Cortens, Andrew. 1999. *Global Antirealism.* Boulder, CO: Westview Press.

Cuneo, Terence. 1999. 'An Externalist Solution to "The Moral Problem"'. *Philosophy and Phenomenological Research* 59: 359–80.

———. 2002. 'Reconciling Realism with Humeanism'. *Australasian Journal of Philosophy* 80: 465–86.

———. 2003. 'Moral Explanations, Minimalism, and Cognitive Command'. *Southern Journal of Philosophy* 41: 351–65.

———. 2003a. 'Reidian Moral Perception'. *Canadian Journal of Philosophy* 33: 229–58.

———. 2006. 'Saying What We Mean: An Argument against Expressivism'. In Russ Shafer-Landau, ed., *Oxford Studies in Metaethics,* 1. Oxford: Oxford University Press.

———. 2006a. 'Moral Facts as Configuring Causes'. *Pacific Philosophical Quarterly* 87: 141–62.

———. Unpublished. 'Humanity as a Source of Value'.

———. Unpublished a. 'From Speech Acts to Moral Facts: How to Talk Yourself Into Moral Realism'.

———. Forthcoming. 'Nonnaturalism, Quasi-realism, Skepticism'. In John Greco, ed., *The Oxford Handbook of Skepticism.* Oxford: Oxford University Press.

Dancy, Jonathan. 1993. *Moral Reasons.* Oxford: Blackwell.

———. 2000. *Practical Reality.* Oxford: Oxford University Press.

———. 2000a. 'The Particularist's Progress'. In Margaret Little and Brad Hooker, eds., *Moral Particularism.* Oxford: Oxford University Press.

———. 2004. *Ethics without Principles.* Oxford: Oxford University Press.

———. 2004a. 'On the Importance of Making Things Right'. *Ratio* 17: 229–39.

D'Arms, Justin and Daniel Jacobson. 1994. 'Expressivism, Morality, and the Emotions'. *Ethics* 104: 739–63.

David, Marian. 2001. 'Truth as the Epistemic Goal'. In Matthias Steup, ed., *Knowledge, Truth, and Duty*. Oxford: Oxford University Press.

——. 2001a. 'Truth as Identity and Truth as Correspondence'. In Michael P. Lynch, ed., *The Nature of Truth*. Cambridge, MA: MIT Press.

——. 2004. 'Theories of Truth'. In Illka Niinuiluoto, Matti Sintonen, and Jan Woleński, eds., *Handbook of Epistemology*. Dordrecht: Kluwer.

Dodd, Julian. 2000. *An Identity Theory of Truth*. London: Macmillan.

Donagan, Alan. 1977. *The Theory of Morality*. Chicago, IL: University of Chicago Press.

Dorr, Cian and Gideon Rosen. 2002. 'Composition as Fiction'. In Richard Gale, ed., *The Blackwell Guide to Metaphysics*. Malden, MA: Blackwell.

Dreier, James. 1999. 'Transforming Expressivism'. *Noûs* 33: 558–72.

——. 2002. 'Troubling Developments in Metaethics'. Review of Mark Timmons's *Morality without Foundations*. *Noûs* 36: 152–68.

——. 2002a. 'The Expressivist Circle: Invoking Norms in the Explanation of Judgment'. *Philosophy and Phenomenological Research* 65: 136–43.

——. 2004. 'Meta-ethics and the Problem of Creeping Minimalism'. In John Hawthorne, ed., *Philosophical Perspectives, 18: Ethics*. Oxford: Blackwell.

Enoch, David. 2003. 'An Argument for Robust Metanormative Realism'. Ph.D. Dissertation, New York University.

Fantl, Jeremy. 2006. 'Is Metaethics Morally Neutral?' *Pacific Philosophical Quarterly* 87: 24–44.

Feldman Richard. 1988. 'Epistemic Obligations'. In James Tomberlin, ed., *Philosophical Perspectives, 2: Epistemology*. Atascadero, CA: Ridgeview.

——. 2000. 'The Ethics of Belief'. *Philosophy and Phenomenological Research* 61: 667–95.

——. 2001. 'Voluntary Belief and Epistemic Evaluation'. In Matthias Steup, ed., *Knowledge, Truth, and Duty*. Oxford: Oxford University Press.

Field, Hartry. 2001. *Truth and the Absence of Fact*. Oxford: Oxford University Press.

Fine, Kit. 1985. 'Plantinga on the Reduction of Possibilist Discourse'. In James Tomberlin and Peter van Inwagen, eds., *Alvin Plantinga*. Dordrecht: D. Reidel Publishing Company.

——. 2001. 'The Question of Realism'. *Philosophers' Imprint* 1. Available on the worldwide web at: www.philosophersimprint.org/

FitzPatrick, William. 2004. 'Reasons, Value, and Particular Agents: Normative Relevance without Motivational Internalism'. *Mind* 113: 285–318.

——. 2005. 'The Practical Turn in Ethical Theory: Korsgaard's Constructivism, Realism, and the Nature of Normativity'. *Ethics* 115: 651–91.

FitzPatrick, William. Forthcoming. 'Robust Ethical Realism, Non-Naturalism and Normativity'. In Russ Shafer-Landau, ed., *Oxford Studies in Metaethics*, 3. Oxford: Oxford University Press.

Foley, Richard. 1987. *The Theory of Epistemic Rationality*. Cambridge, MA: Harvard University Press.

Foot, Philippa. 2002. *Virtues and Vices*. Oxford: Clarendon Press.

——. 2002a. *Moral Dilemmas*. Oxford: Oxford University Press.

Frankena, William. 1973. *Ethics*, 2nd edn. Totowa, NJ: Prentice-Hall.

——. 1976. 'Obligation and Motivation in Recent Moral Philosophy'. In Kenneth Goodpaster, ed., *Perspectives on Morality: Essays by William K. Frankena*. Notre Dame, IN: University of Notre Dame Press.

Geach, Peter. 1960. 'Ascriptivism'. *Philosophical Review* 69: 221–25.

——. 1965. 'Assertion'. *Philosophical Review* 74: 449–65.

Gibbard, Allan. 1990. *Wise Choices, Apt Feelings*. Cambridge, MA: Harvard University Press.

——. 1992. 'Reply to Blackburn, Carson, Hill, and Railton'. *Philosophy and Phenomenological Research* 52: 969–80.

——. 1999. 'Morality as Consistency in Living: Korsgaard's Kantian Lectures'. *Ethics* 110: 140–64.

——. 2003. *Thinking How to Live*. Cambridge, MA: Harvard University Press.

Giere, Ronald. 1989. 'Scientific Rationality as Instrumental Rationality'. *Studies in History and Philosophy of Science* 20: 377–84.

Goldman, Alvin. 1979. 'What Is Justified Belief?' In George Pappas, ed., *Justification and Knowledge*. Dordrecht: D. Reidel Publishing.

——. 1986. *Epistemology and Cognition*. Cambridge, MA: Harvard University Press.

Gowans, Christopher. 2000. 'Introduction'. In Christopher Gowans, ed., *Moral Disagreements: Classical and Contemporary Readings*. London: Routledge.

Greco, John. 2000. *Putting Skeptics in Their Place*. Cambridge: Cambridge University Press.

Griffin, James. 1986. *Well-Being*. Clarendon: Oxford University Press.

Grover, Dorothy. 1992. *A Prosentential Theory of Truth*. Princeton, NJ: Princeton University Press.

Haack, Susan. 1993. *Evidence and Inquiry*. Oxford: Blackwell.

Hacking, Ian. 1975. *The Emergence of Probability*. Cambridge: Cambridge University Press.

Hale, Bob. 1986. 'The Compleat Projectivist'. Review of Simon Blackburn's *Spreading the Word*. *The Philosophical Quarterly* 36: 65–84.

Hampton, Jean. 1998. *The Authority of Reason*. Cambridge: Cambridge University Press.

Hare, John. 2001. *God's Call*. Grand Rapids, MI: Wm. B. Eerdmans.

Hare, R. M. 1981. *Moral Thinking*. Oxford: Oxford University Press.

Harman, Gilbert. 1975. 'Moral Relativism Defended'. *Philosophical Review* 85: 3–22.

——. 1977. *The Nature of Morality*. Oxford: Oxford University Press.

——. 1984. 'Is There a Single True Morality?' In David Copp and David Zimmerman, eds., *Morality, Reason, and Truth*. Totowa, NJ: Rowman and Littlefield.

——. 1986. *Change in View*. Cambridge, MA: MIT Press.

——. 1996. 'Moral Relativism'. In Gilbert Harman and Judith Jarvis Thomson. *Moral Relativism and Moral Objectivity*. Malden, MA: Blackwell.

Hasker, William. 1999. *The Emergent Self*. Ithaca, NY: Cornell University Press.

Horgan, Terry. 1989. 'Attitudinatives'. *Linguistics and Philosophy* 12: 133–65.

——. 2001. 'Contextual Semantics and Metaphysical Realism: Truth as Indirect Correspondence'. In Michael P. Lynch, ed., *The Nature of Truth*. Cambridge, MA: MIT Press.

——. 2002. 'Replies to Papers'. *Grazer Philosophische Studien* 62: 303–41.

—— and Mark Timmons. 1990/91. 'New Wave Moral Realism Meets Moral Twin Earth'. *Journal of Philosophical Research* 16: 447–65.

——. 1992. 'Troubles on Moral Twin Earth: Moral Queerness Revived'. *Synthese* 92: 221–60.

——. 2000. 'Nondescriptivist Cognitivism: Framework for a New Metaethic'. *Philosophical Papers* 99: 121–53.

——. 2006. 'Morality without Moral Facts'. In James Dreier, ed., *Contemporary Debates in Moral Theory*. Malden, MA: Blackwell.

——. 2006a. 'Expressivism, Yes! Relativism, No!' In Russ Shafer-Landau, ed., *Oxford Studies in Metaethics*, 1. Oxford: Oxford University Press.

Horwich, Paul. 1993. 'Gibbard's Theory of Norms'. *Philosophy and Public Affairs* 22: 67–78.

——. 1998. *Truth*, 2nd edn. Oxford: Clarendon Press.

——. 1998a. *Meaning*. Oxford: Clarendon Press.

Hudson, Hud. 2001. *A Materialist Metaphysics of the Human Person*. Ithaca, NY: Cornell University Press.

Hursthouse, Rosalind. 1991. 'Virtue Theory and Abortion'. *Philosophy and Public Affairs* 20: 223–46.

——. 1999. *Virtue Ethics*. Oxford: Oxford University Press.

Jackson, Frank. 1998. *From Metaphysics to Ethics*. Oxford: Oxford University Press.

—— and Philip Pettit. 1995. 'Moral Functionalism and Moral Motivation'. *The Philosophical Quarterly* 45: 20–39.

Jackson, Frank. Graham Oppy, and Michael Smith. 1994. 'Minimalism and Truth-Aptness'. *Mind* 103: 287–301.

Joyce, Richard. 2001. *The Myth of Morality*. Cambridge: Cambridge University Press.

Kalderon, Mark. 2005. *Moral Fictionalism*. Oxford: Oxford University Press.

Kim, Jaegwon. 1993. *Supervenience and Mind*. Cambridge: Cambridge University Press.

Kornblith, Hilary. 1993. 'Epistemic Normativity'. *Synthese* 94: 357–76.

Korsgaard, Christine. 1996. *The Sources of Normativity*. Cambridge: Cambridge University Press.

––––. 1997. 'The Normativity of Instrumental Reason'. In Garrett Cullity and Berys Gaut, eds., *Ethics and Practical Reason*. Oxford: Clarendon Press.

––––. Unpublished. 'Normativity, Necessity, and the Synthetic a priori: A Response to Derek Parfit'.

Kripke, Saul. 1982. *Wittgenstein on Rules and Private Language*. Oxford: Oxford University Press.

Künne, Wolfgang. 2002. 'Disquotationalist Conceptions of Truth'. In Richard Schantz, ed., *What is Truth?* New York: Walter de Gruyter.

Kupperman, Joel. 1987. 'Moral Realism and Metaphysical Anti-Realism'. *Metaphilosophy* 18: 95–107.

Lammantra, Markus. 1988. 'The Normativity of Naturalistic Epistemology'. *Philosophia* 26: 337–58.

Laudan, Larry. 1987. 'Progress or Rationality? The Prospects for Normative Naturalism'. *American Philosophical Quarterly* 24: 19–31.

––––. 1990. 'Normative Naturalism'. *Philosophy of Science* 57: 44–59.

––––. 1990a. 'Aimless Epistemology'. *Studies in History and Philosophy of Science* 21: 315–22.

––––. 1996. *Beyond Positivism and Relativism*. Boulder, CO: Westview Press.

Leeds, Stephen. 1978. 'Theories of Reference and Truth'. *Erkenntnis* 13: 111–19.

Lehrer, Keith. 1986. 'The Coherence Theory of Knowledge'. *Philosophical Topics* 14: 5–25.

––––. 1997. *Self-Trust*. Oxford: Oxford University Press.

Leiter, Brian. 2001. 'Moral Facts and Best Explanations'. In Ellen F. Paul, Fred D. Miller, and Jeffrey Paul, eds., *Moral Knowledge*. Cambridge: Cambridge University Press.

Lemos, Noah. 1994. *Intrinsic Value*. Cambridge: Cambridge University Press.

Lewis, David. 1983. 'New Work for a Theory of Universals'. *Australasian Journal of Philosophy* 61: 343–77.

––––. 1983a. *Philosophical Papers*. Oxford: Basil Blackwell.

Lewis, David. 1986. *On the Plurality of Worlds*. Oxford: Blackwell.

———. 1995. 'Should a Materialist Believe in Qualia?' *Faith and Philosophy* 12: 467–71.

———. 2005. 'Quasi-Realism as Fictionalism'. In Mark Eli Kalderon, ed., *Fictionalism in Metaphysics*. Oxford: Oxford University Press.

Little, Margaret. 2000. 'Moral Generalities Revisited'. In Margaret Little and Brad Hooker, eds., *Moral Particularism*. Oxford: Oxford University Press.

Loeb, Don. 1998. 'Moral Realism and the Argument from Disagreement'. *Philosophical Studies* 90: 281–303.

Lowe, E. J. 2001. 'Identity, Composition, and the Simplicity of the Self'. In Kevin Corcoran, ed., *Soul, Body, and Survival*. Ithaca, NY: Cornell University Press.

McDowell, John. 1985. 'Values and Secondary Qualities'. In Ted Honderich, ed., *Morality and Objectivity*. New York: Routledge, Kegan, Paul.

McGinn, Colin. 1993. *Problems in Philosophy*. Oxford: Blackwell.

———. 2000. *Logical Properties*. Oxford: Oxford University Press.

McGrath, Matthew. 2003. 'What the Deflationist May Say About Truthmaking'. *Philosophy and Phenomenological Research* 66: 666–88.

MacIntyre, Alasdair. 1999. *Dependent Rational Animals*. LaSalle, IL: Open Court.

Mackie, J. L. 1977. *Ethics: Inventing Right and Wrong*. New York: Penguin.

———. 1982. *The Miracle of Theism*. Oxford: Clarendon Press.

McNaughton, David. 1988. *Moral Vision*. Oxford: Blackwell.

Maffie, James. 1990. 'Recent Work on Naturalized Epistemology'. *American Philosophical Quarterly* 27: 281–93.

———. 1990a. 'Naturalism and the Normativity of Epistemology'. *Philosophical Studies* 59: 333–49.

Majors, Brad. 2005. 'Moral Discourse and Descriptive Properties'. *Philosophical Quarterly* 55: 475–94.

Marshall, Leonard. 1987. *The End of the Line*. New York: Penguin.

Milo, Ronald. 1995. 'Contractarian Constructivism'. *Journal of Philosophy* 92: 181–204.

Moore, G. E. 1953. *Some Main Problems of Philosophy*. London: Allen & Unwin.

Murphy, Mark. 2002. *Divine Authority*. Ithaca, NY: Cornell University Press.

Nagel, Thomas. 1986. *The View from Nowhere*. Oxford: Oxford University Press.

Nussbaum, Martha. 1990. *Love's Knowledge*. Oxford: Oxford University Press.

Oddie, Graham. 2005. *Value, Reality, and Desire*. Oxford: Oxford University Press.

O'Leary-Hawthorne, John and Graham Oppy. 1997. 'Minimalism and Truth'. *Noûs* 31: 170–96.

Plantinga, Alvin. 1979. 'De Essentia'. In Ernest Sosa, ed., *Essays on the Philosophy of Roderick Chisholm*. Amsterdam: Rodopi.

——. 1985. 'Self-Profile'. In James Tomberlin and Peter van Inwagen, eds., *Alvin Plantinga*. Dordrecht: D. Reidel Publishing Company.

——. 1987. 'Two Concepts of Modality'. In James Tomberlin, ed., *Philosophical Perspectives, 1: Metaphysics*. Atascadero, CA: Ridgeview Press.

——. 1993. *Warrant: The Current Debate*. Oxford: Oxford University Press.

——. 1993a. *Warrant and Proper Function*. Oxford: Oxford University Press.

——. 2000. *Warranted Christian Belief*. Oxford: Oxford University Press.

——. 2002. 'Reply to Beilby's Cohorts'. In James Beilby, ed., *Naturalism Defeated? Essays on Plantinga's Evolutionary Argument against Naturalism*. Ithaca, NY: Cornell University Press.

Pollock, John and Joseph Cruz. 1999. *Contemporary Theories of Knowledge*, 2nd edn. Lanham, MD: Rowman and Littlefield.

Putnam, Hilary. 1983. *Realism and Reason: Philosophical Papers*, vol. 3. Cambridge: Cambridge University Press.

——. 1987. *The Many Faces of Realism*. LaSalle, IL: Open Court.

——. 1990. *Realism with a Human Face*. Edited and introduced by James Conant. Cambridge, MA: Harvard University Press.

——. 2002. *The Collapse of the Fact/Value Dichotomy and Other Essays*. Cambridge, MA: Harvard University Press.

——. 2004. *Ethics without Ontology*. Cambridge, MA: Harvard University Press.

Quine, W. V. O. 1960. *Word and Object*. Cambridge: Cambridge University Press.

——. 1969. 'Epistemology Naturalized'. In *Ontological Relativity and Other Essays*. New York: Columbia University Press.

——. 1970. *Philosophy of Logic*. Englewood Cliffs, NJ: Prentice-Hall.

——. 1986. 'Reply to White'. In L. Hahn and P. A. Schilpp, eds., *The Philosophy of W. V. Quine*. LaSalle, IL: Open Court.

Quinn, Warren. 1993. *Morality and Action*. Cambridge: Cambridge University Press.

Railton, Peter. 1986. 'Moral Realism'. *The Philosophical Review* 95: 163–207.

——. 1992. 'Some Questions about the Justification of Morality'. In James Tomberlin, ed., *Philosophical Perspectives, 6: Ethics*. Atascadero, CA: Ridgeview Press.

——. 1996. 'Moral Realism: Prospects and Problems'. In Walter Sinnot-Armstrong and Mark Timmons, eds., *Moral Knowledge?* Oxford: Oxford University Press.

Rawls, John. 1980. 'Kantian Constructivism in Moral Theory'. *Journal of Philosophy* 77: 512–72.

Rea, Michael. 2002. *World Without Design*. Oxford: Oxford University Press.

Reid, Thomas. 2002. *Essays on the Intellectual Powers of Man*. Ed. Derek R. Brookes. Edinburgh: Edinburgh University Press.

Rorty, Richard. 1984. *Philosophy and the Mirror of Nature*. Princeton, NJ: Princeton University Press.

———. 1985. 'Solidarity or Objectivity?' In J. Rajchman and Cornell West, eds., *Post-Analytic Philosophy*. New York: Columbia University Press.

Rosenberg, Alex. 1999. 'Naturalistic Epistemology for Eliminative Materalists'. *Philosophy and Phenomenological Research* 59: 335–58.

Rosenberg, Jay. 2002. *Thinking about Knowing*. Oxford: Oxford University Press.

Ross, W. D. 1939. *The Foundations of Ethics*. Oxford: Clarendon Press.

Russell, Bertrand. 1956. *Logic and Knowledge*. Ed. Robert C. Marsh. London: Allen & Unwin.

———. 1997. *The Problems of Philosophy*. Oxford: Oxford University Press.

Russell, Bruce. 1984. 'Moral Relativism and Moral Realism'. *Monist* 67: 435–51.

Sayre-McCord, Geoffrey. 1988. 'Moral Theory and Explanatory Impotence'. In Geoffrey Sayre-McCord, ed., *Essays on Moral Realism*. Ithaca, NY: Cornell University Press.

———. 1996. 'Coherentist Epistemology and Moral Theory'. In Walter Sinnott-Armstrong and Mark Timmons, eds., *Moral Knowledge?* Oxford: Oxford University Press.

Scanlon, T. M. 1998. *What We Owe to Each Other*. Cambridge, MA: Harvard University Press.

Schantz, Richard. 2002. 'Truth, Meaning, and Reference'. In Richard Schantz, ed., *What is Truth?* New York: Walter de Gruyter.

Schiffer, Stephen. 1987. *Remnants of Meaning*. Cambridge, MA: MIT Press.

Schroeder, Mark. 2005. 'Realism and Reduction: The Quest for Robustness'. *Philosopher's Imprint* 5. Available on the worldwide web at: www.philosophersimprint.org/

Searle, John. 1983. *Intentionality*. Cambridge: Cambridge University Press.

———. 1992. *The Rediscovery of Mind*. Cambridge, MA: MIT Press.

———. 1995. *The Construction of Social Reality*. New York: Free Press.

Shafer-Landau, Russ. 2003. *Moral Realism: A Defence*. Oxford: Oxford University Press.

——— and Terence Cuneo, eds. 2007. *The Foundations of Ethics: An Anthology*. Oxford: Blackwell.

Skorupski, John. 1999. 'Irrealist Cognitivism'. *Ratio* 12: 436–59.

Slote, Michael. 1997. 'Virtue Ethics'. In Marcia Baron, Philip Pettit, and Michael Slote, eds., *Three Methods of Ethics*. Oxford: Blackwell.

Smith, Christian. 1998. *Christian America?* Berkeley, CA: University of California Press.

Smith, Michael. 1994. *The Moral Problem.* Oxford: Blackwell.

Soames, Scott. 1997. 'The Truth about Deflationism'. In Ernest Sosa and Enrique Villanueva, eds., *Philosophical Issues,* 8: *Truth.* Boston, MA: Blackwell.

Sosa, Ernest. 1991. *Knowledge in Perspective.* Cambridge: Cambridge University Press.

———. 1993. 'Epistemology, Realism, and Truth'. In James Tomberlin, ed., *Philosophical Perspectives,* 7: *Language and Logic.* Atascadero, CA: Ridgeview Press.

———. 2001. 'Epistemology and Primitive Truth'. In Michael P. Lynch, ed., *The Nature of Truth.* Cambridge, MA: MIT Press.

———. 2003. 'Beyond Internal Foundations to External Virtues'. In Laurence Bon-Jour and Ernest Sosa. *Epistemic Justification: Internalism vs. Externalism, Foundations vs. Virtues.* Malden, MA: Blackwell.

Steup, Mathias. 2001. 'Epistemic Duty, Evidence, and Internality'. In Matthias Steup, ed., *Knowledge, Truth, and Duty.* Oxford: Oxford University Press.

Stevenson, C. L. 1963. *Fact and Value.* New Haven, CT: Yale University Press.

Stich, Stephen. 1990. *The Fragmentation of Reason.* Cambridge, MA: MIT Press.

Strawson, P. F. 1950. 'Truth'. *Proceedings of the Aristotelian Society,* suppl. 24: 129–56.

Sturgeon, Nicholas. 1985. 'Moral Explanations'. In David Copp and David Zimmerman, eds., *Morality, Reason and Truth.* Totowa, NJ: Rowman and Allanheld.

———. 1986. 'Harman on Moral Explanations of Natural Facts'. *Southern Journal of Philosophy,* suppl. 24: 69–78.

———. 1994. 'Moral Disagreement and Moral Relativism'. In Ellen Paul, Fred Miller, and Jeffrey Paul, eds., *Cultural Pluralism and Moral Knowledge.* Cambridge: Cambridge University Press.

———. 1995. 'Critical Study: Gibbard's *Wise Choices, Apt Feelings'. Noûs* 29: 402–24.

Swanton, Christine. 2003. *Virtue Ethics.* Oxford: Oxford University Press.

Thomson, Judith Jarvis. 1990. *The Realm of Rights.* Cambridge, MA: Harvard University Press.

———. 1996. 'Moral Objectivity'. In Gilbert Harman and Judith Jarvis Thomson. *Moral Relativism and Moral Objectivity.* Malden, MA: Blackwell.

Timmons, Mark. 1996. 'Moral Constructivism'. In Donald M. Bouchert, ed., *The Encyclopedia of Philosophy,* suppl. New York: Macmillan.

———. 1999. *Morality without Foundations.* Oxford: Oxford University Press.

van Cleve, James. 1999. *Problems from Kant.* Oxford: Oxford University Press.

van Cleve, James. 1999a. 'Epistemic Supervenience Revisited'. *Philosophy and Phenomenological Research* 59: 1049–56.

van Inwagen, Peter. 1990. *Material Beings*. Ithaca, NY: Cornell University Press.

——. 2001. *Ontology, Identity, and Modality*. Oxford: Oxford University Press.

——. 2005. 'Existence, Ontological Commitment, and Fictional Entities'. In Michael Loux and Dean Zimmerman, eds., *The Oxford Handbook of Metaphysics*. Oxford: Oxford University Press.

——. Forthcoming. 'McGinn on Existence.' *The Philosophical Quarterly*.

Velleman, David. 2000. *The Possibility of Practical Reason*. Oxford: Oxford University Press.

Wedgwood, Ralph. 1997. 'Non-cognitivism, Truth and Logic'. *Philosophical Studies* 86: 73–91.

Wiggins, David. 1990/91. 'Moral Cognitivism, Moral Relativism and Motivating Moral Beliefs'. *Proceedings of the Aristotelian Society* 91: 61–85.

——. 1991. *Needs, Values, Truth*. 2nd edn. Oxford: Blackwell.

——. 2002. 'An Indefinabilist cum Normative View of Truth and the Marks of Truth'. In Richard Schantz, ed., *What is Truth?* New York: Walter de Gruyter.

Williams, Bernard. 1981. *Moral Luck*. Cambridge: Cambridge University Press.

——. 1985. *Ethics and the Limits of Philosophy*. Cambridge, MA: Harvard University Press.

——. 1995. *Making Sense of Humanity*. Cambridge: Cambridge University Press.

Wittgenstein, Ludwig. 1969. *On Certainty*. Eds. G. E. M. Anscombe and G. H. Wright. New York: Harper Torchbooks.

Wolterstorff, Nicholas. 1970. *On Universals*. Chicago, IL: University of Chicago Press.

——. 1980. *Works and Worlds of Art*. Oxford: Clarendon Press.

——. 1994. 'John Locke's Epistemological Piety: Reason is the Candle of the Lord'. *Faith and Philosophy* 11: 575–91.

——. 1995. *Divine Discourse*. Cambridge: Cambridge University Press.

——. 1997. 'Obligations of Belief: Two Concepts'. In Lewis E. Hahn, ed., *The Philosophy of Roderick Chisholm*. LaSalle, IL: Open Court.

——. 2001. *Thomas Reid and the Story of Epistemology*. Cambridge: Cambridge University Press.

——. Unpublished. 'From Presence to Practice: The Gifford Lectures of 1994/95'.

Wong, David. 1984. *Moral Relativity*. Berkeley, CA: University of California Press.

——. 1986. 'On Moral Realism without Foundations'. *Southern Journal of Philosophy*, suppl. 24: 95–113.

Wrenn, Chase. 2004. 'Hypothetical and Categorical Epistemic Normativity'. *Southern Journal of Philosophy* 42: 273–90.

Wright, Crispin. 1992. *Truth and Objectivity*. Cambridge, MA: Harvard University Press.

———. 1995. 'Truth in Ethics'. *Ratio* 8: 209–26.

———. 2001. 'On Being in a Quandary'. *Mind* 110: 45–98.

Zagzebski, Linda. 1996. *Virtues of the Mind*. Cambridge: Cambridge University Press.

———. 2001. 'Recovering Understanding'. In Matthias Steup, ed., *Knowledge, Truth, and Duty*. Oxford: Oxford University Press.

———. 2004. *Divine Motivation Theory*. Cambridge: Cambridge University Press.

Zangwill, Nick. 1992. 'Quietism'. In Peter French, Theodore Uehling, and Howard Wettstein, eds., *Midwest Studies in Philosophy* 17: 160–76.

Zimmerman, David. 1985. 'Moral Realism and Explanatory Necessity'. In David Copp and David Zimmerman, eds., *Morality, Reason and Truth*. Totowa, NJ: Rowman and Allanheld.

Index